Absolute Beginner's Guide to

Cable Internet Connections

que®

201 West 103rd Street,
Indianapolis, Indiana 46290

Absolute Beginner's Guide to Cable Internet Connections

International Standard Book Number: 0-7897-2705-6

Library of Congress Catalog Card Number: 20-01096310

Printed in the United States of America

First Printing: December 2001

04   03   02   01   4 3 2 1

Trademarks

Warning and Disclaimer

Associate Publisher
Greg Wiegand

Executive Editor
Rick Kughen

Acquisitions Editor
Rick Kughen

Development Editor
Todd Brakke

Managing Editor
Thomas F. Hayes

Team Coordinator
Sharry Lee Gregory

Project Editor
Karen S. Shields

Production Editor
Candice Hightower

Indexers
Mandie Frank
Ken Johnson

Technical Editor
Johannes Ullrich

Interior Designer
Kevin Spear

Cover Designer
Ann Jones

Page Layout
Rebecca Harmon

Contents at a Glance

Table of Contents

About the Author

Mark Edward Soper is president of Select Systems and Associates, Inc., a technical writing and training organization.

Mark has taught computer troubleshooting and other technical subjects to thousands of students from Maine to Hawaii since 1992. He is an A+ Certified hardware technician and a Microsoft Certified Professional. He has been writing technical documents since the mid-1980s and has contributed to many other Que books, including *Upgrading and Repairing PCs, 11th, 12th, and 13th Editions*; *Upgrading and Repairing Networks, Second Edition*; *Special Edition Using Microsoft Windows Millennium Edition*, *Special Edition Using Microsoft Windows XP Home Edition* and *Special Edition Using Microsoft Windows XP Professional Edition*. Mark coauthored both the first and second editions of *Upgrading and Repairing PCs, Technician's Portable Reference*, *Upgrading and Repairing PCs Field Guide* and *Upgrading and Repairing PCs: A+ Study Certification Guide, Second Edition*. He is the author of *The Complete Idiot's Guide to High-Speed Internet Connections* and coauthor of *TechTV's Upgrading Your PC*.

Mark has been writing for major computer magazines since 1990, with more than 140 articles in publications such as *SmartComputing*, *PCNovice*, *PCNovice Guides*, and the *PCNovice Learning Series*. His early work was published in *WordPerfect Magazine*, *The WordPerfectionist*, and *PCToday*. Many of Mark's articles are available in back issues or electronically via the World Wide Web at www.smartcomputing.com. Select Systems maintains a subject index of all Mark's articles at http://www.selectsystems.com.

Mark welcomes comments at mesoper@selectsystems.com.

Dedication

This book is dedicated to my father, Stuart Soper, and my stepmother, Elaine Soper; they are among the many new Internet users this book is designed to help. Thank you for your love and support.

Acknowledgments

First of all, as always, I thank God for the talents and skills He has provided me. We all have "talent on loan from God," and I am grateful for the opportunity to use the gift He's given me.

A writer with a family cannot write without the support of his family. I thank Cheryl for her love and encouragement: her decade-long campaign to get me to share what I know with others has paid off in a big way. To our children, Kate, Edward, Ian, and Jeremy and their spouses: thanks for learning about computers and the Internet along with me. I've learned a lot from listening to your questions, comments, and round-table discussions. Many writers' work never escapes the file cabinet to be read by anyone. For the opportunity to share this book with you, I want to thank the terrific publishing team at Que. The first computer book I ever read was published by Que, and it's a great joy to be working with them today. In particular, big thanks to:

Greg Wiegand, who keeps the Que team pointed in the right direction and fields your questions.

Rick Kughen, whose vision for this book helped guide it from start to finish.

Todd Brakke and Johannes Ullrich, whose questions and comments always make the book better.

Thomas, Karen, and Candice, who make sure that the words and pictures line up properly and that no grammatical rules were killed during the production of this book.

Sharry, who keeps those payments coming.

The design, illustration, and layout team, who turn my rough sketches into finished artwork and incorporate them into a coherent design. The proofreaders, who exterminate any spelling errors that survived my edits.

Tell Us What You Think!

As the reader of this book, *you* are our most important critic and commentator. We value your opinion and want to know what we're doing right, what we could do better, what areas you'd like to see us publish in, and any other words of wisdom you're willing to pass our way.

As an Associate Publisher for Que, I welcome your comments. You can fax, e-mail, or write me directly to let me know what you did or didn't like about this book—as well as what we can do to make our books stronger.

Please note that I cannot help you with technical problems related to the topic of this book, and that due to the high volume of mail I receive, I might not be able to reply to every message.

When you write, please be sure to include this book's title and author as well as your name and phone or fax number. I will carefully review your comments and share them with the author and editors who worked on the book.

Fax:	317-581-4666
E-mail:	feedback@quepublishing.com
Mail:	Greg Wiegand
	Que
	201 West 103rd Street
	Indianapolis, IN 46290 USA
Fax:	317-817-7448
Email:	office@mcp.com
Mail:	Executive Editor
	General Desktop Applications
	Macmillan Computer Publishing
	201 West 103rd Street
	Indianapolis, IN 46290 USA

INTRODUCTION

Do You Need This Book?

Until recently, virtually all home and small-office Internet connections were made with a dial-up modem running over the same line as your telephone, fax machine, and voicemail systems. Unless you spent the money to install additional phone lines, you could either be online or use your phone for normal tasks, but not both at the same time. With the increased emphasis on e-mail and Internet-based information sources and the need to stay in touch by phone in times of crisis, tying up the telephone line with a dial-up Internet connection became a big problem for many online users.

Even if you had a phone line dedicated to your Internet connection, the speed of dial-up connections did not keep pace with the changes in online content. When the World Wide Web (the portion of the Internet you navigate with a Web browser) was new in the early 1990s, text abounded online and pictures were rare. Rarely was animation or music used, and video was unheard of. Modems of the time connected at a maximum speed of 28.8Kbps (28,800 bits per second or 3,600 characters per second).

Today, the Internet has become a truly multimedia world, with full-motion videos of movie trailers and music videos, Internet radio stations with continuous music in your choice of formats, and Web sites with colorful, animated interfaces as commonplace online content. However, although the typical speed of today's dial-up modems has increased, the speed increase is less than twice what it was a few years ago. Today's modems (based on the V.90 or V.92 standards) can download data at a maximum rate of just 53Kbps or 6,625 characters per second (an FCC regulation prevents these so-called "56Kbps" modems from exceeding 53Kbps). Whether you want full-time, always-on Internet access that doesn't tie up your phone line or speed that's more than adequate for today's rich Internet experience, a dial-up modem is no longer the right way to go online.

Instead, more and more computer users are looking to broadband Internet connections. Broadband connections provide speeds that are much faster than dial-up modems, and most broadband connections also allow the telephone to be used at the same time as the Internet connection. Although several types of broadband connections are on the market, the favorite of most users at present is cable Internet service, also referred to as cable modem service.

This book shows you how to locate a source for cable Internet service, how to make sure your computer is ready to use it, and how to have the service installed (or install it yourself). After you have cable Internet service, this book will teach you how to use the speed it provides to enjoy features such as Webcams and online storage, how to share the service among multiple users, and how to keep your computer and its contents safe from intruders. Cable Internet service comes from a variety of companies, but regardless of whether your provider is @Home, RoadRunner, or another vendor, *Absolute Beginner's Guide to Cable Internet Connections* will help you maximize your enjoyment of this broadband Internet service type, increase your online productivity, and stay safe while you're online.

What You Need to Begin

To use this book to its maximum benefit, you need to have cable Internet service already installed or be in a market served by cable Internet service (check with your local cable TV operators). Although I use a Windows-based PC, I know that many cable Internet users have MacOS computers, such as iMac, G3, or G4. This book is intended for both Windows and MacOS users.

This book covers both basic cable Internet service as well as the many optional free and commercial products and services you can use with it, such as media players, Webcams, security, and connection-sharing products. You will learn what these products do, how to use them effectively, and how to choose the best product for your needs.

How This Book Is Organized

This book is organized into seven parts and 22 chapters:

- In Part I, "Understanding Cable Modems," (Chapters 1 and 2), you will learn how your PC connects with the Internet and how cable modems differ from conventional dial-up modems.

- Part II, "Getting Cable Modem Service," (Chapters 3 and 4) covers the process of making sure your computer is ready for cable Internet service and how cable Internet service is installed.

- Part III, "Using Your Cable Modem Service," (Chapters 5 and 6) covers the basics of using cable Internet service.

- Part IV, "Enhancing Your Cable Modem Service," (Chapters 7–12) introduces you to popular hardware and software enhancements to cable Internet service.

- Part V, "Securing Your Cable Modem Service," (Chapters 13 and 14) discusses the tools you need to keep your computer and its information secure against intruders and computer viruses.

- Part VI, "Sharing Your Cable Modem Service," (Chapters 15–18) provides details on popular methods of sharing your Internet connection.

- Part VII, "Troubleshooting Your Cable Modem," (Chapters 19–22) helps you troubleshoot your cable Internet connection and services.

Each chapter is described in detail next:

- Chapter 1, "The Internet and Your PC," introduces you to the various ways that computers can connect to the Internet and shows you why cable Internet service is faster and better than a conventional dial-up modem connection.

- Chapter 2, "What Is a Cable Modem?," discusses how the different types of cable Internet service work.

- Chapter 3, "Making Sure You're Ready for Cable Internet Service," shows you how to make sure your computer's hardware and operating system are ready for cable Internet service. You will also learn what types of network cards to purchase, and which to avoid, to provide a place to attach your cable modem.

- Chapter 4, "Ordering and Installing Cable Modem Service," covers the processes of a brand-new cable Internet installation, how to add cable Internet to an existing cable TV installation, and how to self-install your cable Internet service.

- Chapter 5, "Setting Up Your Software to Use Your Cable Modem," shows you how to adjust the configuration of your Web browser, e-mail client, and popular multimedia software. These adjustments are sometimes required to use your service, and in other cases help your computer to take full advantage of your cable Internet connection.

- Chapter 6, "Ten Ways Cable Modems Make the Internet Better," lists exciting new ways you can use your cable Internet service, including easy computer updates, online shopping, online music, and others.

- Chapter 7, "Adding Multimedia Features to Your Cable Modem Service," covers the process of adding a Webcam to your system, popular uses for Webcams, and the types of media players you can use for online multimedia content.

- Chapter 8, "Using Internet Multimedia and Messaging," shows you where to get software such as NetMeeting, media players, and instant messaging services. You will also learn how to use them to bring audio/video conferencing, voice and text chat, Internet radio, and streaming video to your cable Internet connection.

■ Chapter 9, "Using a Webcam," teaches you the basics of using a Webcam for video e-mails and live video chat. You will also learn how video e-mail software can be used to convert existing videos for e-mailing.

■ Chapter 10, "Using Photo and Data-Storage Services," shows you how to print and share your pictures through online photofinishing services. You will also learn where to find and how to use online storage services for backup and easy access to data while you're away from your office.

■ Chapter 11, "Playing Internet Games," introduces you to the world of Internet gaming and shows you how to fine-tune your game's configuration for best online performance.

■ Chapter 12, "Speeding Up Your Cable Internet Service," discusses various configuration changes and system tweaks you can perform to help your system achieve even greater download speed.

■ Chapter 13, "Firewalls and Your PC," shows you why your cable Internet connection is vulnerable to hackers and how you can defend yourself with firewall software. You will also learn how to test your system's security.

■ Chapter 14, "Stopping Computer Viruses," introduces you to the wide variety of threats posed by modern computer viruses, worms, and Trojan horse programs to your computer and your confidential data. You will also learn how to choose and use anti-virus software and online anti-virus scanning services.

■ Chapter 15, "Using Microsoft Internet Connection Sharing," describes how recent versions of Windows can be used to share an Internet connection with other Windows and non-Windows computers. You will learn how the different versions are installed and configured, and also discover the limitations of Internet Connection Sharing.

■ Chapter 16, "Using Other Computer-Based Internet Sharing Programs," introduces you to major third-party Internet sharing programs for Windows PCs and MacOS computers and describes how they differ from Microsoft's Internet Connection Sharing and from each other. You will also learn where to locate free trial versions of the software and how some programs can provide safer online experiences for families.

■ Chapter 17, "Router Your Way to Internet Sharing," discusses how routers can be used to add Internet sharing and enhanced security to all types of networks. You will also learn how to incorporate a router into a new network and how to add it to an existing network.

- Chapter 18, "Setting Up a Home Network for Sharing Your Internet Connection," describes the hardware and software you need to set up popular types of networks, such as 10/100 Ethernet, Wi-Fi Wireless Ethernet, HomePNA, and HomeRF, to permit Internet and resource sharing.

- Chapter 19, "Troubleshooting Your Connection to the Internet," shows you how to troubleshoot problems with your cable modem, your network wiring, your TCP/IP configuration, and your cable Internet setup software.

- Chapter 20, "Troubleshooting Internet Sharing," provides you with the information you need to fix problems with both software and hardware-based Internet sharing methods. You will also learn where to find Web-based sources for solutions and how to apply them.

- Chapter 21, "Troubleshooting Internet Multimedia and Instant Messenger Software," describes how to solve problems with Webcams, media players, and instant messaging programs. You will also learn how to make sure your multimedia software is configured to update itself automatically.

- Chapter 22, "Keeping Your Cable Internet Service Up-to-Date," discusses how to change to a new computer or network card without disrupting your cable Internet service. You will also learn why browser updates might be necessary and how to perform them.

How to Use This Book

If you're completely new to cable Internet service, relax! This book is designed to be read from cover to cover, with introductory material early in the book and more advanced material later. This allows you to build your knowledge of cable Internet service in an orderly fashion.

Even if you already have some knowledge of cable Internet service, you will find this book a useful guide to various elements with which you might need help. For example, if you want to share your cable Internet service, Chapters 15–18 will provide you with information about the software and hardware you need to build or modify a network for that purpose. To learn about complete security for your Internet connection, you will want to read Chapters 13 and 14 to see how firewalls and anti-virus software work together to secure your system. If you're thinking about a Webcam, be sure to read Chapters 8 and 9. Even if you're experienced with the normal operation of most cable Internet software and hardware, Chapters 19–22 will be vitally important to you when disaster strikes. No matter where your interests lie, be sure to read Chapters 1–6 to provide you with a solid foundation before you proceed to chapters of special interest.

Conventions Used in This Book

Commands, directions, and explanations in this book are presented in the clearest format possible. The following items are some of the features that make this book easier for you to use:

- Notes—Information related to the task at hand, or "inside" information is provided in this format to make it easy to find.

- Tips—Pieces of information that are not necessarily essential to the current topic but that offer advice or help you to save time are presented as Tips.

- Warning—Notes explaining the need to be careful when performing a particular procedure or task are presented as Warnings.

- Web sites—These online resources are provided whenever they will help you understand a topic more easily or provide a source for hardware or software you must have to perform a task.

PART I

UNDERSTANDING CABLE MODEMS

THE INTERNET AND YOUR PC

*C*HAPTER HIGHLIGHTS:

- The size and scope of the Internet today
- How information travels from a Web site to your computer
- The varying speeds of different parts of the Internet
- Why your computer has a slow connection to the Internet, and the options you have for speeding it up

From Your Desktop to the World—Connecting to the Internet

The Internet is the world's largest network of computers. A computer *network* is what you have when at least two computers share information, printers, or other types of hardware with each other over some type of a wired or (sometimes) wireless connection. Although most networks link computers in a single building, a campus, or a city, the Internet connects millions of computers in hundreds of countries. The most recent estimates of Internet users suggest that over 410 million people go online frequently, and millions more go online occasionally. That's a lot of users!

Although some users of the Internet are solo users, connecting from a home or office computer directly, others use a network to make the connection. Behind the scenes, networks of computers provide the connection between your computer and the Web page you want. Because the Internet depends on different networks cooperating and connecting with each other, a better name for the Internet is really the network of networks.

How does the Internet work to bring you the information you want?

How the Internet Works—Simply Put

When you type a page request or click a hyperlink to view a Web page, how does the request get from your computer to the remote computer, and how does the information get back to your computer? Although the details are complex, essentially, the request and the page you requested are transferred from computer to computer, similar to how the old Pony Express carried mail across the United States in 1860.

The Pony Express riders rode between St. Joseph, Missouri and Sacramento, California for 18 months in 1860 and 1861, carrying mail between the East and West. The first rider received a bag of mail from the postmaster and carried it on horseback about 10 miles to a meeting point with the next rider, who took over the mailbag and carried it to the next meeting point, and so forth. Eventually, the last rider received the mailbag and delivered it to its destination, where the mail was distributed to its recipients, which required even more transfers of mail from one post office employee to another until each letter was delivered. Similarly, a chain of computers and networks carries your page requests from your computer to the remote computer with the information you want.

For example, if you had sent a love letter in 1860 with a proposal of marriage from California to your sweetheart in Virginia, you wouldn't be satisfied until you got a letter back saying "yes" or "no." Similarly, clicking a Web page hyperlink (a highlighted word or picture that displays another page or site) or typing the Web page address (the *Uniform Resource Locator,* or *URL)* is only half the issue when you use the Internet. The information you want has to come back to you. Unlike those who sent mail via the Pony Express, knowing it would take weeks to receive a reply, society today wants a reply in just seconds.

Of course, the comparison with the Pony Express is a simplified way to describe how the Internet works. With the Pony Express, everyone who carried the mail was paid by the United States Post Office (the ancestor of today's U.S. Postal Service) and traveled fixed routes between California and Missouri. In contrast, the Internet uses many different computers and networks to carry messages between your computer and another computer, even if the Web page you want to see is located in the same city that you are. In addition, the files you receive from the Internet might follow a completely different path from the one taken by your original page request.

What Makes the Internet Fast—and Smart

The Internet is an incredibly intelligent and fast network for two reasons:

- Devices called *routers* are used to transfer information between computers on the Internet. A router is about what you would have if your AAA road map could also drive your car and receive real-time updates on traffic jams, highway construction, and where to get the best breakfast along the way. Routers not only select the best way for information to get from one computer to another across a network, but they also make sure that they send only the exact information that needs to make the trip.

- The connections between major parts of the Internet are called *backbones*, and the amount of information that backbones can carry is truly remarkable. The biggest, fastest backbone connection currently in use is called an OC-192, which transmits data at 10Gbps (more than 10 billion bits per second), which is enough to carry 700,000 simultaneous regular modem connections at the same time!

Although your computer doesn't connect directly to an OC-192 backbone, the connections used by Internet service providers (ISPs)—the folks you pay to provide you with Internet service—are still impressively fast:

- Smaller ISPs use one or more T-1 lines running at 1.5Mbps per line to connect to backbones. Telephone companies refer to a T-1 line as DS1.

- Larger ISPs use one or more T-3 connections to backbones. Each T-3 line runs at 45Mbps. Telephone companies refer to T-3 lines as DS3.

Table 1.1 compares the speeds of Internet backbones and ISP connections to back-bonesto typical connection speeds endured by home and small-office users.

Table 1.1   Internet Connection Speeds

Connection Type	Used for	Speed
OC-192	Internet backbone	10Gbps
OC-48	Internet backbone	2.5Gbps
OC-12	Internet backbone	622Mbps
T-3	ISP to backbone	45Mbps
T-1	ISP to backbone	1.5Mbps
Broadband Connections	user to ISP	128Kbps to 1.5Gbps
analog modem	user to ISP	53Kbps

1Gbps equals 1,000Mbps or 1,000,000Kbps

1Mbps equals 1,000Kbps or 1,000,000bps

bps equals bits per second

As you can see from Table 1.1, most of the Internet is very fast. However, the individual user's connection to the Internet ("user to ISP" in Table 1.1) is much slower than either the backbones or the ISPs' connections to backbones. What effect does this have on how quickly you get information from the Internet?

How Your PC Connects to the Internet

The speed that you experience on the Internet is primarily affected by how fast your personal connection is to the Internet. The vast majority of home and small-business users of the Internet (people just like you) connect through a device called a *modem* by using the same connection that your telephone and fax machine use.

Note

Another name for telephone modems or analog modems is *dial-up modems* because you must dial the telephone number of the ISP's modem at the start of the call process. If the ISP doesn't have enough modems to handle all the callers in a particular time period, you might hear a busy signal when you make the call, and you won't be able to make your Internet connection.

How fast is a telephone modem? You would be better off to ask, "How *slow* is a telephone modem?" To help understand the answer, you need to understand how modems work.

Modem is short for modulate-demodulate. *Modulate* is the process of changing one kind of signal into another, whereas *demodulate* is the process of changing the signal back into its original form. Why do you need to change signal types to enable your computer to communicate with other computers over the telephone line? The reason is that telephone lines are designed to carry *analog* signals, which vary in loudness, pitch, and tone (enabling you to tell your mother's voice from your spouse's voice), and computers use digital signals (on or off and no hedging about it!). Figure 1.1 compares digital and analog signals.

FIGURE 1.1

Computers use digital signals (top), and telephones use analog signals (bottom).

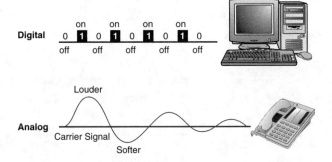

For computers to connect with each other via telephone lines, digital signals must be converted to analog for sending and back to digital when received.

Telephone modems are also called *analog modems* because the modem on your computer converts digital signals into analog signals to make the connection to the Internet. The modem at the other end then converts the analog signal back into a digital signal for transmission via routers and backbones to the remote computer with the Web page you want (see Figure 1.2).

Because dial-up modems must use a low-frequency carrier over a system that was never designed for transporting data, the speed of an analog modem connection is low compared to even a T-1 connection. Conventional modems can send and receive data at just 33.6Kbps (33,600 bits per second). Even the more recent so-called *56K* modems, which set up a faster digital connection for downloading data (receiving data from the remote computer), can't go faster than 56Kbps (and are limited to just 53Kbps by an old FCC regulation that's still in effect). No matter how fast your computer is, whether it's a creaky 300MHz Pentium II or the latest 1.5GHz-plus Pentium 4 or Athlon, using a telephone modem will provide you with a slow Internet connection that also ties up your telephone line, preventing you from making or receiving calls.

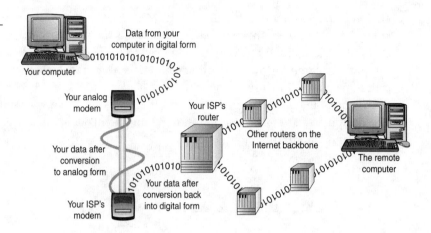

While other types of Internet connections, such as cable modems, which also use a modulated signal, use a much higher frequency to allow much faster data transmission speeds.

Tip

The newest type of 56Kbps service, called V.92, has optional support for call waiting, enabling you to take a voice call without interrupting your Internet connection. However, your ISP must also support all V.92 features to allow you to use this feature. In addition, the duration for which you can sustain an Internet connection and a phone call is still quite limited.

Fast Alternatives to Analog Modems

Much of the most enjoyable and useful content on the Internet, including Internet radio, streaming video, animated maps and others, are so slow and so difficult to use that analog modem users seldom take advantage of them. Fortunately, several faster alternatives to analog modems are now available, including those listed in Table 1.2, which lists typical speeds for different types of Internet connections.

Table 1.2 Analog Modems Compared to Broadband Internet Connections

Connection Type	Download (Receive) Speed	Upload (Send) Speed	Ties Up Telephone Line?	Provider
ISDN (Integrated teleDigital Network)	64Kbps or 128Kbps	Same	No	Local Services phone company (telco)

Table 1.2   (continued)

Connection Type	Download (Receive) Speed	Upload (Send) Speed	Ties Up Telephone Line?	Provider
DSL (Digital Subscriber Line)	Up to 1Mbps	Up to 128KBps	No	Telco or specialized ISP
Satellite	Up to 400Kbps	Up to 128KBps	Telco Return—Yes Two-Way—No	DirecPC, StarBand, others
Fixed Wireless	Up to 1.5Mbps	Up to 256Kbps	Telco Return—Yes Two-Way—No	Sprint Wireless, wireless cable TV companies
Cable modem	Up to 1.5Mbps	Up to 256Kbps	Telco Return—Yes Two-Way—No	Cable TV companies

Note

Telco Return is a type of Internet service that uses your telephone line and an analog modem to send page requests and e-mail from your computer. Downloads use the broadband connection.

Two-way is a type of Internet service that uses a broadband connection for both sending and receiving information. This type of service allows you to use your telephone line for normal calling, faxing, and similar services.

As you can see from Table 1.2, you have plenty of choices that beat analog modems for speed and that don't tie up your telephone line. Of these choices, my personal favorite (and the one I use at home) is two-way cable Internet service, also called cable modem service. I'm not alone in my preference. In the United States alone, more than 3.8 million Internet users were cable modem subscribers in the year 2000, and that number is expected to rise sharply in the future.

Why are cable modems so popular with so many users? Following are some of the reasons:

- Always-on connection—With most two-way cable modem services, the connection is always on whenever your computer is running. You don't have the 15 to 30-second delay necessary with dial-up modems before you can check your e-mail or surf to your favorite Web site.

- High speed—You can expect to achieve 400Kbps–500Kbps sustained speeds with a two-way cable modem service (far and away the more prevalent service type), which is about 8 to 10 times faster than the best analog modem. Sometimes you can come close to the 1.5Mbps that is the theoretical limit of today's services. This level of speed makes downloading large files, viewing streaming video, and listening to high-quality Internet radio possible—and enjoyable.

■ One-stop shopping—Unlike some other high-speed services, cable modem service can be ordered with a single call and can usually be installed in just a few days after you place your order (even if your home isn't currently connected to cable TV).If you already have cable TV, you might even be able to install the additional cabling needed for cable Internet service yourself. While some forms of DSL offer self-install options, other high-bandwidth services might require two or more visits to your home or office and take weeks (or even months!) to install.

■ Reliability—Because two-way cable modem service uses the same fiber-optic cables installed by cable TV networks that have upgraded to digital cable, reliability is higher than with telephone-based Internet solutions, which often are hampered by the age and variable quality of existing telephone lines. Of course, outages are possible with both types of service, but cable Internet service isn't degraded by rain, line noise, or other types of problems which can affect satellite-based and phone-line based Internet connections.

Whether you currently have cable modem-based Internet service, are about to have it installed, or are just considering it, the remainder of this book will help you learn how you can get the most from cable modem Internet services.

Note

Depending upon where you live, you may not have all the choices listed in Table 1.2, because different types of services are available in different areas. However, if you have cable TV service available in your area, you may also have cable Internet service available from the same provider(s).

Summary

The Internet is a "network of networks" which connects your computer with millions of other Internet users around the world. While high-speed connections called backbones connect major portions of the Internet to each other, analog modem connections used by most household and small-business users are very slow by comparison, making your Internet connection very slow.

Depending upon the service offerings in your market, you may have a wide variety of broadband Internet services to choose from for faster connections. Two-way connections also free up your phone line. The most popular broadband connection type is cable Internet (cable modem) service, which is the subject of this book.

WHAT IS A CABLE MODEM?

2

Cable Modems and Your Friendly Cable Provider

A cable modem is a somewhat inaccurate name for the device that enables your TV cable to bring you www.Discovery.com as well as the Discovery Channel and enables you to search with www.Google.com as well as stare goggle-eyed at the latest TV programs. A cable modem, unlike an analog modem, doesn't convert between digital and analog signals. Instead, it's really just a specialized type of tuner that is more akin to the set-top box that many cable TV providers have used for a long time. Just as the set-top box allows you to select from different cable TV channels, the cable modem picks up only the frequencies that are designated by your cable Internet provider for cable modem traffic.

 Note   Cable TV systems use a very wide range of carrier frequencies, ranging from 50MHz or 90 MHz to 860 MHz. This wide band of frequencies is divided into channels that are 6MHz wide. The high speed of cable TV frequencies is the main reason why cable Internet connections are so much faster than dial-up connections, and also explains why you can watch over a hundred channels on cable TV while surfing the Web: there's plenty of room for all the signals.

Cable modem service is much more widespread than its chief competitor, DSL (Digital Subscriber Line), because the multifrequency nature of cable TV is a perfect match for cable modem service. Unlike DSL and its predecessor, ISDN, which might require rewiring of your telephone service to support a high-quality signal, most cable networks, especially those that have been upgraded for digital cable service, work nicely with cable modems.

However, not every cable TV provider offers cable modem service. To find out why, you need to understand the two different types of cable modem service that can be offered, and what cable TV companies must do if they want to offer any type of cable-based Internet service.

The two major types of cable modem service are

- One-way (also called *Telco Return* by some vendors)
- Two-way

Although both types of service provide much faster downloading of information to your computer than what a dial-up modem can provide, they are much different in their operation.

One-Way Cable Service

One-way cable modem service is designed to allow older cable networks that use coaxial cable for their entire network to offer cable-based Internet service. Because coaxial cable can't carry nearly as many channels as fiber-optic cable and isn't as fast as fiber-optic cable, an all-coaxial cable network can only handle Internet data going to your computer.

One-way cable modem service must still use an analog modem (either built into the cable modem or an external analog modem like the ones available in computer stores) to send e-mail and page requests. The end result is that you get much faster downloads, but uploading takes the same amount of time and still ties up your telephone line. I don't recommend one-way cable modem service if you have two-way alternatives, but if you need fast download speed (and who doesn't?) and you can't get a two-way broadband service installed at your location, one-way cable Internet service may be a satisfactory replacement for your existing dial-up service.

Two-Way Cable Service

Two-way cable modem service, on the other hand, is pure broadband Internet service: The coaxial cable running into your home connects to a high-performance fiber-optic network that carries many more TV channels than all-coax networks can carry and has enough bandwidth to handle Internet traffic in both directions. Two-way cable modems don't use your telephone line, so you can surf the Web, chat with your friends, and watch cable TV, all at the same time. Figure 2.1 compares one-way and two-way cable modem operation.

Note

Broadband Internet—Refers to Internet access that receives data at more than 500Kbps, although some discussions of broadband include ISDN (which can run at up to 128Kbps).

Bandwidth—Technically refers to the use of a single physical line to carry multiple frequencies, but is also commonly used to refer to the amount of data that a network connection can carry in a given amount of time, normally expressed in bits per second (bps).

Adding Cable Internet Service to a Cable TV Network

Before you can get cable Internet service at home, be it one or two-way, your friendly cable TV company has to make some major investments to make it possible.

Your cable TV operator needs to work with an ISP (Internet service provider) to bring Internet service to its cable network. The two biggest national players are Excite@Home and RoadRunner, but your cable TV operator might choose another vendor. The vendor installs a router to connect the cable TV network to the Internet, installs the hardware necessary to transmit data from the Internet to the cable TV network, and installs modems for use with one-way cable modem service.

FIGURE 2.1

Both two-way and one-way cable Internet service use the CATV network for received (downloaded) data. Two-way service (top) also sends (uploads) data through the same fiber-optic lines, while one-way service (bottom) uses a modem and your telephone line for uploads.

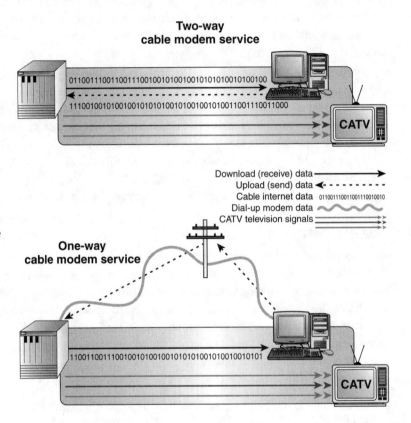

As you learned earlier in this chapter, two-way cable modem service is much better in terms of speed and convenience than one-way service, but the traditional all-coaxial cable TV network can't work in two-way mode.

Fiber-optic cables are necessary for two-way cable modem service as well as digital cable TV, so if your cable TV company offers digital service, ask them if they offer two-way cable modem service now or whether they plan to offer it in the future.

When a cable TV network is upgraded to provide digital service (more than 100 channels, CD-quality music stations, and similar high-end features), part of the upgrade process involves pulling down the network of coaxial cables and replacing them with fiber-optic cables. The only place that coaxial cable continues to be used is in the individual cable drop to your home.

Note Because fiber-optic cable TV networks still use coaxial cable to connect the network to individual homes and businesses, this type of cable TV connection is often called a *hybrid* fiber-optic/coaxial network.

How Cable Modems Connect to Your Computer

Depending on which type of cable modem service your cable TV operator provides, your computer can be connected to a cable modem in several different ways:

- Two-way service usually requires a type of add-on card called a 10BaseT Ethernet *Network Interface Card (NIC)*. Some recent computers have a built-in Ethernet port, negating the need for a separate NIC.

 Tip Most stores no longer carry 10BaseT Ethernet NICs, but a Fast Ethernet 10/100 NIC available at stores for $20–$40 can be used as either a 10BaseT Ethernet or a Fast Ethernet card.

- Some two-way services can use an external Ethernet to a USB port adapter so that you won't need to open your computer to install a NIC.

- Some of the latest cable modems can also connect directly to your computer's USB port, eliminating the need for any type of Ethernet adapter.

- A few two-way cable modem systems may also use a PCI card, which fits into an internal expansion slot.

- One-way cable modem service might use either a proprietary cable modem add-in card which fits into a PCI slot and contains both cable modem and analog modem connections or a 10BaseT Ethernet NIC to connect to an external cable modem.

- A one-way cable modem service that uses an external cable modem also requires your computer to have a serial port to connect to an analog modem for making the dial-up connection and for sending page requests and e-mail.

If you decide to create a home network for sharing your cable Internet service, you might need an additional network card for the connection to the home network. See Chapter 18, "Setting Up a Home Network for Sharing Your Internet Connection," for details.

You can get the full details about making sure your computer is ready for cable modem service in Chapter 3, "Making Sure You're Ready for Cable Internet Service."

Note

Bundled one-way cable modems include an internal analog modem. *Unbundled* one-way cable modems require the use of a standard external modem. If you have a choice of modem types with a one-way service, go with the bundled variety—it's easier to share the connection with other users in a home or small-office network.

Regardless of the type of service (two-way or one-way) and cable modem you use, if you also have cable TV, part of the installation typically includes a splitter (see Figures 2.2 and 2.3) to prevent cable modem signals from interfering with cable TV reception. In some cases, you may get a separate cable for the cable Internet service, and in such cases a filter may be installed on the new cable to prevent it from being used for cable TV service.

Figure 2.2 compares two-way cable modem connections that use a NIC and a USB port, and Figure 2.3 compares one-way cable modem connections that use a bundled analog modem and those that use a separate (unbundled) analog modem.

FIGURE 2.2

If you have a 10BaseT or 10/100 Ethernet card, you can connect directly to most cable modems; some also permit a direct connection with your USB port (top). If your cable modem requires an Ethernet connection, but you have no slot available for an Ethernet card, you can use a USB Ethernet adapter to connect to your cable modem (bottom).

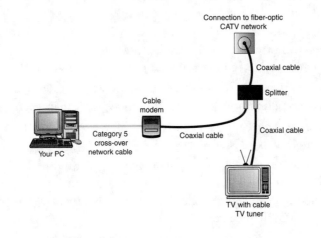

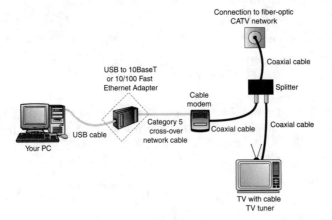

Some one-way cable modem services use an internal cable modem rather than the external cable modem (see Figure 2.3), but this is not common anymore.

FIGURE 2.3

Some one-way cable Internet connections require an external analog modem to handle page requests, e-mail, and uploads (top), whereas others use a cable modem with a built-in analog modem (bottom).

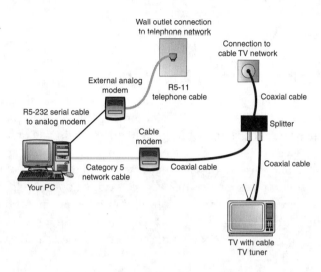

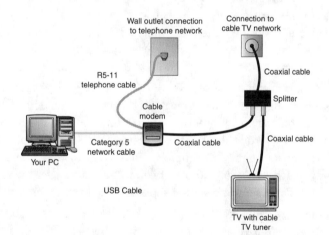

Speeds of Cable Modem Service

Theoretically (which means, in plain English, "Don't count on it!"), cable modem service should allow downloads as fast as 1.5Mbps. This is the figure often used in comparisons that call cable modem service "50 times faster than a dial-up (analog) modem." This is the top speed that the hardware can support, but in reality, a lot of other factors will prevent your cable modem from hitting speeds this fast. These factors include the following:

■ Built-in delays as data is transmitted between your system

■ The many hops required to get your page requests to the remote computer (and back again)

■ Local network congestion

Your Friendly (?) Neighborhood Network

In some cases, the earlier you decide to opt for cable modem service in a new area, the faster the service you'll have, at least for awhile. This is why: cable modem users in the same neighborhood share bandwidth. In other words, you and your neighbors are sharing the speed potential of the cable modem service whenever more than one user is connected. As your neighborhood gets more and more users of the same cable modem service, performance can drop, especially at peak usage times of the day. A well-designed cable modem service will minimize the impact on your speed, but cyber "traffic jams" can occur if everybody on a particular part of a cable modem network is online at the same time checking movie listings, stock exchange results, or anything else.

Traffic slowdowns can also be caused by multiple users trying to reach the same Web site. Many cable modem service providers use *caching servers* (which retain a copy of recently downloaded data) to enable multiple users of their service to share a single page. Figure 2.4 shows you how caching servers (also called *proxy servers)* work to reduce Internet traffic and give you the data you want—fast.

Do you need to worry about sharing your cable modem connection with other users, as Figure 2.4 illustrates? Not much, especially if your cable modem complies with the Data Over Cable Systems Interface Specification (DOCSIS) standard, which is supported by most two-way cable modem systems. DOCSIS cable modems use encrypted data transfer to prevent simple snooping by nosy neighbors. In other words, although each user's cable Internet connection flows over the same fiber-optic cable, each user's data is scrambled in a different way from other users.

What about one-way cable modems? Many of these older systems don't use encryption, so cable Internet providers must use other methods, such as disabling the features built into your Internet connection for file sharing with other users on your home network, to help protect your system.

However, whether you have a two-way or one-way system, especially if you use File and Print Sharing (to allow other users at home or the office to share your drives or printers), you have a potential security risk.

FIGURE 2.4

Caching servers (bottom) allow multiple users to view the same page and reduce traffic o and from the Internet by fetching a Web page just once. Cable Internet systems without caching servers (top) request the page once for every user, increasing traffic to popular pages and slowing down access for everyone.

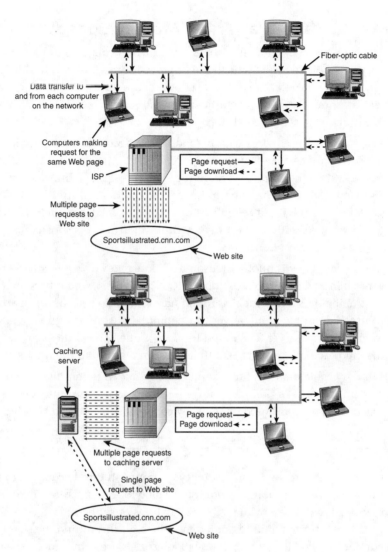

To learn how to protect your system against intruders, see Chapter 13, "Firewalls and Your PC." To learn how to protect your system against computer viruses, worms, and Trojan Horse programs, see Chapter 14, "Stopping Computer Viruses."

Two-Way Versus One-Way Cable Modem Speeds

Although two-way cable modems should theoretically run at higher speeds than one-way cable modems (due to the improved speed and bandwidth of fiber-optic versus coaxial cable), the differences in practice for downloading are minimal. Both services should give you overall performance of around 500Kbps, with bursts of much higher speeds (near 1Mbps) at times.

The real differences come with uploading page requests and e-mail, and with gaming performance. One-way cable modems send information at just 33.6Kbps maximum, and might drop to even lower speeds if telephone line quality isn't top-notch. Two-way cable modems can, in theory, send data just as quickly as they receive it (500Kbps or faster), but might be limited by some cable modem vendors to 128Kbps or 256Kbps. Nevertheless, a two-way cable modem is both faster for uploads and avoids using your phone line.

Online gameplay is another reason to choose two-way cable modems over their one-way siblings. Games such as *Tribes 2*, *Quake III Arena*, and others are popular online. Your ability to survive the first round has a lot to do with how fast your computer can send data to a game server (the computer hosting the game) and get data back from the game server. The round-trip rate is often called the *ping rate*, and the faster the ping rate, the closer to real-time you can respond to the moves of other players.

Two-way cable modems have a huge advantage in ping rate over one-way cable modems because of their advantage in how data is transmitted to the game server. The analog modems used by one-way cable modems have a very high *latency*.

Latency—The delay between when a signal is sent and received.

One-way cable modems have latency of around 100ms because of the time necessary to convert the digital signal into analog for transmission. Two-way cable modems have very low latency (around 10ms or so) because they don't need to convert signals from digital to analog form before transmitting the signal back to the gaming server. Although their download speeds are comparable, the sending advantage of two-way cable modems provides a big boost to online gameplay.

If you suddenly notice a big drop in online speed, you may be experiencing *packet loss*, which takes place when a data packet you send is not received at its destination. It can take your computer as long as two seconds to resend a lost packet. Very heavy traffic online can cause occasional packet loss, but sometimes the problem can be closer to home. Contact your cable Internet operator if slowdowns persist regardless of the site you visit or the time of day. The operator may need to check signal quality or readjust their head end equipment (which processes signals which run between your cable modem and the Internet).

Summary

Cable Internet service runs down the same cable which brings cable TV service to your home. You can have cable Internet service, even if you prefer not to have cable TV. Two-way cable Internet service uses the CATV network for both sending and receiving data, while one-way service uses a modem to upload data via the telephone line, just as with dial-up Internet service.

Most cable modems are external devices which connect to a 10BaseT or 10/100 Ethernet card, but some also connect via the USB port. Internal cable modems are also used by some providers, primarily for one-way service.

Traffic slowdowns can be caused in part by shared bandwidth and by heavy demand for a particular Web page. Proxy servers are used by cable Internet providers to speed up access to popular Web pages.

Most two-way cable modems are DOCSIS-certified, and have encryption features to prevent casual snooping by other cable modem users. However, this is no substitute for security features such firewalls or antivirus software. Two-way cable modems are superior for gaming because of their low latency, which leads to faster connections to gaming servers.

PART II

GETTING CABLE MODEM SERVICE

MAKING SURE YOU'RE READY FOR CABLE INTERNET SERVICE

CHAPTER HIGHLIGHTS:

- Making sure your computer's operating system is "cable-modem friendly"
- Making sure your computer has the hardware components it needs to support cable Internet service
- Discovering where you can connect your cable modem

3

Prerequisites for Any Cable Modem Connection

If you have decided that cable Internet service is the way to go, you need to make sure that you have the three basic elements needed to work with a cable modem:

- An operating system that's supported by your cable Internet provider
- A computer that's fast enough to run cable modem service
- A place to connect the cable modem

Note *Operating system*—The software which tells your computer what to do. Windows XP is an operating system, as is MacOS 9. Office XP, on the other hand, is an *application suite*, a group of application programs which work together to create and modify information. When you work with your computer's desktop icons or print a document, you are using the operating system. When you create a document or make a budget, you are using application software.

If you find that your computer needs a newer version of Windows or MacOS, more RAM memory or a faster processor, or a new card to connect a cable modem, you can upgrade your computer to make it capable of handling cable Internet service. However, if your computer is more than four years old and needs two or more changes to be compatible, the cost to make these changes may not be worthwhile. You may find it more cost-effective to buy a new computer at today's low prices.

Can Your Operating System Speak "Cable Modem"?

First, start with the operating system. Table 3.1 lists what the "Big Two" cable Internet service providers want you to have:

Table 3.1 Operating System Requirements for Major Cable Internet Service Providers (ISPs)

Cable Modem Provider	Windows Versions Supported	Mac OS Versions Supported
@Home	Windows 9x[1]	Mac OS 8.5
	Windows 2000	
	Windows Me	
	Windows NT 4.0	

Table 3.1   (continued)

Cable Modem Provider	Windows Versions Supported	MacOS Versions Supported
RoadRunner	Windows 95[2]	MacOS 8.6 through MacOS 9.x
	Windows 98	MacOS X[3]
	Windows NT 4.0[4]	
	Windows 2000	
	Windows Me	

1 Windows 95 or 98

2 "Best effort" support by RoadRunner because Microsoft no longer offers Windows 95 tele-phone support; Windows 98 or Me recommended

3 "Best Effort" support by RoadRunner

4 Requires that Service Pack 3 or above be installed; Service Pack 5 or above recommended

By the time you read this book, Windows XP should also be on the officially-approved list; because it is based on Windows 2000, it should not be difficult for cable Internet operators to support it. If you're already using Windows XP, contact your cable Internet operator to see if you need any special settings to use your computer with a particular cable Internet service.

If you have a choice of methods for connecting your cable modem to your computer, go with a PCI 10BaseT or 10/100 Ethernet card whenever possible. Ethernet cards have been around for a very long time and are well-supported by all modern operating systems. Internal cable modems may lack support in the latest operating systems, and USB support is inconsistent.

Learning What Operating System Your Computer Is Using

Although most recent PCs will have the right types of operating system and hardware to work with cable Internet service, you might still have some questions about the details of your operating system. To find out which version of Windows you use, click Start, Settings, Control Panel, and then double-click the System icon to open your System Properties sheet. By default, you should see the General tab, which displays the PC's current version of Windows (9x/Me/NT/2000/XP). See Figure 3.1 for a typical example.

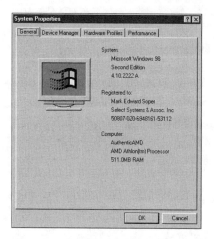

If you're using NT 4.0, keep in mind that some cable Internet providers won't support early releases of Windows NT 4.0. To determine the exact release of NT 4.0 you're using, log in as Administrator or as someone with Power User rights, and click Start, Administrative Tools (common), Windows NT Diagnostics. The Version tab displays the version of the service pack (if any) that is installed on your system.

The latest (and last) service pack for Windows NT 4.0 is Service Pack 6a. If you need to install a service pack to make Windows NT 4.0 compliant with a particular cable Internet service, you can download or order the service pack on CD-ROM from the following Web page: www.microsoft.com/ntserver/nts/downloads/recommended/SP6/allSP6.asp.

If you are a Mac or iMac user, click the desktop to make it active, and then click the Apple menu shown at the top-left corner of your screen. Select About This Computer to display the MacOS version number.

Handling Unsupported Operating Systems

What should you do if you find out that your cable Internet provider's compatibility lists aren't displaying your new PC's operating system?

If you have a new Windows PC with Windows XP pre-installed, contact your cable Internet provider to see if you should expect any problems in using your new system with a cable modem. Chances are you will be fine because Windows XP is based on Windows 2000, and most service providers do support Windows 2000. Macs and iMacs are currently preinstalled with both MacOS 9 and MacOS X, so you can boot the system with MacOS 9 when you want to go online if your cable Internet provider doesn't yet support MacOS X.

If you're planning to upgrade to Windows XP and your cable Internet provider won't be supporting it until later, install it as a *dual-boot* operating system. A dual-boot installation means that Windows XP will be installed to an unused portion of your hard disk or to a separate hard disk. If your current hard disk has at least 5GB of empty space, you have more than enough room to install Windows XP and still keep your current version of Windows.

For more information about installing Windows XP, see *Special Edition Using Windows XP Home Edition* or *Special Edition Using Windows XP Professional*. Both books are written by well-respected authors, Robert Coward and Brian Knittel. Both are published by Que.

As noted previously, MacOS X is already configured as a dual-boot operating system.

Making Sure Your Computer Has the Correct On-Board Hardware

After you find out if your computer's operating system will work with your cable Internet service, it's time to find out whether you have a fast enough processor, enough memory, and enough disk space to handle the cable Internet connection.

First, Tables 3.2 and 3.3 list the hardware recommendations from @Home and RoadRunner, the "Big Two" cable Internet providers. Only the recommended values are listed. You won't be happy with the service if your system barely meets the minimums, and hard disk and memory upgrades (the most common shortcomings of older systems) are inexpensive to perform these days.

Table 3.2 Recommended Hardware for Windows-Based Systems

	RoadRunner	@Home
Processor	Pentium-class 166 MHz or faster	Pentium-class 200MHz or faster
Memory (RAM)	64MB or more[1]	64MB or more[1]
Free Hard Drive Space	50MB	56MB
Other Hardware	CD-ROM drive[2]; 800×600 (SVGA) or higher graphics with 16-bit color or higher; sound card with speakers	CD-ROM drive[2]; 800×600 (SVGA) or higher graphics with 16-bit color or higher; sound card with speakers

1 *Systems with a built-in video adapter borrow up to 11MB of your system RAM for video, reducing the amount of RAM available to your operating system. If your monitor plugs into your computer's motherboard instead of into a separate card, you might want to upgrade to 128MB RAM or more.*

2 *CD-RW and DVD drives also function as CD-ROM drives.*

How can you find out what equipment you have on-board? The General tab in Windows (refer to Figure 3.1) displays the amount of RAM you have. To display the resolution and color settings of your Windows system, open the Display icon in Control Panel (or right-click the desktop and select Properties). Click the Settings tab to see the screen resolution and color settings you're using. See Figure 3.2, and compare them to the recommendations in Table 3.2. If you need to adjust the number of colors onscreen or the resolution, use the slider controls to adjust the settings and reboot if required.

FIGURE 3.2

This computer is set to use 16-bit color (65.536 colors) and a resolution of 800 pixels (horizontal) by 600 pixels (vertical). These settings will allow most Web pages to be viewed without horizontal scrolling.

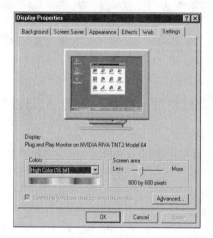

To determine the amount of free hard disk space you have on a Windows PC, open the Windows Explorer through your Start menu, right-click the C: drive icon, and select Properties (see Figure 3.3). Compare the value for free space to the Free Hard Drive space requirements in Table 3.2.

If you need more hard drive space and your system features a Disk Cleanup button, click it to remove files which take up space, but are not needed. Otherwise, you may need to remove programs you don't use or install a larger hard drive.

Table 3.3 lists hardware requirements for Mac-based systems.

Table 3.3   Recommended Hardware for Mac and iMac Systems

	RoadRunner	@Home
Processor	Power PC 75MHz or faster	Power PC 603 200MHz processor or faster
Memory (RAM)	64MB or more	32MB
Free Hard Drive Space	50MB	56MB

Table 3.3   (continued)

	RoadRunner	@Home
Other Hardware	CD-ROM drive[1]; 16-bit color graphics; sound card with speakerss	CD-ROM drive; 16-bit color graphics; sound card with speakers

1 CD-RW and DVD drives also function as CD-ROM drives.

FIGURE 3.3

This computer has more than 980MB of free disk space, which is far more than enough for the software used by typical Cable Internet connection services. However, music, media, and program downloads could use up this space in a hurry.

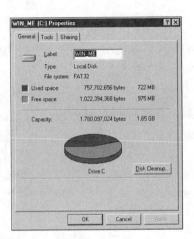

If you don't have the documentation for your Mac handy, you can determine the needed details about your computer by using the following methods:

- MacOS version and total RAM—Check the Applications menu (upper right corner) and verify that you are using the Finder. Go to the Apple Menu and click About This Computer... or About This Macintosh ...

- Speed and type of CPU—Download and run the free Gauge PRO program to determine this information if your documentation doesn't list this information. Get it from the following Web site: www.versiontracker.com/moreinfo.fcgi?id=7313

- Display settings (color depth and resolution)—Open the Monitors Control Panel

- Hard disk size and free space—Click the drive's icon in Finder, go to the File menu and select Get Info

If you bought your computer new in 1998 or later, your system should exceed these recommendations by a wide margin. However, if you're trying to use an older PC as your cable Internet connection, you could run into problems.

If you'd like a one-stop solution to determining the on-board hardware and operating system, you can obtain and run a hardware reporting program. Many are available for Windows and Mac systems. In Tables 3.4 and 3.5, you'll find a listing of some of the more popular options that exist. (This listing is only a small sampling and is in no way comprehensive.)

Table 3.4 lists sources for Windows reporting programs.

Table 3.4 Windows Hardware Reporting Programs

Program Name	Source	Web Site	Program Type
Norton System Information	Included in Norton Utilities or Norton System Works	www.symantec.com	Sold at retail
SiSoft Sandra	Download from vendor	www.sisoftware.demon.co.uk/ sandra/	Standard vesion free for personal use; Professional version with additional options also available for sale
Belarc Advisor	Download from vendor	www.belarc.com (click Download/Try Link)	Demo version of corporate support tool

Table 3.5 lists sources for Mac OS-compatible reporting tools.

Table 3.5 Mac Operating System Hardware Reporting Programs

Program Name	Source	Web Site	Program Type
Norton System Information	Included in Norton Utilities or Norton System Works for Macintosh	www.symantec.com	Sold at retail
TattleTech 2.8x	Download from vendor	www.users.qwest.net/ ~mjohn5/index.htm	Shareware

If you discover that your older Windows-based PC needs a processor, memory, or other upgrade to be compatible with cable Internet service, get on the fun, painless road to a better system by picking up a copy of Que's *TechTV's Upgrading Your PC* by Mark Soper with Patrick Norton.

If you're on a budget, check out the www.scrounge.org Web site for tips on how to get by with low-cost computer hardware and where to find it.

Connecting Your Cable Modem: I/O Slots and Ports

The last step you need to take to make sure your system is ready for cable Internet service is to make sure you have somewhere to attach the cable modem. Depending on the cable Internet vendor and service type (one-way or two-way), you will need the following connections, as listed in Table 3.6.

Table 3.6   Cable Modem Connections

Cable Modem Service Type	Modem Type	External Slot	Internal Connector
One-Way	Internal	N/A	ISA[1]
	External	Serial (COM) Port and USB or 10BaseT Ethernet[2]	N/A
Two-Way	Internal	N/A	PCI
	External	USB or 10BaseT Ethernet[2]	N/A

1 ISA-based cable modems also contain a built-in analog modem for uploading through the telephone line.

2 Some vendors can use the USB port for a direct connection to the cable modem, whereas others will require you to use a USB-to-Ethernet adapter or install an internal Ethernet card, depending on the cable modem provided. You can use a 10/100 Ethernet card in place of a 10BaseT Ethernet card.

What do these external connectors look like? Figure 3.4 shows the back panel of a system that has all three connectors built-in.

You need a serial (COM) port only if you have one-way cable Internet service using a separate analog modem, but you need a USB or Ethernet port with either one-way or two-way cable Internet service unless your service uses an internal cable modem.

Adding an Ethernet Card

If you don't have USB ports, or if you are using Windows 95 or Windows NT 4.0 (which don't support USB ports), you will need to install an Ethernet card inside your computer to connect to your external cable modem. You might also prefer to use an Ethernet card with newer versions of Windows, especially if you attach other devices to your USB ports, such as printers, Web cameras, keyboards, mice, or scanners.

FIGURE 3.4

This recent computer has a built-in Ethernet port as well as the USB and serial (COM) ports that are common on other systems built since about 1998.

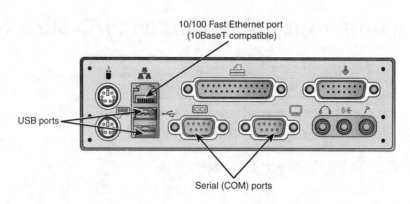

10/100 Fast Ethernet port
(10BaseT compatible)

USB ports

Serial (COM) ports

Note

Regardless of your available ports, if it's an option, I recommend that you use an Ethernet card. Although the maximum speed of a current USB port (USB 1.1) is 12Mbps, which is more than fast enough to support a cable modem, the effective speed of the port is slower if you attach other USB devices. With an Ethernet card, you know what kind of performance to expect.

Although your cable Internet provider can install an Ethernet card for you for an additional charge of up to $50, you can save money and have your choice of cards if you do it yourself. Ethernet cards come in several types, as listed in Table 3.7, but only a couple are suitable for use with a cable modem.

Table 3.7 Types of Ethernet Cards and Their Suitability to Cable Modem Service

Ethernet Card Type	Connector Type	Speed	Cable Modem Compatible?	Reason
10Base2 (Thin Ethernet)	Round coax	10Mbps	No	Wrong BNC connector
10Base5 (Thick Ethernet)	15-pin	10Mbps	No	Wrong connector
10BaseT Ethernet	RJ-45	10Mbps	Yes	Correct speed and connector
100BaseTX (Fast Ethernet)	RJ-45	100Mbps	No	Wrong speed
10/100 Ethernet	RJ-45	10Mbps/ 100Mbps	Yes	Adjusts to speed of cable modem; has correct connector

Although most computer stores and departments sell only Ethernet 10/100 cards today, older cards might still be available as surplus or giveaway materials from companies that have sent obsolete hardware home with employees or made donations to schools, churches, or charities. Figure 3.5 compares the different port types listed in Table 3.7 so you can make sure you avoid cards that won't work.

FIGURE 3.5

Typical Ethernet cards with both RJ-45 ports and obsolete connector types. Avoid cards that have only BNC or 15-pin connectors because they don't work with cable modems.

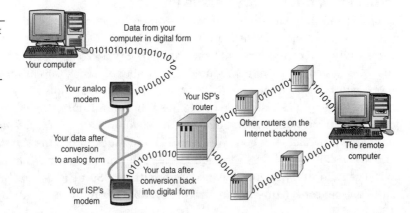

The RJ-45 connectors shown in Figures 3.4 and 3.5 are a bit larger than the RJ-11 connectors used by telephone cabling. The type of cable used with the RJ-45 connector is called Category 5 ("Cat 5") cabling, which is similar to (but thicker than) telephone cabling. Like telephone cable, Cat 5 cable has no metallic shielding; both use groups of paired wires twisted together for better operation. This type of cabling is also called UTP (unshielded twisted-pair); because there is no metal mesh around the data cables, you need to avoid routing the cables near interference sources such as electric motors, cell phone base stations, and alarm systems.

Figure 3.6 compares phone and Cat 5 network cables.

FIGURE 3.6

Telephone cable (left) compared to Cat 5 Ethernet network cable (right).

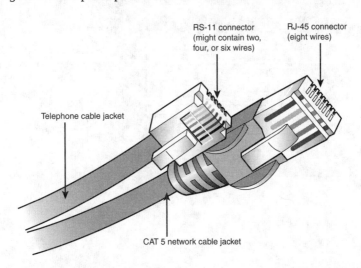

Note	Apple's iMac, G3, and G4 computers all have built-in 10BaseT or 10/100 Ethernet ports, so nothing needs to be added to make them ready to attach to a two-way cable modem.

Which to Choose: ISA Versus PCI Cards

From 1984 until the late 1990s, most PC-compatible computers had several slots that were part of a standard called *ISA* (see Figure 3.7). As Figure 3.5 shows you, Ethernet cards with RJ-45 connectors will work with either type of expansion slot. However, the latest systems have either reduced the number of ISA slots to just one or done away with ISA slots altogether (MACs have never used ISA slots). The standard slot type that replaced ISA is known as *PCI* (also shown in Figure 3.5). PCI offers faster data throughput than ISA and also has the advantage of being *plug-and-play* compatible. It is available in both Windows PCs and Macs, and is the standard type of expansion slot used today. Although ISA Ethernet cards are limited to the 10Mbps speed of 10BaseT, PCI network cards can be either 10BaseT (older cards) or 10/100 Fast Ethernet cards (current store inventory), able to run at either 10Mbps or 100Mbps.

Note	*ISA*—Industry Standard Architecture
	PCI—Peripheral Component Interconnect
	plug-and-play—Cards that are automatically configured with the help of the operating system or the computer, rather than by the user.

Figure 3.7
Although many recent systems still have one or two ISA slots on-board, PCI slots are faster and should be used for most upgrades, including network cards.

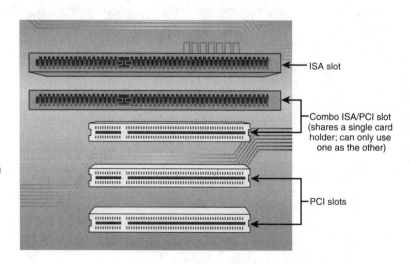

Installing an Ethernet Card

If you need to install an Ethernet card, you need the following:

- An open expansion slot in your PC
- A 10/100 Ethernet (preferred) or 10BaseT Ethernet card to match the slot type
- A driver disk or CD-ROM with drivers for your operating system (should be provided with the card or available for download through the card manufacturer's Web site)

After you have these items, follow this procedure:

1. Shut down your system.
2. Disconnect the power cable from the outlet to cut all power to the system.
3. Use ESD protection equipment, such as a wrist strap, and work mat if available (available at most electronics shops, such as Radio Shack).
4. Open your computer and locate an unused slot (refer to Figure 3.7)
5. Remove the slot cover at the rear of the case that lines up with the empty slot; save the screw for use in reattaching the new card (see Figure 3.8).
6. Insert the Ethernet card into the slot (Figure 3.8).
7. Secure the Ethernet card into place with the screw removed from the slot cover (Figure 3.8).
8. Close the case and plug the power cord into the computer.
9. Restart the computer.
10. Install drivers when prompted. You will also need to provide your Windows CD-ROM for some network software components.
11. Use your new network card.

These instructions assume that you are using a plug-and-play Ethernet card. The settings needed on plug-and-play cards are set by the computer and by Windows.

All PCI cards are plug-and-play, but most ISA cards are not. Because installing a non-plug-and-play card is extremely difficult, avoid problems by using your system's PCI slots.

Now, your system is ready for the installation of a cable modem.

Before you install your cable modem, you should install personal firewall software as discussed in Chapter 13, "Firewalls and Your PC".

FIGURE 3.8

Removing the screw which secures the slot cover (top). Inserting the Ethernet card into the empty PCI slot and then securing it with the screw removed from the slot cover (bottom).

Screw covering slot cover

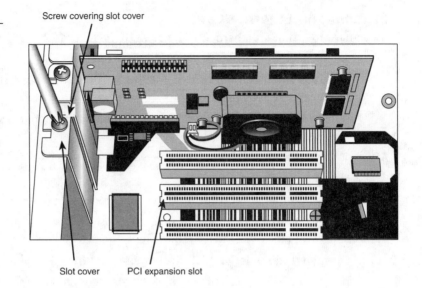

Slot cover   PCI expansion slot

Screw securing card bracket

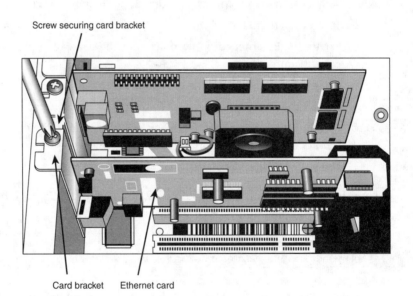

Card bracket   Ethernet card

Summary

Before you order cable Internet service, you should verify that your computer uses an operating system that is supported by the cable Internet service provider. You should also make sure your system has a fast enough processor, enough RAM, and enough free hard disk space to support cable Internet service. Some of this information can be gathered from various operating-system utilities or from the original purchase invoice. If necessary, you can run various system analysis programs to determine your system's hardware.

While most MacOS users already have an on-board Ethernet port, most Windows PC users will need to install an Ethernet card. While a 10BaseT Ethernet card will work, a 10/100 Ethernet card is easier to find new in stores. The process of installing the card requires that you open your system, but modern plug-and-play cards handle the configuration details for you when the card is installed and you restart your system.

ORDERING AND INSTALLING CABLE MODEM SERVICE

CHAPTER HIGHLIGHTS:

- What cable Internet service types and options you might be offered
- What to expect during the installation if you've never had cable TV/Internet service before
- What will change about your existing cable TV installation if you add cable Internet service
- How to make sure your cable Internet service is working before the installer leaves

Service Types and Options

As you know from Chapter 2, "What Is a Cable Modem?," you have two major cable Internet service options:

- One-way service
- Two-way service

The cable Internet operator's cable network configuration determines whether you get one-way or two-way service. If you have two-way service, you might be offered additional options, including:

- Having many IP addresses to have
- Buying or leasing your cable modem

What Is an IP Address, and Why Would I Get More Than One?

The Internet uses a network protocol called TCP/IP to manage Internet connections by all computers and other devices that connect to the Internet.

Note

Network protocol—A series of rules that allow different types of computers to communicate with each other over a network.

Transport Control Protocol/Internet Protocol (TCP/IP)—A suite, or collection, of related network protocols that are used both for Internet and for local area networking.

Each device on the Internet must have a unique IP address to identify it. Currently, IP addresses use four groups of numbers separated by periods, each group ranging from 0–254. Your computer will be assigned an IP address by your cable Internet provider during installation. An IP address looks like this:

192.168.2.134

One common question you might be asking if you have more than one computer at home is whether you need an additional IP address for each computer you want to provide Internet access for. Generally speaking, you don't. Although cable Internet operators would like you to believe that each computer needs its own IP address, you can use a variety of methods covered in Part VI, "Sharing Your Cable Modem Service," to provide Internet access with a single IP address. Not only is this less expensive than paying an extra $5 or so a month for each additional computer, but it's also safer because these other sharing methods discussed in Part VI can provide protection for your network.

Note You might need more than one IP address if you want to use a computer on your home network to connect to your office network over a type of connection called a VPN (virtual private network). The computer using a VPN connection needs a routeable IP address (one which is directly accessible from the Internet), and computers on a home network use non-routeable IP addresses that can't be accessed directly from the Internet.

Not all cable Internet service providers support VPN connections, so if your office network can be accessed through a VPN and you want to use this feature to work from home, be sure to check with your cable Internet provider to see if your cable Internet connection permits this.

For details about protecting your computers, see Part V, "Securing Your Cable Modem Service."

You should wait until your cable Internet service is installed and is working for a few days before you worry about sharing it. Because some cable Internet providers officially frown on sharing, there's no need to discuss the issue with your installer.

Buy or Lease Your Cable Modem?

I've had cable Internet service for about a year now, and when I ordered my service, this was a no-brainer decision. I leased my modem for the following reasons:

- At the time, cable modems cost $300 or more and were not available at retail stores.
- The monthly lease was just $10 and the cable Internet company was responsible for repairs if anything happened.
- I wasn't sure I'd like the service well enough to keep it long enough to make buying the cable modem worthwhile.
- Many cable Internet providers' services weren't compliant with Data Over Cable Service Interface Standard (DOCSIS), meaning that a cable modem bought for one service might not work with another service.

A year later, the cable modem landscape has changed, and I've changed my opinion. This is why:

- Cable modems are now widely available from vendors such as Best Buy, Radio Shack, and others for less than $200. Some vendors such as Toshiba are even advertising cable modems on TV!
- Some cable Internet service providers even offer a self-install option if you already have cable TV from that provider's local cable TV partner.

■ As one-way services are phased out and replaced with DOCSIS-compliant two-way service, the odds are better than ever that if you move and choose cable Internet service at your new address, your cable modem will also be welcome.

■ Cable Internet service has proven itself to be fast and reliable.

If you plan to keep your cable modem service for at least 18 months or longer, it now makes abundant sense to buy a cable modem if the provider will support it and if the cable modem is DOCSIS-compliant.

Avoid buying internal cable modems. Although some of these products might also be DOCSIS-compliant, they're harder to share with other users and use up an expansion slot inside your computer.

Don't buy a one-way cable modem unless it can also be used with two-way service in the future and is DOCSIS-compliant.

Also, don't buy a self-install kit separately from your cable modem unless your cable modem doesn't include the parts you need. Some cable modems provide everything needed for a self-install setup.

To avoid finger-pointing in case of problems, make sure the cable modem you want to buy is exactly the same model as those supported by your cable Internet provider. You might even want to buy your cable modem from your provider if the price is reasonable.

Your Pre-Installation Checklist

After your family or small office finds out that you are planning to order cable Internet service, you'll feel like Santa Claus, ready to bestow fast, always-on Internet access to your home or office mates. Just as Saint Nicholas uses a list and checks it twice to make sure of those who are naughty and nice, you should also have a list to make sure you're ready when the installer shows up.

Before you place your order:

___ Decide where the computer you want to connect to the cable modem will be located; the installer will run coaxial cable to that location. If you live in an apartment, check with the building management for suitable locations, especially if you don't already have cable TV service.

___ Upgrade your computer to exceed the recommended requirements for cable Internet service (see Chapter 3, "Making Sure You're Ready for Cable Internet Service"). If your computer can't be upgraded economically, buy a replacement; any computer available in retail stores will have more than enough punch for use with cable Internet service.

During your ordering process:

___ Decide if the computer will be in a different room from your existing cable TV service, find out if the installer can pull the wire through the wall and if that requires an additional charge.

___ Ask about installation specials, even if the operator doesn't mention them. Remember to play rival cable Internet providers against each other to get the best deal.

___ Ask about discounts for bundled Internet/cable TV service or bundled Internet/cable TV/digital phone service if available.

___ If you're planning to provide the cable modem yourself, find out what brands and models will work with the service before you buy one. Some vendors will support any DOCSIS-compliant cable modem, but others have a preferred list, and still others insist you use their equipment.

___ If your computer doesn't have an Ethernet network card or connection, find out if your cable modem provider will supply it, or if you need to get your own. Which models are recommended or required? How much does it cost if you let the provider install it? Can you use a USB connection or a USB/Ethernet adapter instead? (I recommend using an Ethernet card and Ethernet-compatible cable modem whenever possible).

___ Record the expected time and cost of the installation.

Before the installer shows up, make sure your computer is ready:

___ On a Windows system, run the hard disk error-checking utility (called ScanDisk on some versions of Windows) to test your drives for errors; fix any errors reported. Many technicians run ScanDisk or the equivalent as part of the installation process. If disk errors are reported, some techs won't finish the job, or might make you sign a waiver.

To check your hard drive for errors with ScanDisk, open Windows Explorer, right-click your drive (usually C:) and select Properties, click Tools, and click Error-Checking.

___ Check the Windows Device Manager to see if all your hardware is working correctly. Right-click My Computer, select Properties, and click the Device Manager tab; if you use Windows 2000 or XP, click the Hardware tab, and then click the Device Manager button. If you see hardware marked with a yellow exclamation point (!), the hardware is not working correctly. Some technicians will also make you sign a waiver, or will not finish the installation if these problems aren't corrected.

To find out what's wrong with hardware marked with a yellow exclamation mark, click the device and select Properties. The General tab provides a general description of the problem, which often indicates a driver problem of some kind. Use the Drivers tab to reinstall or update the driver, and the Resources tab to solve a problem with a conflict-ing device.

Installing Cable Internet Service

Depending on whether you're getting brand-new cable service (Internet or Internet plus cable TV) or adding cable Internet service to an existing cable TV installation, the process varies a bit. This section covers both processes, so you will know what to expect.

Installing New Cable Service

When the cable installer arrives at your home or business for the first time, here's what you can expect to happen:

- A coaxial cable tapline will be dropped from the neighborhood cable running by your location to the nearest part of your building.
- The cable will be attached to your electrical box for grounding.
- The installer will put a small hole in your wall for the coaxial cable (and close it up, hopefully, with a cover).
- If you are also getting cable TV service, a splitter must be installed to prevent interference between cable TV and cable Internet equipment.
- Coaxial cables are run from the splitter to the TV/set top box (for cable TV) and to the location for the cable modem.
- The cable modem will be attached to the coaxial cable and turned on. This allows the cable modem to synchronize with the network (a process that can take anywhere from a minute or two to a half an hour). During the synchro-nizing process, the cable modem detects the cable Internet signals and adjusts itself to receive them. Until this process is complete, you can't connect to the Internet.
- While the cable modem is synchronizing, the installer runs the setup pro-gram or manually configures your computer for cable modem service.

See Chapter 19, "Troubleshooting Your Connection to the Internet," for the procedure for recording your computer's Internet configuration.

■ The installer connects your cable modem to your computer, and, after the cable modem is synchronized, should display a few Web pages.

■ After the service is working, you'll be asked to sign the work order and the installer will leave you alone with your fast, always-on Internet service.

The process can take up to two hours, depending mainly on how long it takes to run the cable (my home installation required the installer to drill through the foundation a couple of times) .

If you already have cable TV service, the process takes a lot less time.

Adding a Cable Modem to Your Existing Cable TV Service

If you already have cable TV service, the installation is easier. In fact, some cable Internet providers will even let you do it yourself! Here's a basic outline of the process of upgrading a cable TV installation to provide both cable TV and Internet service. Follow these steps if you perform the installation yourself:

■ The technician installs a splitter on the existing connection to prevent cable TV signals from interfering with cable Internet connections. This splitter should be installed as close as possible to where the cable enters the home, and no other splitters should be installed between the splitter and your cable modem.

■ The technician runs new coaxial cables from the splitter to the existing TV or set-top box connection and to the location for the cable modem.

■ The cable modem is attached to the coaxial cable and turned on. This allows the cable modem to synchronize with the network.

■ While the cable modem is synchronizing, the installer runs the setup program or manually configures your computer for cable modem service.

■ The installer connects your cable modem to your computer, and, after the cable modem is synchronized, should display a few Web pages.

■ After the service is working, you'll be asked to sign the work order and the installer will leave you alone with your fast, always-on Internet service.

Self-Install Cable Internet Service—Why Not?

If you've been inside your computer before, installed a few software programs, or worked with coaxial cable, you can probably handle self-installing your cable modem—if your cable Internet provider will let you and if you already have cable TV service from the provider's local cable TV partner. Follow the basic outline provided in the previous section if you opt for self-installation.

RoadRunner supports self-installation in some markets, and provides a setup kit for your use. Some Excite@Home markets offer a QuickStart installation kit and external cable modem through Radio Shack stores. Check with your cable Internet provider if you would like to perform a self-installation at your convenience.

Cable modems have two types of connections:

- Most external cable modems connect to an Ethernet (RJ-45) jack, which is sometimes built into a computer, but is more often added by means of an internal network card or a USB Ethernet adapter.

- Some cable modems attach directly to the USB connector found on the rear of recent systems.

Figure 4.1 shows you how to attach the Category 5 cable from the cable modem to your computer's built-in Ethernet port. Some newer PCs that run Windows have the port on the rear of the system, as seen in Figure 4.1; iMac computers have the Ethernet port on the side of the computer.

FIGURE 4.1

Lining up the Category 5 cable with the Ethernet port (top); the cable installed in the Ethernet port (bottom).

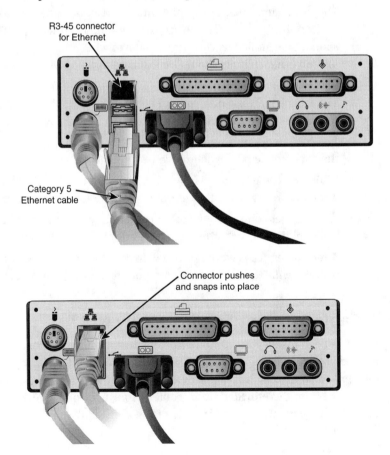

R3-45 connector for Ethernet

Category 5 Ethernet cable

Connector pushes and snaps into place

If your computer already has an Ethernet card, or if you installed an Ethernet card as described in Chapter 3, the RJ-45 connector is found at the rear of the computer. Connect the cable to the port as shown in Figure 4.1.

If your computer doesn't have a built-in Ethernet port and your cable modem requires you to connect it to an Ethernet port, you can do the following:

- Connect a USB Ethernet adapter to your computer's USB port

or

- Install a 10BaseT or 10/100 Ethernet card into an expansion slot (recommended)

Installing an Ethernet card (discussed in Chapter 3) provides you with faster computer performance, but connecting a USB Ethernet adapter is easier than opening your system.

The process of connecting a USB Ethernet adapter consists of doing the following:

1. Connecting the USB cable to the adapter
2. Connecting the adapter to your computer
3. Connecting the Category 5 Ethernet cable from the cable modem to the adapter

Most USB Ethernet adapters have a detachable USB cable. The thicker end of the USB cable is called a Type B USB connector, and attaches to the Type B port on the adapter, as shown in Figure 4.2.

FIGURE 4.2

Line up and connect the USB Type B cable connector with the Type B USB port on the adapter.

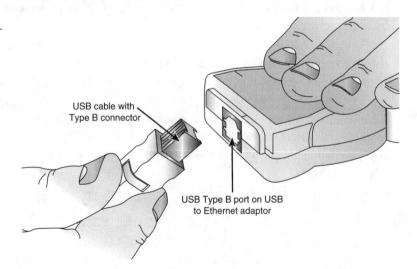

USB cable with Type B connector

USB Type B port on USB to Ethernet adaptor

After the USB cable is attached to the USB to Ethernet adapter, attach the other end of the cable to one of the Type A USB ports on the rear of the computer, as seen in Figure 4.3.

FIGURE 4.3

Line up the USB Type A cable connector with one of the Type A USB ports on your computer.

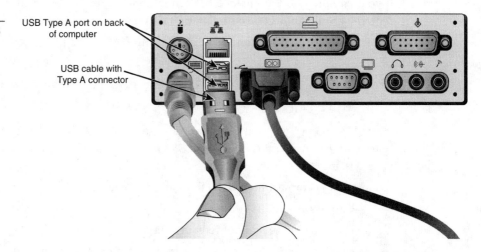

USB Type A port on back of computer

USB cable with Type A connector

After the USB Ethernet adapter is connected to the computer, you can attach the Category 5 Ethernet cable from the cable modem to the other side of the adapter, as shown in Figure 4.4.

After you attach the USB Ethernet adapter to your computer, insert the driver disk or CD-ROM as required to finish the installation; you will also need your Windows CD-ROM to provide network drivers.

If your cable modem connects directly to your computer's USB port, run the USB cable provided with the cable modem from the cable modem's Type B USB connector to the Type A USB connector on the rear of the computer. Refer to Figures 4.3 and 4.4 for examples of the ports and connectors.

After you have attached the cable modem to your system with any of the preceding methods and attached the coaxial cable from the cable network to the rear of the cable modem, you can use the setup software provided to complete the setup and signon process.

Tip

RoadRunner provides online step-by-step instructions with an animated tutorial at the following Web site: http://rrcorp.central.rr.com/cust/selfinstall.asp.

FIGURE 4.4

A Category 5
Ethernet cable
connected to the
RJ-45 Ethernet
port on the USB
to Ethernet
adapter (left).

Troubleshooting Your Initial Installation

After the installer (which could be you!) has connected the cable modem to the network and to your PC, turned on the cable modem and the PC, and installed the setup software, you should be able to view Web sites much faster than before (assuming that you're upgrading from a typical analog modem or ISDN).

Because Web browsers usually store pages you have already visited (if you previously had another type of Internet access), check your cable modem by visiting a site you haven't gone to before. Here are some sites you'll find useful to see how fast your connection is:

- Residential broadband gateway maker 2Wire has a bandwidth (speed) tester on their Web site at:

  www.2wire.com/services/bwm.html

- Corporate broadband Internet access provider Bandwidth Place's speed tester is available at:

  bandwidthplace.com/speedtest/

■ MSN's Internet Speed test is located at:

`tech.msn.com/internet/speedtest.asp`

■ CableModemHelp's Speed Test (which also features an archive of results for your ISP and a speed comparison) is located at:

`www.cablemodemhelp.com/speedtest/`

If you can't connect to any of these pages, check the following:

■ Make sure you have connected the cable modem to the coaxial cable and to your computer.

■ Make sure you use the cables provided with the cable modem or use a compatible replacement; some cable modems use a cross-over Ethernet cable instead of a normal cable. If you don't use the correct cable, the signals can't travel between the cable modem and your Ethernet card or connector.

■ Make sure the other end of the coaxial cable is connected to the splitter for CATV/cable modem connections.

■ If you're using a CATV/cable modem connection, see if you can receive cable TV; if you can't, you might have a bad splitter or the coaxial cable coming from the CATV network might not be properly attached to the splitter.

■ Check the signal lights on the cable modem; blinking or red lights can indicate problems (check the cable modem's manual for details) .

■ If you're using USB or a USB Ethernet adapter to connect to your cable modem and you have never used your computer's USB ports before, make sure they are working correctly if your computer uses Windows. You must have Windows 98 or newer versions, not Windows NT or Windows 95, for full USB support.

For more details, see Chapter 19, "Troubleshooting Your Connection to the Internet."

Note

Cat 5—A type of Ethernet network cable which can handle either 10BaseT (10Mpbs) or Fast Ethernet (100Mbps) traffic. Depending upon how it's installed, it might even be capable of handling Gigabit Ethernet (1000Mbps) traffic. Virtually all network cable sold in stores is Cat 5 or better. The maximum length between stations using Cat 5 cable is 328 feet (100 meters), so you can position your cable modem away from your computer by using a longer cable than the one supplied with the cable modem.

Cat 3—A now-obsolete type of Ethernet network cable which resembled phone cable, but uses the same RJ-45 connector used by Cat 5. Cat 3 can handle 10Mbps traffic only. You can replace Cat 3 with Cat 5.

Coaxial cable—The stiff cable with a threaded end and a center shaft that runs between your cable modem and the splitter. If you need to buy replacement cable, make sure you check the markings on the existing cable and buy the same type (usually RG6). RG58 and RG59 coaxial cables were designed for now-obsolete types of computer networks, and will not work with a cable modem.

Summary

In most cases, you need only one IP address; you can add additional IP addresses at a later date if you discover that your sharing solution won't support a specialized use such as gaming or VPN.

Using a pre-installation checklist helps ensure a smooth installation process, whether you have an installer put in your cable Internet service or you do it yourself. Brand-new cable service requires a service call, but adding cable Internet service to your existing cable TV service is a simpler process you may be able to do yourself.

Depending upon the exact model you choose, your external cable modem can be attached to a built-in Ethernet port or Ethernet card or to your computer's USB port. If you cannot install an Ethernet card and your cable modem lacks a USB port, you can install a USB Ethernet adapter to connect your cable modem to your PC.

After your cable Internet service (hardware and software) is installed, use one or more of the speed test pages available online to check the speed of your connection and verify your new service is working correctly.

If necessary, you can buy longer cables to replace the cables included with your cable modem or self-install kit. Longer cables allow you to position your cable modem away from your computer.

USING YOUR CABLE MODEM SERVICE

SETTING UP YOUR SOFTWARE TO USE YOUR CABLE MODEM

*C*HAPTER HIGHLIGHTS:

- How to change your Internet browser configuration for always-on service
- How to configure your e-mail client
- How to change the configuration of media players and other Internet software to take full advantage of your high-speed connection

Setting Your Browser Configuration

Depending on the company you have selected for cable Internet service, you might find that the cable modem installation program has installed a "new" or "improved" proprietary Web browser on your system that the vendor would like you to use. However, if you have been online for a while, you're probably accustomed to your existing Internet Explorer (IE) or Netscape browser. You probably also have lots of Favorites (IE) or bookmarks (Netscape) that you would like to keep using, now that your service runs faster than ever before.

> If you don't want the installer to add the new browser, just ask them to skip that step of the installation process and just adjust your existing browser configuration instead.

Fortunately, making sure your existing Web browser can work properly with your cable modem connection is simple. In many cases, you don't need to make any changes to your browser configuration. However, if your browser automatically dialed your Internet connection with your modem and you now have a two-way cable modem connection (which requires no telephone modem) or if your previous ISP used special proxy settings, you will need to make changes to allow a proper connection.

> *Proxy settings*—What are proxy settings, and how can they prevent your Web browser from connecting? Some ISPs, particularly those that use filtering software to block client access to objectionable Web sites, might use proxy servers, which are computers which sit between your PC and the Internet.
>
> When you request a page from the Internet, the proxy server receives the message and sends it along to the correct Internet site. On the way back to you, the Web page passes through the proxy server if the server's filters deem it acceptable, or block the page if the server's filters determine that the page's contents or the site are on the blocked list.
>
> Because different ISPs that use proxy servers won't use the same servers and most ISPs don't use proxy servers, leftover proxy server settings in your Web browser can prevent your browser from connecting with the Internet.

The following sections describe what to do to disable automatic dialing with your old telephone modem or to disable proxy-server settings that your former ISP might have used.

Changes to Make with Internet Explorer

If you have two-way cable Internet service, your modem is no longer needed to make a connection. To disable automatic dialing with Internet Explorer, open Internet Explorer and follow this procedure:

1. Start by clicking the Tools menu.

2. Click Internet Options. The Internet Options dialog box appears.

3. Click the Connections tab. This tab controls how your browser connects to the Internet.

4. Click the Never Dial a Connection option (see Figure 5.1).

FIGURE 5.1

Disabling automatic dialing in Internet Explorer.

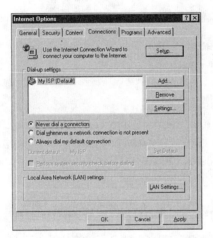

5. Click OK. Your browser will no longer try to connect using your old dial-up connection.

If you are using one-way cable modem service, don't change these settings; your cable modem is used only to receive data, and an analog (telephone) modem is used to send data and page requests. Therefore, you still dial a connection if you have a one-way cable modem.

Because your cable modem connects directly with the Internet, no proxy servers are used. To disable proxy-server settings with Internet Explorer, open IE and follow these steps:

1. Click the Tools menu to get started.

2. Click Internet Options. The Internet Options dialog box appears.

3. Click the Connections tab.

4. Click the LAN Settings button under the Local Area Network (LAN) Settings section.

5. Clear the Use a Proxy Server box (see Figure 5.2).

FIGURE 5.2

Disabling proxy servers in Internet Explorer.

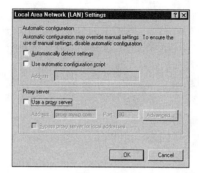

6. Click OK.

These changes make sure that your Internet Explorer browser "knows" that your cable Internet connection is always on and ready to go. When you open your IE browser after making these changes, you should immediately go to the default Web page for your browser.

Changes to Make with Netscape Navigator/Communicator

If you use a system with both Internet Explorer and another Web browser, the steps in the previous section for disabling automatic dialing will also do the trick for these browsers (such as Netscape Navigator).

If you prefer not to open Internet Explorer, or your system doesn't have IE installed, open the Internet icon in the Windows Control Panel and you will see the same Internet options menus shown in the previous section. Follow the same steps given there to turn off automatic dialing.

MacOS users should disable automatic dialing with the PPP Control Panel. Click the Options button and then the Connection tab. Clear the Connect Automatically When Starting TCP/IP Applications and click OK.

You need to use Netscape's own menus to disable proxy settings if they're no longer needed. After opening Communicator or Navigator, do the following:

1. Click the Edit menu to get started.

2. Click Preferences. This is the menu you use to change how Netscape operates.

3. Click the + (plus) sign (4.x) or down-arrow (6.x) next to Advanced. This opens up the Advanced menu so you can choose all the options.

4. Click Proxies.

5. Click Direct Connection to the Internet (see Figure 5.3).

6. Click OK.

FIGURE 5.3

Disabling proxy settings in Netscape Navigator/ Communicator.

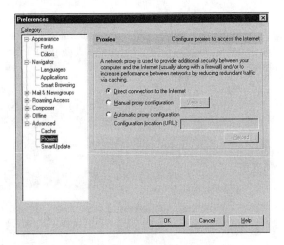

Configuring Your E-Mail Client

Many cable Internet providers use Microsoft Outlook Express as their default e-mail client (after all, it's integrated with Internet Explorer, and it's free!) and might configure Outlook Express for you. However, if you already use a different e-mail program, or if you use multiple e-mail addresses that you plan to keep active, you need the following information to manually configure your preferred e-mail client to handle your new e-mail account:

- Type of e-mail service (POP3, HTTP, IMAP)
- Name of incoming e-mail server
- Name of outgoing e-mail server
- Your username
- Your password

This information might be located on the paperwork you received with your cable Internet service, or you might need to pull it from the default e-mail client provided with your service.

In most cases, you can use a single e-mail client to handle all your e-mail accounts, including the account provided by your cable Internet provider and Web-based accounts such as Hotmail. This is how you use Microsoft Outlook Express to view or change settings for a current e-mail account or add a new account.

 Note Even if you are already using Outlook Express as your default e-mail client, you need to change e-mail server settings to allow you to send e-mail for other accounts you are using through your cable Internet service's e-mail servers rather than your former ISP's mail servers. If you are performing a self-install of your cable Internet service, you will need to add the cable Internet provider's e-mail settings to Outlook Express or any other e-mail client you prefer.

This is how to access the setup menus in Microsoft Outlook Express to allow you to view, add, or change e-mail configurations.

To add your cable Internet provider's e-mail account to Outlook Express:

1. Open Outlook Express.

2. Click the Tools menu to get started.

3. Click Accounts. Outlook Express can be used for e-mail, newsgroups, and directory services, so you may see a large list.

4. Click Mail.

5. To add a new account, click Add, Mail.

6. Enter your name as you want it to be displayed on the From field. Click Next.

7. Enter the e-mail address assigned you by your cable ISP. Click Next.

8. Select the e-mail server type (the default, POP3, is used by most cable Internet providers) and enter the incoming and outgoing mail server names used by your cable ISP. The server names might be the same, or might be different (see Figure 5.4). Click Next.

9. Enter the username and password assigned to you by your cable ISP. Select the option for Secure Password Authentication (SPA) only if your cable ISP requires you to use this to logon to your mail server. Click Next.

10. Click Finish. The Internet Accounts window will list your account under the mail tab when you're finished.

You probably have e-mail already waiting from any number of senders. To read it, click Tools, Send and Receive, and select the e-mail account you just configured.

FIGURE 5.4

FIGURE 5.4

Configuring
incoming and
outgoing e-mail
servers in
Outlook Express.

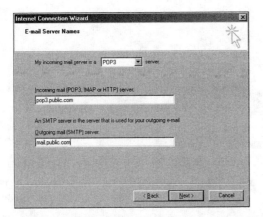

What if you absolutely, positively, can't stand Outlook Express and prefer to use another e-mail client? Here's how to find out the settings you need to set up another program to get your e-mail.

1. Open Outlook Express.

2. Click the Tools menu to get started.

3. Click Accounts.

4. Click Mail to see just the mail accounts.

5. Click the name of your current e-mail account.

6. Click Properties to see the names of the e-mail servers and other settings used for your e-mail account.

7. Click the General tab to see user information (see Figure 5.5).

FIGURE 5.5

Viewing the
General tab in
Outlook Express.

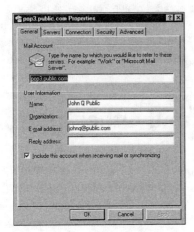

8. Click the Servers tab to see mail server types, names, and passwords (see Figure 5.6).

FIGURE 5.6

Viewing the Servers tab in Outlook Express.

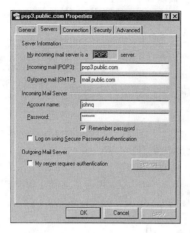

9. Click Cancel after recording the information you need to set up your preferred e-mail client; this assures that accidental changes will not be kept.

Tip

If you are managing multiple POP3 e-mail accounts, you usually must use the outgoing (SMTP) mail server provided by your cable Internet ISP for all accounts. Follow the steps listed above for viewing the settings for your current e-mail account to access the Servers screen. Change only the outgoing (SMTP) mail server entry to the mail server used by your cable ISP. Remember, once you drop your old dial-up Internet service, you can't use its e-mail servers anymore.

By default, Hotmail and other Web-based e-mail accounts use the same e-mail account for both sending and receiving mail, but you can manually select your cable Internet outgoing mail server for sending e-mail with most e-mail clients. See your e-mail client software manual for setup details.

Tweaking Media Players and Other Internet Software

Most Internet users, regardless of how fast (or how slow!) their Internet connections, have some sort of a media player installed, such as the following:

- RealPlayer
- Microsoft Media Player
- Apple QuickTime

If you installed and configured these players when you used your old dial-up analog modem connection, you set them up for slow-speed connections that sacrificed sound and video quality to run at acceptable speeds. Now that you have a cable modem, it's time to reset them to take full advantage of your fast connection.

If you don't have these media players installed on your system, see Chapter 7, "Adding Multimedia Features to Your Cable Modem Service" and Chapter 8, "Using Internet Multimedia and Messaging" to learn where to locate these programs and how to install them.

Configuring RealPlayer 8 for Cable Internet Connections

RealPlayer 8 can be configured for a wide range of connection speeds. Because you probably had a low-speed dial-up connection when you installed it, it won't take full advantage of your fast cable Internet connection until you change its connection preferences.

This is how you configure RealPlayer 8 for high-speed connections:

1. Open RealPlayer from the Start menu or desktop shortcut.

2. Click View.

3. Click Preferences. The Preferences dialog box appears.

FIGURE 5.7

Configuring RealPlayer 8 for high-speed connections.

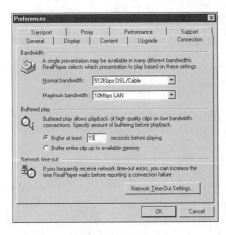

4. Click the Connection tab (see Figure 5.7).

5. Click Normal Bandwidth and select 512Kpbs DSL/Cable.

6. Click Maximum Bandwidth and select 10Mbps LAN; this allows RealPlayer to use all the bandwidth it finds for even better performance.

7. Click Buffer at Least __ Seconds Before Playing; change the value listed to 15 seconds. By buffering (storing) 15 seconds of content before playing, you should enjoy smooth streaming audio or video through your fast cable modem. Change the value later if you find that there are pauses in playback.

8. Click OK.

RealPlayer will use the new settings immediately.

Configuring Windows Media Player for Cable Internet Connections

Windows Media Player 7.0 and 8.0 automatically detect your connection speed by default, but you can also manually set the connection speed if you prefer. Because the connection speed could already be set to a low value, you should follow this procedure to check the connection speed settings and change them, if necessary:

1. Open Windows Media Player.

2. Click Tools.

3. Click Options. The Options dialog box appears.

4. Click the Performance tab (see Figure 5.8).

FIGURE 5.8

Configuring Windows Media Player 7.x for high-speed connections.

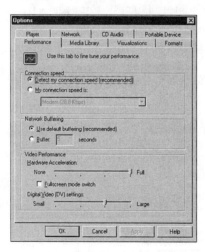

5. Click the option Detect My Connection Speed (default). If you prefer, you can also manually set the speed: Click My Connection Speed Is and select DSL/Cable 384Kbps from the pull-down menu. Select the connection speed manually only if you're not satisfied with the performance of Media Player when it detects the connection speed for you.

6. Click OK.

Even after you configure your player programs to use high-speed connections, some Internet sites that provide media content might still require you to choose a connection speed. Choose the highest speed/quality connection offered to get the best quality possible. For example, if a site offers content at 28.8Kbps, 56Kbps, or 100Kbps, choose 100Kbps. See Figure 5.9 for an example.

FIGURE 5.9

Windows Media Player's choice of Internet radio stations lists different speeds for several stations; for best listening quality, select the fastest speed listed for a given station.

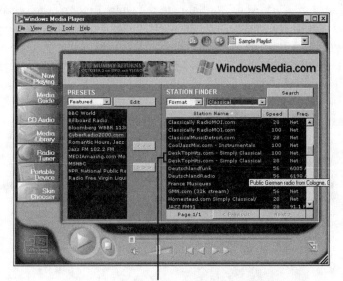

DeskTop Hits.com offers its Simply Classical
broadcasts at two different speeds.

You might need to adjust existing browser and media player configurations for proper operation after you install your cable modem and its software.

Configuring Apple QuickTime for Cable Internet Connections

The QuickTime 5 player can be configured to use a wide range of connection speeds. Because your copy of QuickTime was probably installed before you installed your cable Internet service and QuickTime defaults to assuming you have a 56Kbps dial-up modem, you should manually adjust the player's properties to take full advantage of your fast cable modem connection. Here's how:

1. Open the QuickTime player from the desktop icon or from the Start, Programs menu in Windows.

2. Click the Edit menu.

3. Click Preferences, then QuickTime Preferences to change the settings for QuickTime.

4. Click the down-arrow next to About QuickTime to see a list of settings.

5. Click Connection Speed. Select 512Kbps DSL/Cable to start; you can select other speeds later if you want to try faster playback or more reliable streaming (see Figure 5.10).

6. Click the down arrow next to Connection Speed and scroll down to Streaming Transport. Click Auto Configure to tell QuickTime to test your Internet connection for the best way to receive streaming video. Click OK once the test is completed to save the settings.

7. Close the QuickTime settings window. The new settings you selected will be used immediately.

FIGURE 5.10

Selecting a faster connection speed for the QuickTime player.

The speed setting values in media players assume good performance by the server providing the content. If you find that playback with a particular media player consistently stops or skips frames, use a lower value for the connection speed to improve reliability.

Summary

Your existing Web browser can be used with your new cable modem service, but its configuration should be adjusted to disable any proxy-server settings you previously used. If you have two-way cable modem service, you should also disable the automatic dialing feature, because your Web browser has an always-on connection to the Internet.

You may need to add your new e-mail account settings to your preferred e-mail client. If you want to use a different e-mail client than the one provided by your cable Internet service, you can view the settings within the client and manually configure your preferred e-mail client. No matter how many POP3 accounts you use, you should set all of them to use your cable Internet service's outgoing (SMTP) e-mail server for sending messages.

You should check the configuration of your media players, because most will not be set for best performance with a fast cable modem connection. By adjusting the defaults to a suitable setting, you improve the playback quality of streaming audio and video content.

TEN WAYS CABLE MODEMS MAKE THE INTERNET BETTER

CHAPTER HIGHLIGHTS:

Learn how to take advantage of the extra performance of cable Internet connections for

- Upgrading your system
- Sending e-mail
- Enjoying Internet media
- Searching the Web
- Gaming online
- Storing photos and files online

Better Computer Health Through Easy Access to Software Service Packs and Updates

Because cable Internet service is so much faster than dial-up service, your ability to keep your computer in top working condition is greatly enhanced, especially if you have two-way service. Here's why:

- You can download the huge service packs available for Microsoft Windows and Apple MacOS and applications from Microsoft and Corel in just minutes, instead of hours or days as you would with a dial-up modem. Because you can't afford to tie up a phone line for this long, odds are you have been forced to order the CD-ROM and wait a week or so for your update to arrive. Otherwise, you're left with limping along with software that's not as stable or secure as it ought to be because there's no efficient means for you to keep it up to date.

- It's now practical to take advantage of real-time maintenance features such as Symantec's Live Update (for Norton Utilities, System Works, AntiVirus, and other products), Windows Update, and MacOS Software Update. These maintenance features are more important than ever before, given the increasing incidents of computer viruses and worms (ILOVEYOU and Nimda are just two of the worst to strike in the past couple of years) that take advantage of continuing vulnerabilities in popular browsers and e-mail clients.

- If you have been laggard about keeping your antivirus software updated, you can either download the latest virus signatures fast or, in a pinch, use free or low-cost online virus-checking services. Although online virus checkers work well, they are no substitute for having up-to-date antivirus software installed and running on your computer to protect your system against infection or damage.

Tips for Using Windows Update

If you use Windows 98 or newer versions of Windows, you'll find the Windows Update icon on the Start button (Windows XP has moved this to the All Programs section of the Start menu). Click Windows Update to go to the Windows Update Web site. Click the Product Updates button to download and install updates specific to your computer. You might see a security warning that you're about to install a Windows Update Control Package to allow Windows Update to work, as shown in Figure 6.1. Click Yes.

Figure 6.1 contains an option called Always Trust Content From. In the past, most experts have recommended selecting this option, which turns off security warnings for ActiveX and other active content (such as Java) in Internet Explorer. Selecting this option means that subsequent software installations from a particular vendor won't trigger a warning. However, because of the possibility of forged online credentials being used to install potentially dangerous software on your system, I recommend that you leave this box unchecked. This way, you will receive a warning whenever a Web site wants to install new software on your system, giving you the power to decide whether it's legitimate.

Be sure you download and install the critical updates listed for your system. These provide improved system stability and help prevent security breaches of your system. Review other features offered to you to see if you need to install them.

Because every system is a little different (different versions of Windows and installed software), you need to use Windows Update on each system you use at home or in your office. Updates available for Windows 98, for example, will be different from the ones available for Windows Me or Windows XP. Windows Update tracks the updates already installed on your computer so you won't waste time installing updates you don't need.

Making E-Mail More Exciting with Attachments

E-mail isn't exactly new. It was around even before the Internet, but the extra speed of cable Internet service makes it much easier to send and receive e-mail with richer content.

The key to sending more interesting e-mail is to take advantage of file attachments when they're appropriate. What is a file attachment? It's a file you created with an Office suite (such as Microsoft Works, Microsoft Office, or WordPerfect Suite); graphics program (such as Adobe PhotoShop Elements CorelDraw); or other content-creation program that you can attach to an e-mail message.

Because of the slow upload (transmission) speed of dial-up analog modems, you probably haven't attached many files to your e-mail in the past. However, even though upload speeds for typical cable Internet services are slower than download speeds, you're still talking about upload speeds that are between four and eight times faster than what you have had with your old analog modem.

Before you click the file attachment button in your favorite e-mail client to share favorite photos or other content with friends and family, consider these issues:

- Don't send file attachments unless there's no other way to provide information in your e-mail. For example, instead of sending someone an article you saw online, just send the Web address. You can copy it from the address bar in your browser and paste it into your message.

- As an alternative to sending photos directly to family and friends, consider setting up a Web site for your photos. As you will learn later in this chapter, you can set up password-protected Web sites that let you control who can see pictures of the new baby or the new car.

- Don't send unsolicited file attachments; ask first if it's okay to send attachments. Here's why: Many savvy e-mail users now routinely delete e-mails containing unsolicited attachments, even mail from people they know, because of the insidious work of e-mail viruses such as ILOVEYOU and its many descendents. ILOVEYOU and similar e-mail viruses grab addresses from an infected system's address book and send out fake messages with attachments that, when opened, propagate themselves to more and more systems, and will often erase files or cause other damage to infected systems.

- Even after you get the go-ahead to send the attachment, you might want to send a separate message first that specifies the name and size of the attachment you will be sending. This helps protect your recipient against opening a message that really isn't from you.

- When you send files to others, keep in mind the size of the files. Many non-corporate e-mail servers, including both free e-mail sites such as Yahoo! and Hotmail, as well as e-mail servers used by cable Internet and other ISPs, limit incoming and outgoing e-mail messages to 1MB (1024KB) in size, including attachments. In addition, some also limit the number of files you can attach to a single message. You can send one or more large files to a recipient easily by creating a compressed archive file with a program such as WinZip, PKZip, or StuffIt. See "Overcoming File-Attachment Limits with Zipping Programs," later in this chapter.

■ When you send attachments, you need to be sure that the recipient can read the file. Because different programs create different types of files, you need to send files that users can read without special software (unless you know that they have and can use that software).

"Safe" File Types to Send

If you're going to the trouble to send e-mail attachments to your friends, family, or co-workers, it's best to find out what programs they use, so you can save messages in the correct format. However, if you don't know what they will be using to send files, here are some file types that virtually everyone can read:

■ Documents (letters, reports, memos)—Save them in .RTF (Rich Text Format), which can be read by both low-powered programs such as WordPad that are found on nearly all Windows-based systems as well as full-featured word-processing programs and office suites for various platforms, including Windows, MacOS, Linux, and others.

Why not use the default Microsoft Word .DOC format? Different versions of Microsoft Word save .DOC files in different ways, making interchange difficult between Word XP, Word 2000, and Word 97, not to mention older versions that some people might still have. Also, a popular type of computer virus known as a macro virus attacks Microsoft Word .DOC documents in particular, so you could send an infected file to a friend if you're not careful.

■ Photographs and graphics—Save them as .JPG (JPEG) files, which can be viewed in Web browsers as well as by most photo editors. Because JPEG files shrink in size when saved by discarding fine detail, save your pictures as .TIF or .BMP files first to preserve all the detail possible. Then, resize them to fit in a browser window. I recommend 640 dots wide (the length will adjust automatically if you use the Constrain Proportions option) for the new size.

If you would like to view virtually every file that somebody sends you, whether you have the "right" program or not, get a copy of QuickView Plus from Jasc Software (www.jasc.com). The latest version lets you scroll through a folder and view hundreds of different types of graphics, documents, spreadsheets, and other types of files. You can download a trial copy from the Jasc Web site.

■ Other types of files—If you use programs that can export Adobe Acrobat (.PDF, or Portable Document File) files, you can create files that anyone with Adobe Acrobat can read. Corel's WordPerfect Suite 2000 and 2002 can export documents as Adobe Acrobat files from the WordPerfect word processor. Other programs with built-in Acrobat support include recent versions of CorelDraw, Adobe Photoshop, Adobe PageMaker, and other programs. If you have Adobe Acrobat 4 or Acrobat 5 (which create Acrobat files), you can make an Acrobat .PDF file within virtually any program.

Overcoming File-Attachment Limits with Zipping Programs

How can you send multiple files to an e-mail recipient whose e-mail service can accept only one file attachment per message? What can you do if you need to send 2.5MB worth of files to a recipient whose e-mail service limits total message size to just 1MB, including attachments? The answer to both of these problems is to create a compressed archive file, often called a Zip file, from your files and use it for the attachment.

Note

The term "Zip file" has nothing to do with the popular Iomega Zip drive, but instead is a reference to PKWare's PKZip, the first program that could create Zip-compatible archive files.

The native file format used by Windows-based file compression programs is .ZIP, although the native Macintosh file format is .SIT, which is supported by both Mac and Windows versions of StuffIt.

If you have versions of Windows earlier than Windows Me, or if you use a Mac, you don't have the ability to create compressed archive files unless you install a file-compression utility. In addition to the pioneering PKZip program available from www.pkware.com for Windows, DOS, Unix, and OpenVMS, other leading file-compression programs include the following:

■ WinZip—For Windows, available from www.winzip.com

■ StuffIt—For Windows, Macintosh, Sun Solaris, and Linux, available from www.stuffit.com

■ QuickView Plus 6.x—For Windows, available from www.jasc.com

■ PowerDesk4 Plus, available separately or integrated as part of Ontrack System Suite 3.x—For Windows, available from www.ontrack.com

Many freeware and shareware programs are also available online from other vendors.

The Microsoft Windows 98 Plus! program, available at computer stores, adds support for compressed archive files to Windows 98 and Windows 98SE.

Specific features vary between programs, but most programs allow you to select the files you want to zip (compress) from the Windows Explorer or Mac Finder and create the compressed file immediately; you also can view the contents of a compressed file with all of these programs.

After you create the compressed file, you should view the size of the file to be sure it will be less than 1MB in size. The amount of compression you can expect varies widely with the type of file you store in a compressed archive. However, you can expect to reduce the size of a typical Microsoft Word .DOC file by up to 75% and a .BMP or .PCX graphics file by up to 80% or more. .GIF graphics files are stored in an efficient manner, but can still be compressed for modest space savings. Already compressed files such as .JPG graphics and .ZIP or .CAB archives don't compress any further, but you can still use a compression program to store multiple compressed files in a single archive, enabling you to e-mail several files with a single attachment. You can see how much smaller each file is when compressed by opening the compressed archive file in a typical compression program, as in Figure 6.2. Note that already compressed files are stored or have minimal shrinkage, although other types of document and graphics files can be reduced substantially in size.

FIGURE 6.2

A .ZIP archive created by WinZip 8.1 from files found on a typical Windows Me system, with files sorted by compression ratio.

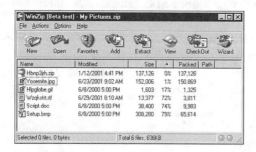

Many file-compression programs for Windows give you the option to create either a .ZIP file (which must be opened with a separate unzipping program) or a self-extracting .EXE file (which opens automatically when you run it or double-click it). Although the .EXE file is easier for recipients to open, it could be mistaken for an e-mail virus and deleted by your recipient. The self-extracting file is also larger than a .ZIP file would be. Therefore, I recommend that you skip this option and use the default .ZIP file option. Add a note to your e-mail reminding users to get an unzipping program if necessary.

View Multiple Web Sites

Cable Internet service is fast enough that you can take advantage of a feature you have probably "accidentally" discovered already: You can have multiple Web browser windows open at the same time.

Many link-based Web sites use this feature to create so-called "child" windows to display content in a browser window separate from the main browser window. To do this manually, all you need to do is launch your browser for each window you want open, and then enter or select a URL from the Favorites or Bookmarks option to display the sites you want to see. You can click back and forth between browser windows, or shrink the windows to allow you to see multiple windows at the same time.

To open a new window for a link on a Web page you're visiting, right-click the link and select Open in New Window.

The one disadvantage this has for users of Netscape or Internet Explorer browsers is that each browser window is a separate instance of the program running, consuming memory and other resources. This can be a serious issue for Windows 9x/Me users in particular because Windows 9x/Me can become unstable when too many programs are opened. Eventually your system could crash. To free up some of the memory and resources used, be sure to close browser windows when you don't need them open anymore, save your work periodically, and keep an eye on your free system resources by installing the Windows Resource Meter, which is an optional component of Windows 9x/Me. When you run the Resource Meter, it displays a gas gauge onscreen, and can be minimized to your system tray (the area near your onscreen clock). When it displays yellow as in Figure 6.3, it's time to close some programs; when it displays red, it's time to shut down your system and reboot!

FIGURE 6.3

This Windows 98 computer is running low on resources, thanks to multiple browser windows and a couple of other running applications.

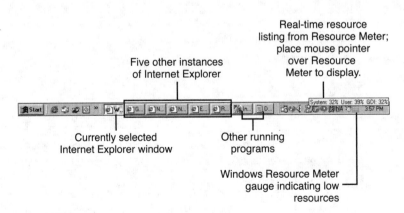

Five other instances of Internet Explorer

Real-time resource listing from Resource Meter; place mouse pointer over Resource Meter to display.

Currently selected Internet Explorer window

Other running programs

Windows Resource Meter gauge indicating low resources

If you want to use a browser that can display multiple windows without running multiple copies of itself, check out Opera Software's Opera browser. It's much faster than either Microsoft or Netscape browsers, and works on Windows, Mac, and other systems including Linux. Get more information and try it free at www.operasoftware.com.

Listen to Internet Radio

As you learned in Chapter 5, "Setting Up Your Software to Use Your Cable Modem," you can tune your system for faster, better Internet-based media by adjusting your media players to use the faster speed. Because two-way cable modems are always-on services, you can take full advantage of the wide world of Internet radio without limiting your ability to surf the Web and perform other types of work.

Windows Explorer 5.x and above work with the Windows Media Player to supply Internet radio stations, which you can search by format, language, location, or other options. Just click Favorites, Media, Internet Radio Guide after opening IE to get started.

Netscape users can install Netscape Radio or use the radio capabilities of add-on media players such as WinAmp or Real Player.

The volume controls built into most media players can't work beyond the limits of your system's main volume control, which on Windows systems is found in the form of a speaker icon in the system tray. Click the icon to bring up a master volume slider that you can adjust. Set it up to about three-quarters of maximum, then reduce the volume, as necessary, with your media player's volume control.

To learn more about installing and configuring media player software, see Chapter 7, "Adding Multimedia Features to Your Cable Modem Service," and Chapter 8, "Using Internet Multimedia and Messaging."

Watch Streaming Video

The same media players that supply Internet radio can supply streaming video to your system. Unlike high-bandwidth Internet radio, which, although it can't really challenge CD-quality music, sounds pretty good, the huge bandwidth demands of streaming video mean that your TV set has nothing to fear at the moment; you won't be turning off the TV to watch the Internet any time soon. The small viewing window used by major media players such as RealPlayer and Microsoft's Windows Media Player is no accident: Creating streaming video of adequate quality (and speed) is easier to do if the target is a small window rather than a full screen.

The speed adjustments suggested in Chapter 5 for your media players will help both audio and video run more quickly. As with streaming audio, you can normally choose both high-bandwidth and low-bandwidth versions of a given video feed on major entertainment and news Web sites. Unlike high-bandwidth audio, which puts little stress on your system, high-bandwidth video won't view very well if you're running a lot of other programs at the same time. Close other browser windows and other programs if you want to see skip-free video, or choose the low-bandwidth version and sacrifice some viewing quality.

If the video clip you're trying to watch has a lot of skips in it, wait until it downloads completely to your system before watching it, or select the low-bandwidth version.

Use Multiple Search Engines at the Same Time

No matter what search engine is your favorite (Google at www.google.com and Northern Lights at www.northernlights.com are two of mine), no search engine can access the entire Web. Naturally, you can open each search engine manually (in separate browser windows if you like) and perform the search, but so-called metasearches, which can search multiple search engines for you and find more results for you than any single search can, are easy and fast with high-speed cable Internet access.

If you use Internet Explorer 5.5 or above, its search tool is actually a metasearch tool. Enter a search term, and IE will use four or more major search engines to locate the information you're looking for.

To customize the IE Search tool, click Search, then Customize. Add or remove checkboxes under the Find a Web Page section to select the search engines that you want IE Search to use. This tool can also be used to customize other search types, including address, e-mail address, business, dictionary, map, and picture searches.

Other popular metasearch sites and tools include these:

- Dogpile—Can be customized to use your choice of up to 15 different search engines in the order you prefer and has prespecified searches; www.dogpile.com

- GoSearch—Acts as a portal to your choice of nine different search tools, but you must select one at a time; www.gosearch.com

- MetaCrawler—Can be customized to use up to 12 different search engines, and also offers filters for domains, site speed, and sort order; www.metacrawler.com

- Copernic 2001 Basic—Unlike others, you download this one and install it on your system to search more than 80 major search engines at once; available from Copernic Technologies, Inc. at www.copernic.com

Exchange Messages, Files, and More Via Instant Messaging Services

Instant messaging (IM) services, which provide immediate chat between two or more users, have become among the most popular uses of the Internet, especially for users with always-on cable Internet or similar broadband connections. If you're wondering why your teenagers are no longer tying up the phone line after you install cable Internet service, they're probably "chatting" online with their friends with an IM program.

Although you can use IM products such as AOL Instant Messenger (AIM), Microsoft's MSN Messenger (MSNN) or Yahoo! Messenger (YM) with any speed of Internet connection for keyboard chatting and messaging, high-speed Internet makes it easy to use their advanced features, such as

- File transfer
- PC-to-PC voice chat
- Live video from Webcams

Although the industry is striving to develop an open architecture for IM software, at this point in time, you and your friends need to decide on a particular IM product, install it, and share your screen names with each other. In most cases, it is not possible to use one IM software product to communicate with users of a different product.

For basic keyboard chat and file transfer, all you need is an account with the appropriate IM service, but voice chat requires that each user has a sound card and microphone. Webcams also require that a Webcam (a small live-video camera that connects to the USB or IEEE-1394 port) be attached to your computer.

All IM products listed in Table 6.1 support text and voice chat, file transfer, online gaming, and exchange of user lists; all are available for Windows and Macintosh. Table 6.1 shows you where to find the leaders, and their special features.

Table 6.1 Major IM Software and Features (for Microsoft Windows Versions)

IM Product	Vendor	Web Site	Additional Features
MSN Messenger	Microsoft	messenger.msn.com	Free international and low-cost PC-to-phone calls, Hotmail new-message notification, NetMeeting support (for video chat and shared whiteboards), paging, news ticker
AOL Instant Messenger	AOL	www.aol.com/aim/homenew.adp	Low-cost PC-to-phone calls, IM greetings, AOL or POP3 e-mail new-message notification, news ticker
Yahoo! Messenger	Yahoo!	messenger.yahoo.com	Storage of text chats, Web cam support, file sharing
ICQ	ICQ	www.icq.com	Spell checking, file sharing, send ICQ messages by e-mail, IP telephony, SMS support for GSM cell phones, wireless paging

After you download and install any of these IM programs, the program loads automatically at startup and is ready for you to use immediately.

To learn more about installing and using a Webcam with IM and other services, see Chapter 9, "Using a Webcam."

Play Online Games

Online gaming and high-speed Internet access have revolutionized the PC gaming business. Instead of blasting away at computerized armies of limited intelligence and maneuvers, you can safely participate in the "most dangerous game" by playing against other PC users around the country and around the world.

Online gaming requires that you own a game with online features (a feature found in the majority of games sold today), or one that is designed strictly for online gaming. Some of the most popular online games include

- *Everquest*
- *Tribes* and *Tribes 2*
- *Quake* series (*Quake*, *Quake 2*, and *Quake III Arena*)
- *Half-Life*
- *Counter-Strike*
- *Unreal Tournament*
- *Diablo II*

Two-way cable Internet service is one of the best choices for online gaming for two reasons:

- High speed
- Low latency (also called ping rate)

Note   *Latency* describes how long it takes for information to go from your computer to a remote computer and back again.

Because multiplayer games are hosted on specialized game servers, the round-trip time should be as short as possible so that you get up-to-date information onscreen about the location and current activities of other online game players. In other words, you want to know who's shooting at you and where the other players on your side are. Two-way cable modems have a low latency rate compared to satellite-based broadband Internet solutions and dial-up modems, meaning that you're more likely to stay "alive" through any given round.

To get started, check your favorite games for online access configuration and searches for game servers. The following third-party Web sites provide online gaming news and help:

- www.gamespy.com—Covers all types of gaming, with specialized sites for most major online games
- www.stratics.com—Covers multiplayer and online games with articles, reviews, and specialized coverage of major strategy-based games
- www.cprextreme.com—Gaming news for the extreme player with lots of links to other sites, add-ons, and reviews

To learn more about playing games online, see Chapter 11, "Playing Internet Games."

Print and Share Your Photos Online

Although cardboard photo albums with decorative photo corners are making something of a comeback among hobbyists who want to pass around family snapshots, PC users with friends and family across the country need a more high-tech way to share photos with others. Whether your pictures began life as pixels or you've scanned film into digital form, online photo services provide lots of ways for you to print and share your photos.

Typically, online photo services offer the following services:

- Photo processing—Process your film with online vendors and they'll scan and store your pictures for free as long as you're an active customer

- Photo cropping and enhancements for both existing and newly processed film—Reduce red-eye, fix up faded colors, and crop away extraneous detail to make your pictures better

- Secure photo albums—To share with family and friends e-mail them the custom URL mailed to you by the processor or use your special login

- Custom greeting cards and other specialty items—Some companies even let you order mouse pads and mugs

The speed of two-way cable Internet service makes transferring digital photos to online photo services fast and easy, while both one-way and two-way cable Internet service provides great speed for viewing photo albums online.

Some of the leading services include the following:

- Kodak's Ofoto—www.ofoto.com

- Photoworks—www.photoworks.com

- Shutterfly—www.shutterfly.com

- PhotoFun.com, Inc.—www.photofun.com

- Snapfish.com—www.snapfish.com

 Tip

Before you decide to settle on a single service for processing your file online, shoot a roll of film and send it to the service you're considering. Order prints and evaluate their quality. There can be a lot of difference between services, so test them first to see who does the best job with your pictures.

For best results when you choose online processing, be sure to specify high-quality or high-resolution scans of your film if the processor offers you a choice of scanning quality. You can always reduce image size (and quality), but detail that was never present because of inadequate scan resolution can never be replaced.

To learn more about installing and using online photo services, see Chapter 10, "Using Photo and Data-Storage Services."

Store Files Online

Online file storage provides an additional level of security in the case of fire or disaster, and also makes it possible for you to work on big projects away from your normal office.

Although some online file storage continues to be "free" to the end user (supported by advertising revenues), others charge a modest monthly or annual fee. Some of the companies that originally provided online storage service have now transformed themselves into technology suppliers for corporations who need online storage and ISPs who can either use this technology as a value-added feature or an extra-cost option for their customers.

The extra speed of cable Internet service makes pulling files from online storage fast and quite practical, and two-way cable Internet service also makes uploading data to online storage space very practical.

Some of the major providers of online storage include

- Xdrive Plus—$4.95/month for 75MB; upgrades available; contact `plus.xdrive.com` for details
- SwapDrive—$7.50/month for 100MB SwapDrive FilesShare service; discounts for annual rates and upgrades available; online backup service also available; contact `www.swapdrive.com` for details
- bigVAULT—$36.00/year for 100MB; upgrades available; contact `www.bigvault.com` for details
- Yahoo! Briefcase—15MB free to Yahoo! ID holders (signups are free); contact `briefcase.yahoo.com` for details
- iTools iDisk—20MB of free personal storage for Apple Macintosh users; additional space can be purchased; contact `itools.mac.com` for details
- @Backup—50MB of scheduled or on-demand online backup for $50/year; additional capacity and CD-ROM option also available at additional charge; contact `www.atbackup.com` for details

To learn more about using online storage services, see Chapter 10.

Summary

A wide variety of services, hardware, and software can be added to your cable Internet-connected system to enhance your Web-browsing experience.

Keep your computer healthy with automated update, online storage, and backup services. Make your e-mail more interesting by adding file attachments. Make those attachments smaller and easier to manage by using compressing and archiving programs. Develop, print, and share your photos online with friends and family.

Open multiple browser windows, change to a different browser, or try a metasearch tool to find more information fast. While you surf, enjoy Internet radio and streaming video content, and chat with friends by using instant messaging programs.

PART IV

ENHANCING YOUR CABLE MODEM SERVICE

ADDING MULTIMEDIA FEATURES TO YOUR CABLE MODEM SERVICE

7

*C*HAPTER HIGHLIGHTS:

- How to choose and install a Webcam to your system for e-mail and chat
- The benefits of using NetMeeting for conferencing, audio chat, and video chat
- The media players you need for Web-based audio and video content

Web Cameras

Cable Internet connections do much more than provide faster Web surfing and downloads; their incredible speed (especially if you have two-way service) opens up a new world of interactive entertainment. One of the most enjoyable features you can add to your computer is a Webcam, also referred to by some users as a Netcam. A *Webcam* is a small camera that is usually placed atop the monitor to provide a fixed angle view of you, your office, or whatever you point it toward.

Whatever you call it, a Webcam really enhances live chatting, giving you and your PC a real-life, very affordable counterpart to the Jetsons' picture phone. You can also use a Webcam to create video e-mail files to send to friends and family.

Choosing a Webcam

You should keep several criteria in mind if you want to add a Webcam to your system:

- Interface—Most Webcams plug into the USB port, but a few high-perform-ance models can attach to the IEEE-1394 (FireWire/i.Link) port available on some add-on cards and as part of some recent PCs.

- Resolution—Most low-end Webcams have a resolution of 320×240 or 352×288 pixels, which is the CIF (common interchange format) standard, but better models support resolutions up to 640×480, which will provide better viewing quality, even in a smaller-sized window.

- Frame rate—30 frames per second (fps) is the frame rate needed for so-called *full-motion video*, but most low-end Webcams can sustain this frame rate only when a small window (under 400 pixels wide) is used. Using a larger window drops the frame rate and causes jerky video display. Faster, higher-end Webcams can support 30fps at 640×480 resolution.

- Additional features—You need a microphone for voice/video chat, and some high-end Webcams include one. Others can be used as digital cameras, and a few Webcams even have provision for additional flash memory storage.

- Operating system support—Most USB Webcams include Windows software, whereas IEEE-1394–based Webcams usually include both Windows and Mac software.

Note

I recommend that you choose a Webcam which supports a frame rate of 30 fps, but don't be surprised if your real-life results are lower. The speed of the connection between you and the receiver has a lot of effect on the frame rate. Even with a cable modem, you might prefer to improve your frame rate by using a smaller capture window when you use your camera for chats, especially with users who have a dial-up Internet connection. Using a smaller capture window reduces the effective resolution of your Webcam, but also reduces the amount of data you must capture for each frame and makes faster frame rates easier to achieve.

Some of the major Webcam vendors include the following:

- Logitech—USB; www.Logitech.com
- Intel—USB; www.intel.com
- Creative Labs—USB; Webcam.creative.com
- Orange Micro—IEEE-1394; www.orangemicro.com
- ADS Technologies—IEEE-1394; www.adstech.com

If you use a Mac, and the Webcam you want to use doesn't include Mac software in the package, check the Webcam manufacturer's Web site. Some vendors, such as Creative Labs, offer both Windows and Mac software and drivers for download.

Installing a Webcam

Installing a Webcam is easy, especially if you select a USB model. Because most computers have working USB ports, the process is similar to this:

1. Attach the Webcam to a USB port on your PC.
2. Install the software. The Webcam is now ready to work.

Depending on the Webcam and the platform (PC/Windows or Mac), you might need to install the software before you plug in the Webcam.

If you opt for the faster, more expensive IEEE-1394 Webcam and your computer lacks an IEEE-1394 port, you will need to install an IEEE-1394 card before you can attach the Webcam to your system.

To save money, look for bundles that include an IEEE-1394 card and Webcam.

After your Webcam is installed, you can use its software to create video e-mail and simple movies. However, if you want to conduct video-enabled chat, you might need to install third-party software.

Installing NetMeeting

Microsoft NetMeeting is among the most popular video chat software products for Windows users. It can be downloaded free from Microsoft's Web site, and is part of the full Internet Explorer download, along with Microsoft's free e-mail product, Outlook Express.

Depending on the version of Windows you use, a shortcut to NetMeeting will be available under the Accessories section of the Start menu, either in the Communications or Internet Tools section.

Get the latest version of NetMeeting as well as updates, links to companion products and services, and other help from the Microsoft NetMeeting home page at www.Microsoft.com/windows/netmeeting.

NetMeeting is not available for Windows XP; it has been replaced with Windows Messenger, an enhanced version of MSN Messenger.

The first time you run NetMeeting, you will be asked to supply the following:

- Your name
- Your e-mail address
- Your location

After you go online with NetMeeting, you can choose whether to reveal this information to other users. NetMeeting supports directory servers, which list your name and make you available for calls from others, but the primary way that NetMeeting users make calls is through your MSN Messenger buddy list. You can opt to log on to a directory server or block your information from appearing. Next, you specify the speed of your connection: Choose Cable (modem) to set NetMeeting for the correct speed. If you plan to use NetMeeting frequently, you can add shortcuts to your desktop and your QuickLaunch bar (the icons near the Start button).

Next, the audio tuning wizard appears (if you have onboard sound, which virtually all systems have). Adjust the volume of your speakers or headphones, and then set the recording volume of your microphone. If your video playback window displays the Microsoft NetMeeting logo instead of live video, close NetMeeting, turn on your Webcam, and restart NetMeeting. After you see the NetMeeting interface as in Figure 7.1, you're ready to chat. See Chapter 9, "Using a Webcam," for details.

If other people can't hear you, if the level of background noise in the room changes, or if you change to a different type of microphone, speakers, or headset, run the Audio Tuning Wizard again.

FIGURE 7.1

Microsoft
NetMeeting 3.01
provides
audio/video chat
and other fea-
tures for
Windows users.

Video E-Mail

As you learned in Chapter 6, "Ten Ways Cable Modems Make the Internet Better,"
cable Internet connections make more exciting e-mail easy. Just as the high-speed
connection makes sending and receiving large e-mails with attachments easier, it
makes sending and receiving video e-mails easier and faster as well.

What is video e-mail? *Video e-mail* (also called vmail) is full-motion video that has
been saved as a file. Webcams are the most popular way to create vmail, but you
could also convert DV camcorder or standard analog camcorder video into a vmail
message.

Vmail can be sent as a file attachment with a conventional e-mail client, with special e-mail software, or by a link within a text message to a video e-mail server.
Because vmail files, even when created with a low-resolution Webcam at high compression, are much larger than still pictures or documents, it's useful to have another
way to send and receive them rather than the normal file attachment method.

Some of the most popular vmail products and services include the following:

■ Video-Express (www.imagemind.com)

■ iVISTA (www.inetcam.com)

■ MaxxNote (www.summus.com)

■ VideoLiveMail (www.gocyberlink.com)

Most Webcams also include video e-mail software.

For more information about using video e-mail services, see Chapter 9.

The Software You Need for Online Audio and Video Content

Web content has changed dramatically from what it was in the mid-1990s, when the World Wide Web was new, text ruled, and photo content was rare. In the days of slow 14.4Kbps and 28.8Kbps dial-up modems, there was little place for live audio or video media online. Cable Internet and other types of broadband connections make the Internet more interesting because they're fast enough to help you enjoy full-motion video and on-demand music, but only if you have the correct software installed.

With so many different products used online, it's impossible to list every product you need to install to be ready for multimedia playback, but this section will discuss the most common player products you need to handle the most common types of online content.

Many browsers include some of these add-on programs already, but changes in versions might require you to install updated versions in the future.

How can you tell when you need to install new multimedia software? Depending on the browser you use and the Web site you're trying to access, you might see a warning such as "Sorry, but this site requires the _____ plug-in" or you might see a screen similar to the one shown in Figure 7.2.

Click the link provided (an icon of a puzzle piece in this case) to install the helper program. Microsoft Internet Explorer normally detects the type of program required and prompts you to install a helper program, as in Figure 7.3.

Depending on the multimedia program, it might install automatically, or you might need to confirm or modify the default installation options. After the program is installed, you can view Web content that uses that helper program.

Netscape Navigator and Netscape Communicator use plug-ins, whereas Internet Explorer uses ActiveX controls. If you use both browsers, many multimedia program installers will automatically update both browsers when you run the setup program.

FIGURE 7.2

If you don't have the Apple QuickTime media player installed, you'll see a blank screen with a puzzle piece in the Netscape browser window in place of the QuickTime content you are trying to view.

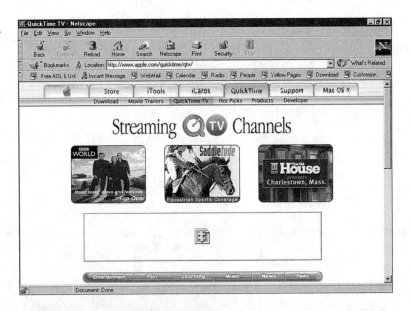

FIGURE 7.3

Microsoft Internet Explorer prompts you to accept the QuickTime installer if you try to view a page using QuickTime and don't have the proper version installed.

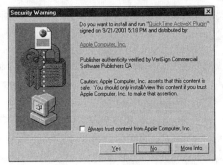

The most common multimedia content you will encounter online is listed in Table 7.1. If you install these programs before you go online, you won't need to stop as often to install additional helper programs.

Table 7.1 Multimedia Content and Required Programs

Content Type	Program Needed for Playback	Major Uses	Download From
Flash	Macromedia Flash Player	Web animations and user interfaces	www.macromedia.com/downloads
Shockwave	Macromedia Shockwave Player	Web animations	www.macromedia.com/downloads

Table 7.1 (continued)

Content Type	Program Needed for Playback	Major Uses	Download From
Windows Media Audio	Microsoft Media Player	Streaming audio and digital rips from prerecorded CDs	www.Microsoft.com/windows/windowsmedia
QuickTime	Apple QuickTime Player	Streaming and downloaded video; optional support for still images and audio	www.apple.com/quicktime
Real Audio, Real Video	RealPlayer	Streaming video and audio	www.real.com
Portable Document Format (.PDF)	Adobe Acrobat	Documents and presentations	www.adobe.com

To learn more about using multimedia players, see Chapter 8, "Using Internet Multimedia and Messaging."

Internet Radio

Internet radio, which is available through the latest Microsoft and Netscape browsers, provides a fast way to locate your favorite types of online music. Essentially, Internet radio provides links to stations with different formats, and uses the same streaming music players used to play back other types of online content (normally Windows Media Player or RealPlayer). Thus, you need to install and properly configure the correct player(s) before you can listen to Internet radio.

For configuration details for Internet media players and Internet radio, see Chapter 8.

Summary

Your high-speed cable Internet connection needs specialized hardware and software to provide you with complete enjoyment of online content, chatting, and e-mail opportunities.

Webcams can be used for live chats and video e-mail, and are typically connected through the USB port. NetMeeting provides a way for Windows 9x/Me/2000 users to have live audio and video chats and collaborate on projects.

Streaming audio and video content, Web animations, and print-ready documents can be displayed in your Web browser only when the appropriate add-on software has been installed on your system. The most common media players for audio and video content include RealPlayer, Windows Media Player, and QuickTime. Internet radio depends on the installation of compatible media player software to work.

Flash is a popular choice for Web animations, and Adobe Acrobat Reader enables Web browsers to display onscreen documents the same way they'll print. Free downloads are available from vendors for most multimedia Web content, and some vendors offer deluxe versions with extra capabilities at a low cost.

USING INTERNET MULTIMEDIA AND MESSAGING

CHAPTER HIGHLIGHTS:

- ▇ How to install, configure, and use Windows Media Player, RealPlayer, and QuickTime

- ▇ How to use media players to listen to Internet radio stations

- ▇ How to install, configure, and use popular instant messaging (IM) clients

- ▇ How to install, configure, and use NetMeeting

Windows Media Player

Because Windows Media Player is bundled with recent and current versions of Microsoft Windows, it is among the most popular streaming media and download-able media players around. Even if you prefer other media players, you will need to configure Media Player and use it to access much of what's available online.

Upgrading and Installing the Latest Version of Media Player

Early versions of Windows Media Player were designed primarily as pop-up helper programs used mainly when a Web site offered you Media-Player–compatible con-tent, as in Figure 8.1.

FIGURE 8.1

Windows Media Player 6.01 being used to play back a radio talk show.

If your Windows Media Player resembles the interface in Figure 8.1, it's out of date and should be replaced; the current version is 7.1 or higher. To see the version of Windows Media Player you're using, click the Help menu, and choose About to see the version number, as shown in Figure 8.1.

Note

Windows Media Player 8.x is also called Windows Media Player for Windows XP, and works only with Windows XP. Version 7.x works with Windows 98 or above; 7.01 is also available for MacOS. Windows 95 and Windows NT 4 users can upgrade to version 6.4 only.

To upgrade Windows Media Player 6.x to the latest version, click the Upgrade button on the menu bar and select Upgrade Now. The Upgrade Now button will open your default Web browser and bring you to the Windows Media Player download page. If you are trying Windows Media Player for the first time or clicking Upgrade Now doesn't display the correct page, set your browser to www.Microsoft.com/windows/ windowsmedia/en/download/.

Select the correct version for your operating system and the language you use, and click Download Now to start the upgrade process. To learn more about the latest features of Windows Media Player, click More Info.

Although Microsoft sometimes uses the Run from Current Location option to install software, you should download the large Windows Media Player program to your computer, save it, and run the program from your hard disk to install it. Run from Current Location is designed to start installations in which the files installed to your computer could vary, depending on the software already installed on your computer; this method is used for Internet Explorer installations. The Windows Media Player installation is the same for all systems installing a particular version, so Microsoft provides a single installation file.

Early in the installation process, Microsoft displays a privacy statement describing the ways that Media Player interfaces with public information sources for music licensing, CD identification, and so forth. If you want to read this information in greater detail and learn how to disable some or all of these features, click the More Info button and save or print the Privacy Statement Web page that will be displayed. After you click I Have Read the Privacy Statement, you can continue the installation process.

The component setup screen allows you to deselect Windows Media Player components (not recommended), but it also allows you to discover new features of the release; click on each component to learn what it does. For example, the Adaptec CD-Burning plug-in allows you to create CDs from content displayed in the Media Player window and use them on a normal CD player.

As is typical with most programs, Windows Media Player will become the default player for all the media formats it supports. If you prefer to use a different player for MP3 or other non-Windows Media content, clear the checkmarks when prompted before you click Next (see Figure 8.2).

After you complete installation, you must restart the computer. The next time you open Windows Media Player, if upgrading to version 7.x, its interface will appear as it does in Figure 8.3. If you have a two-way cable modem connection, the Windows Media Web site will appear immediately to provide instant links to streaming music and video content and play a sample tune. With a one-way cable modem, connect online and click the Media Guide to view the latest links and content.

FIGURE 8.2

Windows Media Player will be the default player for all formats listed unless you clear the appropriate checkmarks.

FIGURE 8.3

Use the latest version of Windows Media Player with your two-way cable modem for instant access to Windows Media-compatible streaming audio and video media (version 7.x shown here).

Windows Media Player for XP has an almost identical user interface (see Figure 8.4), but offers additional buttons along the left side of the screen for support of its new CD-creation feature.

Using the Windows Media Player to Explore Online Content

As soon as Windows Media Player starts, you can immediately sample online media content. As Figure 8.3 indicates, you have a wide variety of streaming audio and video available to you. To play content, just click on the link. After the audio or video stream is received, it will start playing. A separate browser window might appear with album or artist information, but if you want to rewind or pause the playback, use the VCR-style remote controls displayed at the bottom of the Windows Media Player window.

Tip

For the best-quality audio and video, be sure to click the speed option beneath the content title. If you click the content title, you will need to choose the speed, or the player might default to playing the low-bandwidth version of the content.

Low-bandwidth audio lacks brilliance in the treble. Low-bandwidth video plays back in a very small portion of the Windows Media Player screen, and will look fuzzy because of the high level of data compression used to make the video.

While a track is playing, you can click the File menu and add it to your media library, which you can later transfer to CD-R or CD-RW media if you have a CD-RW drive.

As with previous versions, Windows Media Player will pop into action if you're surfing the Web and click on a link that requires the Media Player. By default, the Media Player displays a visualization that changes with the music or audio, as in Figure 8.4. To switch to a different visualization, click View and select Visualizations. To display the visualization full-screen, click View, Full Screen, or hold down the Alt key and press Enter; press Alt+Enter again to return to normal view.

FIGURE 8.4

The Windows Media Player provides intriguing visualizations when you play audio content (version 8.x shown here).

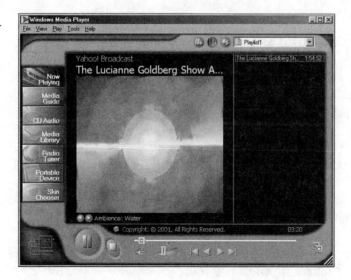

The visualizations don't require any additional bandwidth—they are played from a library of effects included with the player.

Normally, Windows Media Player will automatically tune itself for fastest connection speed and network settings. If you need to change these options, see Chapter 5, "Setting Up Your Software to Use Your Cable Modem," for details.

RealPlayer

Although Windows Media Player has made major inroads into online media support, RealPlayer is still popular. If you prefer the Netscape browser, you probably already have it installed on your system. However, it works with Internet Explorer as well, and can be downloaded from www.real.com.

Unlike Microsoft, which likes to give away most of its online tools, Real's only business is online media. You can get basic tools for free, but its deluxe players will cost you a bit of money.

Not sure whether you need to pony up for RealPlayer Plus? Try the free RealPlayer Basic and see if it meets your needs first. RealPlayer Plus offers better video display, which you can fine-tune; full-screen video playback of some content; and access to more than 2,500 Internet radio stations. Many Web sites offer a choice of either Real or Windows Media-compatible content; try both to see which you prefer.

Downloading and Installing RealPlayer Basic

Follow links from the home page to locate the free basic RealPlayer download page. Enter the required information, select your operating system (various Windows, MacOS versions, and Unix), language, and connection speed (cable modem is one of the options), and click the Download button to start the process.

If you're interested in Internet radio, be sure to select the SPINNER option (for Windows users only) to access more than 140 Internet radio channels in multiple formats).

To get the fastest download, be sure to select a site near you, preferably in the same country in which you live.

As with many other programs today, you will download and start a small download utility that will complete the rest of the setup process. If you're downloading with Internet Explorer, depending on your security settings, you might need to give permission for an ActiveX control to work to enable the process to continue; if your security settings are set to Low, the ActiveX download will take place without notifying you. After the download utility completes the file download, follow the onscreen prompts to complete the installation.

> I recommend that you set your Internet Explorer (IE) settings to at least Medium (the default security setting) so that you will be notified when ActiveX controls try to install themselves on your system. To check or change the security settings for Internet Explorer security, open IE, click Tools, click Internet Options, and click the Security tab. Select the Default level to set the controls to Medium, or click the Custom Level buttons to adjust settings to your preference.

After the installation process is complete and you are personalizing your copy of RealPlayer, you can specify which media types you want to play with RealPlayer. As with Windows Media Player, you should clear checkmarks if you're happy with your current default player for a specified format. Unlike Windows Media Player, which serves up whatever Microsoft thinks you would like to know about entertainment and news, RealPlayer lets you specify just the news and entertainment features in which you're most interested.

The equivalent to Windows Media Player's Media Guide is the Web site realguide.real.com; you can launch it automatically from the Real Guide shortcut on your desktop. Follow the links to your favorite entertainment media. The Real Guide is displayed automatically in the RealPlayer window when you start RealPlayer. Figure 8.5 shows RealPlayer with RealGuide content.

FIGURE 8.5
RealPlayer offers a sampling of current content in the main window (right) and access to specific channels in the channel window (left).

GoldPass content (as shown in Figure 8.5) refers to content available only to RealPlayer Plus users. Although some broadband content can be viewed with RealPlayer Basic, most require RealPlayer Plus.

Fine-Tuning RealPlayer

RealPlayer offers the following options for customizing its appearance and performance:

- Sharpening control during video playback
- Performance options for adjusting CPU usage, Web site playback, sound and video card optimization (in Preferences menu)
- User-defined news and entertainment flash categories (in Preferences menu)
- Accessibility controls (in Preferences menu)
- Three-band graphic equalizer
- Favorites options for storing favorite media Web sites

Why Upgrade to RealPlayer Plus?

If you prefer RealPlayer content over Windows Media Player, you might want to upgrade to RealPlayer Plus. The following are the benefits if you upgrade:

- 10-band graphic equalizer
- Enhanced video playback controls, including brightness, contrast, and others
- Special content, including broadband versions of content available in lower bandwidth versions only if you have just the basic player

For the latest pricing, see the Real Web site (www.real.com).

Apple QuickTime

Apple's contribution to streaming audio and video players, QuickTime, isn't just for Macs. It also works with 32-bit Windows. If you don't have QuickTime already installed on your computer and you open a Web page that requires QuickTime with Internet Explorer, QuickTime will be installed on your computer if you grant permission for the QuickTime ActiveX control as discussed in Chapter 7. If you don't use Internet Explorer, you can manually download the appropriate version of QuickTime from www.apple.com/quicktime/download.

The current version of QuickTime is 5. During installation, you can choose from Minimum, Recommended, and Custom installations. Minimum installs the QuickTime Player, Web browser support, and support for MP3, VR, and Flash animations. Choose Recommended to add PictureViewer (to view graphic files not supported by browsers), digital video (DV) support, media export, and authoring support to the Minimum package. Choose Custom to choose exactly the features you want from those listed in other options, and special features such as QuickTime Diagnostics, QuickTime Capture, and others.

Note

If you want to install QuickTime for Java, you might need to download and install the Sun Java VM first; recent versions of Microsoft Windows don't include it, and the Windows Java VM available from Windows Update won't work with QuickTime for Java. If you get a warning about needing to install the Java VM, close the QuickTime installation and go to the Java 2 Platform Web site at Java.sun.com/j2se. Download and install the Java 2 Runtime Environment, Standard Edition for Windows, and then restart the QuickTime Custom installation.

After QuickTime is installed on your system, the QuickTime Setup Assistant starts. Select the approximate connection speed of your cable modem; I suggest 512Kbps DSL/Cable unless your own speed tests show you're getting consistently faster or slower results. Click through the other options and click Finish when prompted, and QuickTime is ready to go.

Using QuickTime

Once QuickTime is installed, it will be used to view any QuickTime content you find online. Sites offering QuickTime videos often ask you to select the window size you want for playback; generally, you should choose the largest window available because your cable modem has the speed needed for good playback in most cases. However, if you find that the video playback is choppy, choose a smaller window size to improve playback speed.

The QuickTime player window used to view Web-based content has a minimalist design, as you can see in Figure 8.6. The progress bar along the bottom of the playback window moves to indicate the progress of media download; after the content is downloaded to your system, use the controls to play, pause, or move to a particular portion of the content.

FIGURE 8.6

The QuickTime 5 player for Web content.

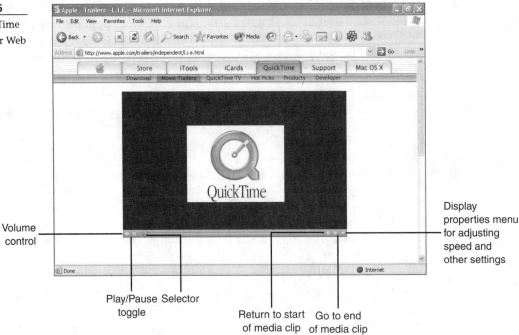

Volume control

Display properties menu for adjusting speed and other settings

Play/Pause Selector toggle

Return to start of media clip   Go to end of media clip

You can also launch the QuickTime player manually from your system's desktop or Start menu to play back current online content or content stored locally or on a network drive. When started by the user, QuickTime provides additional menu options for playback, as in Figure 8.7.

FIGURE 8.7

The QuickTime 5 player for standalone or Web content lets you adjust the size of the playback window and play the current movie in a continuous loop.

Use the File menu to open a file on a local or network drive or a particular URL (Web site). Select a QuickTime TV channel from the QTV menu.

During the QuickTime setup process, you will be asked if you want to upgrade to Apple's fee-based QuickTime Pro player and content development tool. Buy QuickTime Pro to get the following features:

- Full screen video playback
- Resizable movie playback windows
- Ability to save online content on your own system
- Copy, paste, and convert popular media and publishing formats
- Create movie and audio content
- Use effects filters
- Convert video to DV camcorder format for better quality
- Create streaming content for the Web
- Use more advanced compression technologies

For the latest pricing and feature information, click the QuickTime Pro button at www.apple.com/quicktime.

Internet Radio

Internet radio refers to Web sites that offer real-time streaming playback of various music genres, just like AM and FM radio stations do. You need to install a media player such as Windows Media Player or RealPlayer to listen to content available online from Internet radio stations.

While, in theory, Internet radio is available to anyone with an Internet connection, it's a much better choice for two-way cable modem and other types of broadband Internet users than for those who have only a dial-up connection. Because Internet radio provides streaming content (*streaming* means that the music plays continuously, rather than your needing to download the song before you play it), you need an always-on connection to use it full-time. Thus, it's a perfect match for two-way cable modem Internet connections.

Finding Internet Radio Content

There are a variety of ways to locate Internet radio content. The Radio Tuner feature in Microsoft's Windows Media Player offers preset stations or the option to create your own, accessible from the left window. Use the Station Finder tool in the right window to locate stations by format, wavelength (FM, AM, or Web-only), language, location, call sign, frequency, and keyword. Figure 8.8 shows you the results of a search for classical music online.

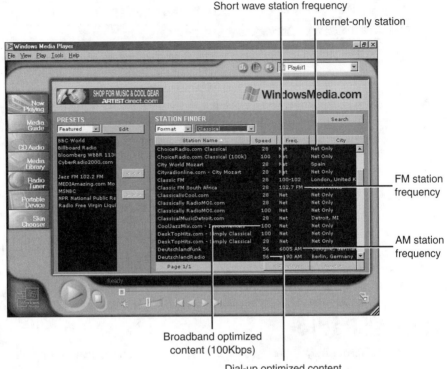

FIGURE 8.8

The WindowsMedia .com station finder after performing a search for classical music online.

Short wave station frequency

Internet-only station

FM station frequency

AM station frequency

Broadband optimized content (100Kbps)

Dial-up optimized content (28Kbps or 56Kbps)

Most stations offer low-bandwidth (28.8Kbps or 56Kbps) content only, but a few offer higher-quality 100Kbps broadband content as well. Higher-bandwidth music takes a few more seconds to start playing than lower-bandwidth options, but the music is less compressed and sounds better. Stations that broadcast over shortwave, FM, or AM bands provide this information under the Freq. heading, and the City listing is also provided so you can tune in while you're on the road and away from your PC. After you click on the station, click the large triangular Play button to start the music.

When you click on a station, Windows Media Player sometimes opens a browser window for the station. You might need to click on additional options or register yourself as a listener before the music starts.

During times of heavy usage, no stations might be accessible; you might get a Server Is Currently Unable to Handle the Request error. Try your station again later. This is a server problem at the Windows Media Player server site, not at the station.

With RealPlayer, click the Radio menu and select Open Radio Tuner to display featured content and formats. Use the Find button to enter keywords such as format or station name to locate stations from the 2,500 stations in the RealPlayer database. Figure 8.9 shows the results of a search for classical-format stations. The speed and language are listed next to the station name. Click the station name to play their current online broadcast, or click the buttons to visit the Web site or add the station to your Favorites list of Web sites.

Opens station Web site

Bandwidth   Adds station to Favorites list

FIGURE 8.9

The RealPlayer Radio search tool after performing a search for classical stations.

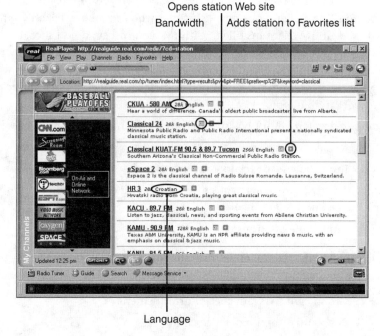

Language

Choose the broadband stations (100Kbps or over) for the best possible sound quality. If only 28Kbps and 56Kbps options are listed, 56Kbps will provide better sound quality than 28Kbps.

Although you can configure RealPlayer to display visualizations while it plays, it shrinks by default to a small player window onscreen when you listen to Internet radio.

Instant Messaging Services

At first glance, instant messaging (IM) services look like a throwback to the early days of online computing. Instead of watching full-motion online video content or listening to lush stereophonic music, IM users spend much of their time typing text messages to each other. Yet, make no mistake: Many industry pundits think IM is the next "killer app." Even though nobody gets a dime in profits from it (at least now), Microsoft and Yahoo! are big competitors to AOL Instant Messenger (AIM), originally developed by Netscape. AOL also owns ICQ, the most powerful IM service, which supports more computer platforms than other IM services.

Why You Need to Use an IM Client

Always-on Internet access should, in theory, give you immediate access to family members, friends, and business associates who are online. It's only a theory unless you have an IM client installed. With IM, you can set up a list of users (often called a "buddy list" or "friends list"), get immediate notification when any member of your list is online, and immediately exchange text messages or files with members of your list. ICQ users can also publish their ICQ code number and receive instant messages from anyone.

Compared to e-mail, IM has the following advantages:

- Immediate access
- Immediate feedback to your messages
- True two-way conversations via keyboard or optional voice and video (depending on IM client)
- Immediate file transfer

Compared to the telephone, IM has the following advantages:

- No busy signals
- Group chats without special arrangements
- Keyboard or optional voice chat
- Optional saving of online transcripts for a permanent record

It's no wonder that IM is becoming so popular for both home and business use.

Choosing an IM Client

As you learned in Chapter 6, "Ten Ways Cable Modems Make the Internet Better," several incompatible IM clients are available free at the current time. AOL Instant Messenger and MSN Messenger are more popular than Yahoo! Messenger, and ICQ, while it's the oldest and most powerful IM client, is better known outside the United States. Each client also has different feature sets. Unfortunately, until the IM industry agrees on common standards, you and your friends, family, or business associates will need to agree on a particular IM client and service. Despite the names, you don't need to be an MSN user to run MSN Messenger, or an AOL member to use AOL Instant Messenger.

Although you need a different IM client for each IM service, nothing can stop you from installing multiple IM clients. You can install AIM and MSN Messenger, for example, on the same machine and have both of them active at the same time. You can use whichever IM client you need to communicate with a given user.

AOL Instant Messenger

You can download versions of AIM for Windows, MacOS, or other operating systems.

When the AIM program first starts after installation, the screen name is set to <New User> and the password field is blank. Enter the correct information for both fields. Figure 8.10 shows how the AIM screen appears during the login process. Click Sign On to start the process.

FIGURE 8.10

The AIM screen during initial user setup.

By default, AIM assumes that you will be using the same PC and be the only AIM user on that PC, so it saves the password for you. If other family members will also use this same PC, clear the Save Password field. If you don't want AIM to be running at startup, clear the Auto-Login field.

A wizard appears to help you complete AIM setup. To review features and uses, click through the Quick Overview screens with the Next button. Click Add a Buddy to enter the screen name(s) of your AOL buddy list; these are the people you want to stay in touch with via AOL. Each buddy can be stored as part of the Buddies,

Family, or Co-Workers group. Use the New Group button to add a buddy to more than one group. Click Finish when you're done.

> If someone you don't want to authorize tries to add you to their buddy list, you can block them with the Privacy dialog box in the Preferences menu or when they first contact you via IM.

Click Create a Profile if you want other AIM users to be able to locate you by searching by location, by areas of interest (five is the maximum), or by e-mail and Web site addresses.

> The Profile information is strictly optional. You don't need to create a profile to use AIM. I would recommend creating a profile only if you want to meet new people online.

Chatting with AIM

Starting a text chat with AIM is simple: Double-click a name in your buddy list and a typing window opens. Enter text and press the Enter key, and it's sent to your buddy.

The first time you receive an IM message from another AIM user, you can accept or block the message. Only your screen name appears during chat. If you accept, a dialog window appears showing the sender's message with a typing area for your reply. Figure 8.11 shows a typical chat in progress.

FIGURE 8.11

The AIM interface (left) and a typical chat in progress (right).

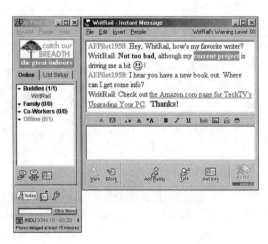

The buttons between the chat area (top) and typing area (bottom) can be used to add smileys (AOL's term for the yellow emoticons in Figure 8.11), text color and other enhancements, and hyperlinks. You can even send an AOL Greeting card electronically.

Need to speak directly? Click the Talk button. You can accept or reject a talk request as well. A volume control appears, and a Disconnect button lets you drop the voice chat and return to text chat. Use the File menu to send a file to your buddy. A warning message appears during file transfers, allowing you to accept or reject the file. The file transfer request is added to your chat window.

Voice chat sets up a direct connection between your computer and the other user's computer, thus creating a security risk. File transfers can display your IP address and also create a potential security risk.

You should install a personal firewall program and up-to-date anti-virus software before using voice chat or file transfer with any IM product. See Chapter 13, "Firewalls and Your PC," for details.

If you want to keep a transcript of your chat, use the File, Save option and select AOL Rich Text Format (saves in HTML for viewing in a browser) or text before you close the chat window. When you're finished chatting, close the chat window.

Use the People button to send chat invitations, play an online game available at AOL.com, or transfer a buddy list to make setting up a new user in your list of buddies faster and easier. Use the My AIM menu to read e-mail from a POP3 mail account, display stock and news alerts, and change your user preferences. You can also stay offline without closing your AIM program.

MSN Messenger and Windows Messenger

MSN Messenger and its Windows XP sibling, Windows Messenger, are relative newcomers to the online chat business, but they offer many features that distinguish them from AIM, including the following:

- Integration with Hotmail—MSN Messenger and Windows Messenger automatically tell you when you have new Hotmail
- Integration with NetMeeting—MSN Messenger contact lists are the easiest way to use NetMeeting
- Free PC-to-PC phone calls with both MSN Messenger and Windows Messenger
- Support for pagers and Pocket PCs with both MSN Messenger and Windows Messenger
- Notification when the other party in a chat is typing a message

The most advanced version of MSN Messenger described in the preceding list is available for Windows 95 and newer versions up through Windows 2000; Windows Messenger is the advanced version of MSN Messenger for Windows XP; it has integrated video chat but will not connect to a PC running NetMeeting. A less advanced version of MSN Messenger is available for MacOS.

When you install MSN Messenger, you must provide a Microsoft .NET Passport or Hotmail address. If you don't have one already, you must create a .NET Passport or Hotmail address before you can continue. You can choose to add yourself to the Hotmail Member Directory during the setup procedure.

Windows Messenger is built into Windows XP, but you must connect to a Windows .NET Passport server before you can use it and enter your current Passport or Hotmail address (or set up a new .NET or Hotmail account) before you can use Windows Messenger. This can take place during installation of Windows XP, or the first time you launch Windows XP.

After you install MSN Messenger or activate Windows Messenger, you need to set up a contact list (comparable to AIM's buddy list). Use the Add button to add contacts by any of the following:

- MSN Messenger username
- E-mail address
- Search of your personal address book or Hotmail Member Directory

The e-mail address need not be a Hotmail address; if the user isn't using MSN Messenger or Windows Messenger already, you can send a personalized e-mail invitation.

If a user adds you to their contact list and you don't want to be there, you can block the user by right-clicking on the contact name and selecting Block.

Chatting with MSN Messenger and Windows Messenger

To open a chat session with either version of Messenger, double-click the user and a chat window opens. A small window appears momentarily onscreen to inform the recipient that you want to chat.

You can add emoticons to your chat, as seen in Figure 8.10, but the process is considerably clumsier than with AIM unless you're accustomed to typing emoticons in the traditional way. For example, to insert the "crazy" emoticon in Figure 8.12, you must type :-p or :p.

To see a complete list of emoticons and other symbols you can use in MSN Messenger, click Help, Help Topics, Use Emoticons. With Windows Messenger, click Help, All Topics, Sending messages, invitations and files, Use Emoticons.

FIGURE 8.12

The MSN Messenger interface (left) and chat window (right) during a typical chat session.

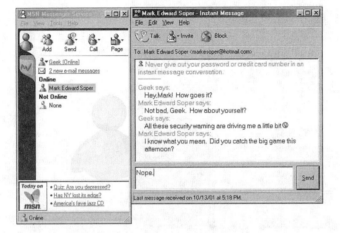

Unfortunately, you can change only the text size, font, font color, and effects in a chat window. MSN Messenger and Windows Messenger don't provide a provision for background colors or hyperlinks.

Click the Talk button to set up voice chat, or Invite to invite another person to join the chat or to use an online program. Use the File menu to send or receive a file.

If you want to capture an MSN Messenger chat transcript, highlight the text, select Edit, Copy, and then paste it into a text editor such as Notepad, WordPad, or a word processing program such as WordPerfect or Microsoft Word. Note that the graphic emoticons will not be converted back into text.

With Windows Messenger for Windows XP, you can also select voice chat (talking) or video chat (camera), as seen in Figure 8.13. Text chats can take place with both Windows Messenger and MSN Messenger users, but video chats require that both users have Windows XP and use Windows Messenger. Audio chats require that users have Windows Messenger 4.5 or MSN Messenger 4.0 or above. Click Help, About to check the version number of Windows Messenger or MSN Messenger. Use Windows Update to download the latest version of Windows Messenger or MSN Messenger.

Advanced Features of MSN Messenger and Windows Messenger

From the main MSN Messenger screen, click Tools to send messages to cell phones, pagers, or Pocket PCs. This requires you to sign up with MSN Mobile. You can also send messages via Hotmail and invite members of your contact list to start an online meeting with NetMeeting.

FIGURE 8.13

The Windows Messenger for Windows XP interface during a typical text and voice chat session.

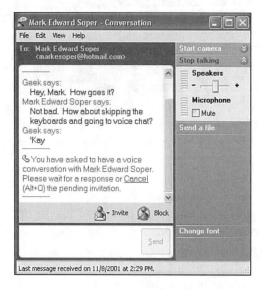

Similarly, the Windows Messenger Tools menu also supports sending messages to different types of devices and sends mail via Hotmail. However, instead of using NetMeeting, it has integrated Webcam, whiteboard, and application sharing support (all features of NetMeeting), and also supports the Windows XP Remote Assistance feature, which allows another user to control your computer for training or troubleshooting purposes.

Yahoo! Messenger

Yahoo! Messenger is the latest major IM player, but it supports the widest range of operating systems and platforms, including all of the following:

- Windows 95 and later
- MacOS
- Java
- Unix/FreeBSD/Linux
- PalmOS
- Windows CE
- Mobile Phone
- RIM alphanumeric pagers

Yahoo! Messenger can be integrated with Yahoo! e-mail and other features during installation.

Chatting with Yahoo! Messenger

Yahoo! Messenger offers three different chat options:

- Instant Message
- Conference
- Chat rooms

Instant messages with Yahoo! Messenger can be sent to one or more friends (equivalent to buddies or contacts), and will be retained in an offline message box if the friend isn't accepting messages at that time.

A conference is designed for up to 10 users to chat with each other, and you also can create a custom chat room in Yahoo! Chat and invite friends to join you there.

The chat interface in Yahoo! Messenger is similar to AIM and MSN Messenger, and features smiley and text-formatting features similar to those in AIM. Click the Voice button to set up voice chatting, and the Webcam button to activate your Webcam.

Tip

You can use Webcams on either or both ends of a chat. Webcams can also be used in a conference.

Figure 8.14 shows various elements of the Yahoo! Messenger service, including its interface, IM window, and Webcam windows.

FIGURE 8.14

A typical Yahoo! Messenger chat with voice and Webcam options enabled.

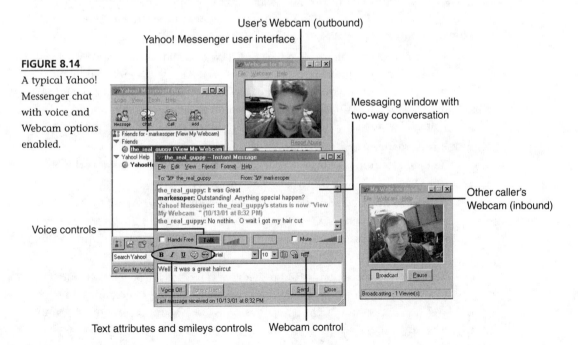

The user interface for Yahoo! Messenger's Conference feature is similar to the IM interface, except that icons representing each participant are displayed.

Webcams can be turned on and off during an IM or conference session, and those actions are displayed as part of the transcript.

Advanced Features of Yahoo! Messenger

Yahoo! Messenger's integrated Webcam and voice features allow you to conduct A/V chats without running additional software. Messenger's ability to automatically archive messages and conferences make it very easy to keep track of information for both personal and business use.

 To create an archive of instant messages and conferences, enable this feature in Properties. You can specify which types of messages to archive and how long to keep them.

ICQ

ICQ is the oldest and most powerful instant messaging product on the market. Although ICQ is unknown to many PC users in the United States, ICQ is very popular in other parts of the world. Although ICQ is now owned by AOL (which also distributes the popular AOL Instant Messenger client originally created by Netscape), ICQ is a distinctly different product. Compared to other IM clients, ICQ has the following differences:

- Wider platform support—Versions of ICQ are available for 32-bit Windows, PowerPC (recent and current MacOS), as well as older or more exotic platforms such as Windows CE, Windows NT 3.5, Windows 3.1, classic (68000-based) Macs, JAVA (for use on PCs and Linux, Unix, and so on), and Palm OS systems.

- Business groupware support—While most other IM products are primarily designed for fun, ICQ also supports business collaboration and workgroup tasks with its ICQ Groupware clients and servers.

- Extensible architecture—While most IM products are designed to provide a closed environment, ICQ works along with NetMeeting, CU-SeeMe, and many other voice and video chat products. ICQ also supports plug-ins for additional integration of basic features into the ICQ client itself.

- Versatile contact options—ICQ provides seven ways for people to contact you via ICQ, from providing each user a unique ICQ code you can put on your Web site to personal ICQ homepages, SMS to ICQ support, e-mail access to ICQ, and others.

■ Web integration—ICQ's Web site provides links to chat rooms, interest groups, and member directories, and you can add applets to your Web site that allow other ICQ users to send you instant messages.

ICQ features vary by operating system; the screen shots in this section reflect version 2001b for Windows 98/2000/Me/NT4/XP.

During the installation process, ICQ displays a reminder that the service is not for use by children under 13 years of age. This warning is there for a reason: While all chat products can be used for both age-appropriate and inappropriate tasks, ICQ has a huge number of communities and chat rooms that specialize in so-called "adult" topics. Both ICQ and Yahoo! Messenger (which also offers chat rooms) should be considered "adults-only" chat products for this reason.

During installation, you can complete as much or as little of the registration form as you like—the less you complete, the harder it is for other ICQers to find you online (ICQ allows strangers to find you via various search tools). ICQ's default allows others to add you to their contact list and see if you're online; if you value your privacy, change the default setting and require your authorization before you show up on a contact list.

Write down the ICQ number that's displayed during registration; it's how you're identified to other ICQ users and to the ICQ client. After the ICQ number is displayed, you can enable or disable options to search your address books to create a customized "My ICQ," set the ICQ homepage as your browser's default homepage, and make yourself available for chats with others who have similar interests, newsletters, and customized e-mail signatures.

Chatting with ICQ

When you open the ICQ client for 32-bit Windows, you will see an interface similar to the one in Figure 8.15; this interface is called simple mode. Click the Add/Invite Users button to open a form that enables you to search for other ICQ users by e-mail, nickname, first or last name, or ICQ number. You can add any or all of the matches to your search to your user list (ICQ's term for its buddy or friend list).

After one or more ICQ users are added to your user list, their icons appear in your ICQ client and are listed by their status. Online means the user has been added to your list and is currently connected to ICQ; offline means that the ICQ user on your list is not currently connected to ICQ; not on a list means that the ICQ user shown is not on your list of users, but has found you by searching the ICQ user list. Click the user's icon to send a message, add the user to your list, delete the user, or change user information.

FIGURE 8.15

The ICQ client
for 32-bit
Windows in sim-
ple mode.

When you select Send Message, the ICQ message window opens. You can specify
whether to send a message by ICQ (chat), by e-mail, or with some versions of ICQ,
by SMS (short message service, which works with GSM-compatible mobile phones).
You can select one or more methods for sending your message, which helps ensure
that your recipient will get the message. Your message and your recipient's replies
are color-coded, as seen in Figure 8.16.

Use the controls displayed in Figure 8.16 to add emoticons, switch to audio chat,
spell-check your text, add smileys or other emoticons, and add text enhancements.

FIGURE 8.16

A typical text
chat with ICQ.
The upper win-
dow displays
your messages
and the other
user's responses,
while the lower
window is used
for entering your
current message.

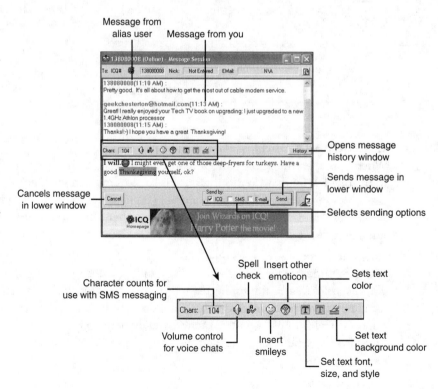

Tip

Because ICQ is a much more powerful tool than other IM products, you should use the "how to start" button on the ICQ client main display to bring up a Web-based tutorial to bring you up to speed on ICQ's many features, even if you're already familiar with IM products in general.

Click the Online button to start chatting with a friend or change the status of your ICQ connection to make yourself invisible to other ICQ users, indicate you're busy, and so forth.

NetMeeting

NetMeeting is a powerful multimedia and collaboration tool for Windows 9x/Me/2000 users. It allows you to do the following:

- Perform audio, a/v, and text chats
- View and optionally control another person's desktop and programs
- Create and share a whiteboard
- Perform file transfers to one or multiple recipients

Originally developed for business users, NetMeeting has also become popular with home users who run MSN Messenger, because MSN Messenger provides one of the primary methods for connecting with other NetMeeting users.

Figure 8.17 shows the major elements of the NetMeeting 3.01 user interface.

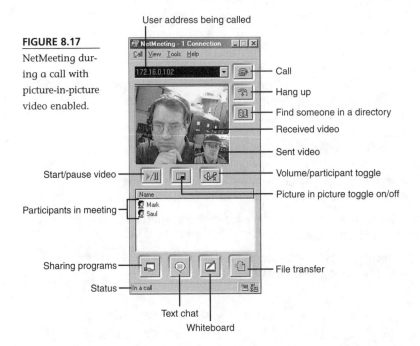

FIGURE 8.17
NetMeeting during a call with picture-in-picture video enabled.

User address being called

Call

Hang up

Find someone in a directory

Received video

Sent video

Start/pause video

Volume/participant toggle

Picture in picture toggle on/off

Participants in meeting

Sharing programs

File transfer

Status

Text chat

Whiteboard

Upgrading NetMeeting

NetMeeting is typically installed as part of an Internet Explorer installation or upgrade. Many Webcams also come with NetMeeting as part of their software bundle. Windows Update may also offer the latest version of NetMeeting for your version of Windows as a recommended update.

If you need to download NetMeeting separately from other programs, upgrade to the latest version, or need more information about NetMeeting, set your browser to www.Microsoft.com/windows/NetMeeting.

Connecting to Other Users

After you've installed the latest release of NetMeeting 3.01 or later, you can use your MSN Messenger contact list to place NetMeeting calls. To call someone on your MSN Messenger list, do the following:

1. Click the Find Someone in a Directory button to display your MSN Messenger contact list.

2. Click the user to start your call, as in Figure 8.18.

FIGURE 8.18

The MSN Messenger Service contact list is used as the primary way to place calls in NetMeeting 3.01 and later.

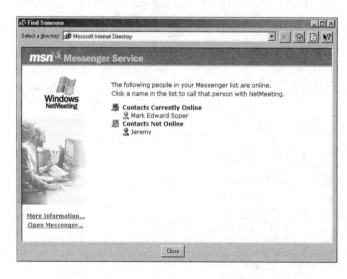

3. The recipient's MSN Messenger window will display your request for a NetMeeting call, and will either Accept or Decline it, as in Figure 8.19.

4. Another dialog box appears on the recipient's screen; the recipient will click Accept to open NetMeeting.

5. After NetMeeting starts, the caller and the person(s) who were called and accepted will be displayed on all users' NetMeeting screens as shown in Figure 8.16.

FIGURE 8.19

NetMeeting won't start the incoming call until you accept the invitation that MSN Messenger issues.

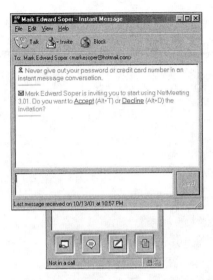

Note

Older versions of NetMeeting used as their default contact method various public and private Internet Locator Service (ILS) servers across the world. If you prefer to use this, your preferred servers can be manually entered into NetMeeting through its Tools, Options menu (General tab). For an up-to-date list of ILS servers where you can chat with other NetMeeting users, go to www.netmeet.com/bestservers.asp.

Many servers require a membership fee; check the ILS server's Web site for details.

Using NetMeeting Features

As Figure 8.17 makes clear, you can use NetMeeting as a videophone system; in fact, many Webcam vendors no longer offer their own software for this task but include NetMeeting instead. NetMeeting is an H.323-compliant program, so it can communicate with other videophone programs.

Note

You can use audio and video features with only one other user at a time.

You can also use NetMeeting to conduct planning meetings with multiple participants by using its Chat feature. By default, text you type in Chat goes to all participants in a call. To chat with only one other party, click that person's icon and select it in the Send To window before you type your message. Users in a call can also add text or graphics to the Whiteboard unless you have locked the Whiteboard (see the View menu).

You can also transfer files between participants in a call and share your desktop and active programs with other users. File transfers, as with Chat, can be sent to just one person or to everyone in the current meeting.

Perhaps the most exciting feature in NetMeeting is also the most potentially dangerous: sharing your desktop. You can use this as a troubleshooting tool by opening a program and displaying the screen to other participants in the call. You can also share an open program, allowing someone else to actually take control of your desktop (see Figure 8.20).

FIGURE 8.20

Sharing the desktop allows other users to see and, optionally, control your desktop. Use the Control feature with care!

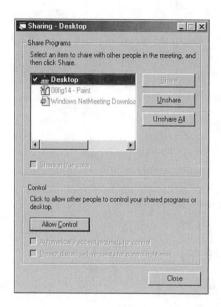

Click the Allow Control button to allow other users to control any programs you selected as shared on your Desktop. After another user double-clicks on their copy of your desktop or shared program, a prompt appears on your screen. If you accept their control, that user is in charge.

A pointer with the user's initials appears on your screen. This feature, especially when combined with voice or text chat, allows NetMeeting to be a useful training and troubleshooting tool.

Tip

If you need to seize control back from other users, just click your mouse and control of your system returns to you.

Troubleshooting NetMeeting

Trying to use older and newer versions of NetMeeting is difficult, especially because older versions don't properly handle the use of the MSN Messenger contact list for call lookups. In addition, some bundled versions of NetMeeting are hard-wired to use a proprietary ILS server instead of the MSN Messenger list, and continue to do so, even if you upgrade your installation.

To cure most problems with NetMeeting, uninstall older versions and install the latest version. Windows 9x/Me users, for example, should install NetMeeting 3.01 with Service Pack 2 or higher. This version uses the MSN Messenger contact list and will no longer display the Can't Logon to Directory Server error that is so frustrating in older versions.

Another major problem comes when you use a router. NetMeeting requires a large number of open TCP ports if you want to use its audio and video features, and typical home and home-office routers don't have provisions for selectively opening those ports. As an alternative, most of these routers have a so-called DMZ (or demilitarized zone) setting for a given IP address, which turns off the incoming firewall protection in the router. Although this allows NetMeeting to work, it's also potentially dangerous.

Don't use the DMZ mode unless you cannot get NetMeeting to work, and be sure you have an effective personal firewall program installed before you use this option. I recommend turning off DMZ and returning to normal firewall mode after using NetMeeting if you use NetMeeting infrequently.

If more than one person on your home network wants to use NetMeeting, be sure your router supports DMZ or H.323 videoconferencing standards for more than one user; some low-cost routers support only a single DMZ user at a time.

If your router or firewall appliance/program has a preset option for H.323 videoconferencing traffic, use this option to allow NetMeeting to work. This setting will open the TCP ports needed by NetMeeting and other H.323-compliant programs but will keep other TCP ports closed to protect your system against intruders.

As an alternative to using NetMeeting, you might also want to try Yahoo! Messenger's Webcam and voice support if you want audio/video chat features or a third-party videophone program.

Windows XP doesn't support NetMeeting; its Windows Messenger combines the video chat and collaboration features of NetMeeting with the text and audio chat features of MSN Messenger. Windows Messenger can connect with MSN Messenger for chats, but not with NetMeeting. If you want to have video chats between Windows XP and other Windows or non-Windows operating systems, you need to use a third-party videophone program such as CU-SeeMe or others that support Windows XP and the other operating systems.

Summary

The major Web-based media players you should consider installing and using on your cable Internet connection include Windows Media Player, RealPlayer, and Apple QuickTime. These programs support the most common formats used for streaming video and audio online. While your computer may have a version of these programs already installed, you might need to upgrade to the latest version for your operating system to fully enjoy online content. For additional features with RealPlayer or Apple QuickTime, consider purchasing their deluxe versions.

If you want to enjoy Internet radio, you need Windows Media Player and RealPlayer to have access to the widest possible choices of online radio programs.

Instant-messaging clients allow you to have instant text chats with old friends and new acquaintances. Depending on your computer's operating system, you might be able to choose from most of the following: AOL Instant Messenger, MSN Messenger, Windows Messenger, Yahoo! Messenger, or ICQ. While each IM client has its own strengths and weaknesses, it is necessary at this time to choose the same client that your friends use to stay in touch, because there are no industry standards for IM clients at this time. Some IM clients also support voice and video chats, or can be integrated with third-party programs that provide these features.

Windows 9x/Me/2000 users can use NetMeeting for text/voice/video chatting and collaboration on business projects. Because NetMeeting is an H.323-compliant video-conferencing program, it can connect with other H.323-compliant programs. However, Windows XP's similar Windows Messenger won't connect with NetMeeting; Windows Messenger 4.5 and later can connect with MSN Messenger 4.0 and later for text and audio chats.

USING A WEBCAM

*C*HAPTER HIGHLIGHTS:

- How to use a Webcam to create a video e-mail message
- How to create compact video e-mails
- Where to find video e-mail services
- How to use a Webcam with services such as NetMeeting and Yahoo! Messenger

9

Creating and Sending Video E-Mail

Webcams can be used for immediate face-to-face communications with popular IM and conferencing tools, but it isn't always feasible to set up such a connection. If you want to use live video with a dial-up connection, for example, be prepared for excruciatingly slow response. And, although nothing can beat live interaction, our memories often preserve the details of phone calls and conversations imperfectly. You can share almost-live video with friends and family and give them a moving, speaking memory that will last by using your Webcam to create video e-mail messages.

Methods for Creating Video E-Mail

The simplest video e-mail is a file containing recorded audio and video. You can create this with video-editing programs such as the simple Windows Movie Maker included with Windows Me and Windows XP or with commercial video-editing programs sold by many different manufacturers or bundled with IEEE-1394 or high-end video cards. This approach makes sense only if the recipient uses the same software you do, or if you can save the video file in a format that is supported by your recipient's video program (such as the Windows Video .AVI format). Otherwise, the recipient wouldn't be able to play back your video.

Because video capture and editing software, not to mention Webcams, are still far from common, it makes more sense in some cases to use software that can create a self-contained file, which the recipient can open and play without additional software or hardware. Such software is included with most Webcams, and this discussion will focus on how to use such programs.

Before sending your intended recipient a video e-mail which uses a self-contained player program, find out if the user's e-mail service will accept .EXE (program) files. For security reasons, some corporate networks block e-mails which have .EXE attachments.

If the recipient's e-mail service won't allow .EXE file attachments, you can still send video e-mail with one of these options:

- As a workaround, you might be able to use an archiving program, such as WinZip, PKZip or StuffIt, to create an archive file which the user can open with a compatible program and then view the video e-mail.

- Save the video e-mail as an .AVI or other file type that is supported by the user's media player software. See Chapter 8 for details.

Using Video E-Mail Recording Software

Most Webcams offer both video capture programs and video e-mail programs. What are the differences between these types of programs?

- Video e-mail programs create files that are more compact in size and might have lower image quality than capture programs.

- Video e-mail programs can create self-contained files that include the player program and the video; video capture programs often lack this option.

- Video e-mail programs can send the file for you; video capture programs use your ordinary e-mail client and require you to manually attach the video file and separate player program (if necessary) to an outgoing file.

Intel Video Email, packaged with Intel Webcams, is a typical example of a video e-mail program (see Figure 9.1). It allows you to record, trim off extraneous portions of the video clip, and e-mail it to recipients.

FIGURE 9.1

Intel Video E-mail after recording a video clip.

The controls on a typical video e-mail recording program, such as the one in Figure 9.1, are similar to those on a VCR, allowing you to start and stop the recording, play back the recording, and move to a specific place in the recording. Unlike a VCR, however, you can remove portions of your recorded video, deleting awkward pauses or other miscues.

Before editing a recording, save the original to a file so you have a backup in case you make a mistake while trimming or editing the recording.

Some programs also display the size of the recorded file during the process.

Adjusting Image and Video Quality

During the video capture process, you might be able to optimize for settings such as the following:

- Low light
- Fast action
- Image quality
- White balance
- Color saturation
- Image sharpness
- Exposure
- Camera zoom, pan, and tilt

Check your video e-mail software for an Adjust Video or Video Properties dialog box if you need to improve the quality of the video you record within the program.

Try making test recordings with different settings to see what effect the settings have before you try sending your first video e-mail. Keep in mind that the default settings are designed to provide the best results in most situations. Before you make changes, see if an option is available to reset the software to its defaults.

Editing the Recording

You can edit video e-mail in two ways:

- Trimming the beginning and end of the e-mail
- Using a separate non-linear editing program, which can combine clips and perform special effects, such as fades and wipes

Simple video e-mail programs such as Intel Video Email have trim capabilities only. However, most commercial video editors (including the ones bundled with many IEEE-1394 cards for connecting with DV camcorders) can edit .AVI (Video for Windows) files, which is the most common file format that Webcams use.

To trim a recording with a typical video e-mail program:

1. Save the recording.
2. Select the Trim tool. Look for a button labeled Trim as in Figure 9.2 or check the program's menus for this option.
3. Position the left tool at the start of the section you want to keep.

4. Position the right tool at the end of the section you want to keep (skip ahead to Figure 9.2).

5. Depending on the program, you might need to remove the trimmed sections immediately, or you might need to remove them when you send or save the file.

Be sure to save the trimmed version with a name different from the original version of your file. Using a different name for the trimmed version enables you to go back to the original version to make other changes if you need to.

Sending Video E-Mail

After you have played back the edited version of your video e-mail file, you can send it. Some programs, such as Intel Video Email, allow you to address the e-mail and send it straight from the program, as shown in Figure 9.2. Others might open your normal e-mail client and use it to send your e-mail.

FIGURE 9.2

Sending a trimmed video clip with Intel Video E-mail.

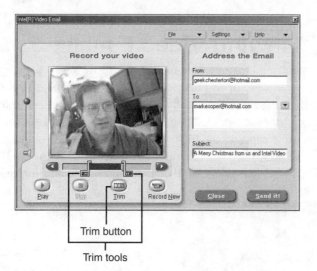

During the sending process, the video clip is compressed to take up significantly less space than the original video file. For example, the original 8-second video clip created for the figures in this chapter occupied 1915KB of disk space as an .AVI file. However, the same video clip required only 544KB of disk space when it was e-mailed, even though the file also contains a self-standing player program.

A great rule of thumb for video e-mail clips is "the shorter, the better." Shorter video clips translate into smaller file sizes.

Clips that are larger than 1MB can't be received by e-mail servers that require file attachments to fall below 1MB. Also, dial-up users' slow modems will take a while to download even a 500KB file.

Keep in mind that you can use the Trim tool to create multiple smaller files from your original video clip if you use a unique name for each trimmed version.

After a video clip has been compressed and combined with a player program for e-mailing, it can no longer be edited. Make sure you save the video before you e-mail it if you want to edit it later.

You can also send pre-existing video clips as video e-mail if your video e-mail program can open the file type used to store the video clip. For example, Intel Video Email can open and save files in .AVI format, so any .AVI file can be converted into a video e-mail file.

Receiving and Viewing Video E-mail

When the recipient receives a video e-mail, it might include a message that provides information about how to open and view the file. If the video e-mail file is attached to a message, the message will typically tell you to save the file and open it from the Windows Explorer or Mac Finder. Some video e-mail services store the file on a special server, instead of sending the file to the recipient. In such cases, the e-mail will provide a special URL where you can go to retrieve and play the file. Figure 9.3 shows the video file playing through its self-contained player program.

FIGURE 9.3

Viewing an Intel Video Email clip with its stand-alone player program.

Even though video e-mail files are highly compressed, even a short greeting can use considerable mailbox space. If you prefer to leave your e-mail messages on your e-mail server (a popular choice if you need to access messages from home and work, or from work and on the road), you could run out of space in your e-mail box after receiving just one or two typical video e-mail messages. Messages which arrive after your e-mail box fills up will bounce back to the sender.

To avoid running out of space in your e-mail box, save video e-mail files or other large file attachments, save the text message sent with the attachment, and delete the message (and its attachment) from your e-mail box. Check with your ISP to determine the maximum size of your e-mail box.

If you want to share the clip with another family member or friend, use the Forward or FW: option in your e-mail client to send along the message. Because many people routinely delete messages with FW in the subject line, change the subject line to delete the FW and make sure to keep the original text explaining how to view the e-mail.

Playing Video E-Mail that Doesn't Include a Player Program

Most video e-mail includes a self-contained player, but if someone sends you a video clip that is not a program file, you will need to use a compatible program to open it. For example, if someone sends you a Video for Windows (.AVI) file, you can play it with RealPlayer or Windows Media Player.

If you are wondering what types of files your media player can use, open the File menu, click Open, and scroll through the file types listed. For example, RealPlayer can also play Active Stream Format, MPEG movie and video files, and Macromedia Flash movies, as well as various types of Real media files and music files. Windows Media Player can play various types of Windows Media files, as well as MPEG files, AVI files, and Windows Movie Maker files. See Figure 9.4.

FIGURE 9.4

Using the Windows Media Player File, Open, Files of Type menu to view supported file types.

Depending on the resolution of the Webcam used, movie files played back in a media player might be displayed in a window larger than that used by a self-contained player program (see Figure 9.5).

FIGURE 9.5

Video size comparison between the original AVI file played in Windows Media Player (left) and the self-contained Intel Video E-mail Player (right).

Using a Webcam with NetMeeting

The Microsoft NetMeeting program discussed in Chapter 8, "Using Internet Multimedia and Messaging," can be used without a Webcam, but when you use it with a Webcam, you can use it as a highly effective videophone. NetMeeting automatically detects a Webcam that you have installed on your system.

Note

In Windows XP, Microsoft has replaced NetMeeting with Windows Messenger. Windows Messenger is compatible with MSN Messenger for text and voice chatting, but offers built-in Webcam support for video chatting with other Windows Messenger users only. Windows XP users who want to have video chat with users of other versions of Windows need to use a third-party chat tool such as Yahoo! Messenger, CUseeMe 5.0 (www.cuseeme.com/support/downloads/index.html), or others.

Most of the video controls that NetMeeting uses are found in the Video tab of the Options menu (see Figure 9.6). Use this tab to determine if you will automatically send or receive video at the start of a call, the sending video window size, the video quality (faster or better-quality), and to select the video camera (if your system has more than one).

Other video controls in NetMeeting include the following:

- The picture-in-picture toggle, which is beneath the main receive window. When enabled, the small video in the lower-right corner of the screen is the video you are sending, whereas the rest of the screen area is used for the video you are receiving (if any).

■ The View menu, which has a picture-in-picture option, as well as a My Video option. The My Video option displays the video you are sending in a separate window that you can move around onscreen (see Figure 9.7).

■ The play/pause button below the main video window, which starts and pauses video sending.

FIGURE 9.6

Using NetMeeting's Video Options menu.

FIGURE 9.7

Comparing the default size of the optional My Video window (left) to the small (top right) and large sizes (bottom right). This is also the size of the window that the receiver will see.

Medium (Default)

Small

Large

Use the chat feature in NetMeeting to determine whether your video settings are satisfactory to the receiver. If your video is too slow at the receiving end, reduce the size of your sending window and adjust the sliding control in the Video Options menu toward Faster Video (see Figure 9.6).

Using a Webcam with IM Services

The four major IM clients (ICQ, AOL Instant Messenger, MSN Messenger, and Yahoo! Messenger) differ in many ways, not the least of which is in their support for Webcams. Of these, Yahoo! Messenger, although it is the youngest of the major IM services, is the only one to build Webcam support into its version of IM. Although MSN Messenger doesn't support Webcams directly, it is tightly integrated with the latest version of NetMeeting (version 3.01), which uses the MSN Messenger contact list to make NetMeeting calls.

AOL Instant Messenger and ICQ have no integrated Webcam support at present, although many third-party Webcam programs can be integrated with ICQ. In ICQ, Webcam programs show up under the Voice/Video/Games or Internet Phone/Games menus displayed after you select someone to call via ICQ. If both parties have the same Webcam software, it starts automatically on both systems enabling video chat.

Some of the popular ICQ-compatible Webcam programs include Webcam 1-2-3 (www.webcam123.com; also works with other IM software), Cybration's ICUII (www.icuii.com), and nanoCom's iSpQ (www.ispq.com). AOL IM doesn't offer a menu option for third-party software support, but third-party add-on programs such asNanoCom's BuddyVision (www.buddyvision.com) are available. You can use BuddyVision even if only one of the parties has a Webcam.

Yahoo! Messenger and Webcams

Yahoo! Messenger's Webcam Preferences page (see Figure 9.8) allows you to adjust the image quality of your Webcam picture, control who can see your Webcam, determine whether chat room participants can view your Webcam, and set the message displayed when you start your Webcam. Click Login, Preferences, and select Webcam to configure these options.

The Tools menu is used to start the Webcam and to invite users to view your Webcam. You can send invitations to individual Yahoo! users to view your Webcam, and you can chat with some users while allowing other users to view your Webcam and vice-versa.

FIGURE 9.8

Yahoo!
Messenger's
Webcam
Properties sheet.

Summary

Webcams can be used for a variety of tasks, including video e-mail and instant messaging. As broadband Internet connections become more widespread and IM services continue to enhance Webcam support, look for Webcams to become a more and more popular addition to computers everywhere.

Because many third-party Webcam applications can be downloaded on a limited-time trial basis, it's easy to find the best Webcam software for your needs. Remember, in most cases you need to use the same Webcam software at both ends of a connection to enable two-way voice chats.

USING PHOTO AND DATA-STORAGE SERVICES

CHAPTER HIGHLIGHTS:

- Learn how to get your photos processed and printed from online vendors
- Display photos online
- Store other types of files online for easy backup and use anywhere

Selecting an Online Photo Service

For years, mail-order photo processors have provided a close-as-your-mailbox alternative to taking your film to a drugstore, camera shop, or discount store for developing, printing, and reprints. Now that the Internet is no longer a curiosity, both traditional mail-order film processors and newcomers have brought this concept online. In addition to traditional services such as developing, printing, and reprinting from color-negative film such as Kodacolor and Fujicolor, you can now get true photo prints from digital scans you do yourself and get your pictures stored and displayed online as part of the deal.

Whether you use a traditional film camera or have switched to digital, online photo services can be useful to you. Here's why:

- Fast, convenient processing and digitizing of color negative film—You won't need an expensive filmstrip scanner to convert your pictures into digital form.

- Higher-quality and more durable prints from digital originals than even the best inkjet printers can perform—Most services use the same high-quality silver-halide based paper that is used by top-quality traditional photofinishers.

- Online photo albums—You don't need to whip up a Web site (or worry about letting the wrong folks see it) with most online photo finishers' online photo album option. Your albums are password-protected so only you or those you trust can see your pictures.

- Easy ordering of photo novelties—Get everything from enlargements to mugs and greeting cards from your photos.

The best online photo service for you is the one that provides a good balance of what follows:

- High scanning quality (for film processing)
- High print quality (from your preferred media—digital images or film)
- Easy-to-access and secure online albums
- Fast service
- Variety of photo-related products
- Reasonable prices

The speed of your cable Internet service will make it easy to move your pictures to an online service; after that, you need to evaluate the leaders and see who does the best job to determine who you want to use for the long haul.

See Chapter 6, "Ten Ways Cable Modems Make the Internet Better," for a partial listing of major online photofinishers.

Getting Your Photos Online

The first step in trying an online photo service is getting your pictures online. Most online photo processors offer a free photo transfer program you can download, or you can use a browser-based process to send copies of your digitized pictures to the processor to be made into online albums or to order prints. Figure 10.1 shows a typical drag-and-drop interface.

FIGURE 10.1

Using PhotoWorks' Upload Photos feature to transfer digital images to the PhotoWorks Web site.

You can transfer pictures online from any drive letter, including your hard drive or picture CDs, or even directly from flash memory cards. Some services, such as PhotoWorks, support multiple picture formats, whereas others, such as Ofoto, require all your pictures to be in the JPEG (.JPG) file format before you can transfer them.

Tip

If you prefer to use the Netscape browser and your photofinisher uses a browser-based interface for uploading pictures, you might want to log on to your preferred photofinishing site with both the Netscape and Microsoft Web browsers. Generally, if you want to use a drag-and-drop interface, you need to use Internet Explorer and install an ActiveX control that the photofinisher provides.

Although most online print services will keep your album online for up to six months, the main reason to transfer pictures is to make prints. Therefore, some photofinishers display a warning message such as the one in Figure 10.2 if you try to upload a low-resolution picture.

FIGURE 10.2

If you try to upload a photo with too low of a resolution for decent prints, PhotoWorks' Upload Photos feature displays this warning and stops the transfer.

Note

In digital photography, resolution refers to the number of dots (horizontal×vertical) in a digital image. 640×480 will fill most of a typical display, but is sufficient resolution for only small snapshot (4×6-inch or smaller) prints. By comparison, most monitors have resolutions of 800×600 up to 1,280×1,024.

Most online processors scan film at 1000×1500 resolution, which can be used for prints up to 8×10 inches. This is comparable to the resolution of a 2-megapixel digital camera.

After you've selected your pictures, click the Upload button and the pictures will be transferred to the online processor's server. From there, follow the prompts onscreen to select the photos you want in an online album, title it, and share it with others.

Figure 10.3 shows a picture from my photo album online at Ofoto. Ofoto displays the photos as a slide show as well as in album format and provides an immediate opportunity to order prints in the most common sizes.

FIGURE 10.3

Viewing an online slideshow created by Ofoto. Photo by Stuart E. Soper (my father).

Ordering Photo Prints Online

After you have uploaded your photos to your preferred online photofinisher, you can order prints. Although available print sizes range from wallet (about 2.5×3.5 inches) to 20×30, image quality in the larger sizes will drop significantly if you submit low-resolution pictures for printing.

For best results when you take digital pictures, do the following:

- Use the highest resolution and quality settings that are available on your camera.

- If you edit your pictures before uploading them, either save them in a non-lossy format such as TIFF (.TIF) or .BMP or use the maximum quality setting for JPEG to avoid loss of detail. For best results when you scan photos, slides, or negatives, follow these guidelines:

    - Create images at least 1,500 pixels wide; some finishers will handle images up to 2,200 pixels wide before reducing the size to their maximum.

    - Save the image in either a non-lossy format such as TIFF (.TIF) or .BMP or use the maximum quality setting for JPEG to avoid loss of detail.

Note Most digital cameras use the Joint Photographic Expert Group (JPEG) file format for storing pictures. JPEG pictures use the .JPG file extension. JPEG pictures use less storage space (and thus take less time to upload) because they use a highly effective form of data compression to shrink the picture to about half the size it would be otherwise. However, JPEG compression is "lossy," meaning that some fine detail is discarded to compress the image; increasing compression to use even less space discards more detail. If you repeatedly save a JPEG picture after making changes to it, even at maximum quality, you will eventually lose noticeable detail. Other picture formats such as TIFF and BMP either don't use compression or use a lossless form of compression that keeps all the detail. Because of this, however, TIFF and BMP files are larger than JPEG files of the same image. GIF files are often used on the Web because they are very small, but they can only display a maximum of 256 colors, making GIF a bad choice for photos.

As you saw in Figure 10.2, some photofinishers will warn you during the initial upload process if a picture is too low of a resolution to make decent-quality prints. Others might wait until you have uploaded your pictures to an album to recommend the maximum print size for each image.

To find out how large of an image you need to upload to create high-quality prints at different sizes, I scanned a photo and saved it in six different sizes. Table 10.1 lists the image sizes and the maximum-size high-quality picture you can print according to leading online photofinisher Ofoto.

Table 10.1 Maximum Print Sizes for Popular Digital Image Sizes

Width in Pixels	Maximum Print Size
640	Wallet
800	4×6 inches
1,024	4×6 inches
1,280	5×7 inches
1,760	20×30 inches
2,200	20×30 inches

As you can see from Table 10.1, higher-resolution digital images can become higher-resolution pictures.

KEEP IN MIND THE BIG PICTURE

Although Ofoto supports print sizes of up to 20×30 inches, very few digital images are sharp and clear enough to be printed this large. And, at prices of about $20 per enlargement, printing an image of marginal quality will hit you in the wallet.

If you want high-quality super-sized enlargements, be sure you do the following:

- Take a very sharp picture to begin with—Image faults such as poor focus, camera shake, or motion blur are magnified with larger prints. Use a tripod, and shoot in bright light outdoors or with a flash indoors to avoid these problems.

- Because lens quality and original picture quality are critical, consider shooting with either a very high-quality (3 megapixel or higher-resolution) digital camera or a 35mm single-lens reflex camera using a fine-grain film such 200-speed or slower color print or slide film. Most point-and-shoot digital or film cameras don't have really high-quality lenses, and fast film introduces unwanted graininess and loss of fine detail.

- If you are scanning negatives or slides to create your digital images, be sure to carefully brush or wipe dust from the film before you scan it.

- Use digital retouching features in photo-editing programs to improve sharpness, color rendition, contrast, brightness, and cropping before you create the digital image. You can also remove dust and scratches from older or damaged images if you're careful.

- Order an 8×10 enlargement (around $4–5) first. If the 8×10 is not of high quality, the larger prints will be even poorer.

As with other forms of online shopping, you will need to supply a credit card for payment and provide shipping information before your order is complete.

Sharing Photos Online

After your photos are online, and even before you place your first print order, most online photofinishers will create an online photo album for you, as you saw earlier in this chapter. It's a great combination of good customer service and better profits, a win-win deal!

The good customer service comes from your ability to specify who can see a given album; most online photofinishers will provide you with a special Web site address (URL) you can e-mail to friends and family members. Some will even save you the trouble of copying it and pasting it into your e-mail client and let you send the invitation directly from their Web site. Because you can create multiple albums (for example, Our Wedding, Our New Home, Our Vacation, and so forth), you can match albums to the people who'd like to see them very easily. All they need is a Web browser and an Internet connection to see your digital masterpieces, even if you're too lazy to make that extra set of prints you always promised to send along.

The better profits part comes in when family and friends view your albums, because most online photofinishers make it easy to purchase prints and enlargements during the viewing process.

With online photo albums, your life in pictures is just a click away from the people you want to see it, and only the people to whom you give access can see those photos.

You can use your online photofinisher as a backup storage site for your digital photos as long as you order prints occasionally. Use this as a backup to your own archive on CD-R or other removable media.

Selecting an Online File Storage Service

You have probably experienced the same problem I have, especially if you work in more than one place. You find yourself sitting down at the computer, only to discover that the data files (documents, images, or whatever) were left at home or at the office. And, maybe you have watched in horror as a system crash destroyed your work because you didn't have a big enough removable-media drive to hold your current project. You might have also received messages informing you that your co-workers can't e-mail you the files you need because they're too large, even after being compressed, to fit within the file-attachment size limits imposed by your cable ISP.

Online storage makes it possible for you to access your information via any Internet connection without worrying about e-mail attachment limits, and the speed of cable Internet service makes it faster than ever to send (and receive) the files you need. If your boss (including the one in the mirror) makes you bring work home from the office, you can use your office's high-speed Internet connection to upload the files you need. And you can use your home's cable Internet service to download your work instead of lugging home a bunch of floppy disks or CDs. When it's time to call it an evening, upload your changes and pick them up at the office the next day.

As you learned in Chapter 6, many providers of online storage services are available, including

- Drive Plus—Fee-based (plus.xdrive.com)
- Swapdrive—Fee-based (www.swapdrive.com)
- bigVAULT—Fee-based (www.bigvault.com)
- Yahoo! Briefcase—Free to Yahoo! users; anyone can sign up for a Yahoo! username and password (briefcase.yahoo.com)
- iTools—Users of MacOS 9 and above can use iTools, including 20MB of free storage through iDisk (itools.mac.com)
- @Backup—Fee-based online backup service (www.atbackup.com)

With a wide variety of fee-based providers and even some free providers, how can you choose the best online storage provider for your needs? The following criteria will help you make the best choice.

Cost factors to consider include

- Cost per MB—If you're looking for economy, the lowest cost per MB might be the most important factor. And, a free service such as Yahoo! Briefcase or iTools will be the winner. However, free services let you store only a few MB of data online. Use fee-based services for larger storage needs.
- Cost per project—This is the cost per MB of the amount of storage you need for your project; most fee-based services let you rent varying amounts of capacity to meet your specific needs.

Usability factors to consider include

- Platforms supported—Most online storage providers support major browsers, and some might also support wireless devices and PDAs. Be sure to check to see whether your operating system or device type is supported before you try a particular service, or be sure you have a free trial period to work out any bugs or questions. Most drag-and-drop options require IE 4.0 or above and a 32-bit version of Windows, though.

- Interface—The simpler the interface to use, the more likely you are to use it. Drag-and-drop options that use Windows Explorer are much easier than browser-based interfaces, but must be installed on each client PC you use.

- Features—If you need features beyond simple online storage (for example, automated backup or CD-creation), be sure your provider supports them.

Speed and capacity factors to consider include

- Upload size limit—If you want to upload large files or a large group of files, check the maximum size of files you can upload. You might need to upload a large project in several phases, or use a compression tool to reduce a single file in size below the maximum size limit.

- Upload speed—The faster your data can be uploaded, the more likely you are to use the service.

- Download speed—Especially if you sometimes will retrieve your data from slow dial-up connections, the faster you get your data, the better.

Security and corporate factors to consider include

- Sharing and workgroup support—If you are considering online storage because you are part of a workgroup or want others to be able to access your files, look for online storage services that support collaborative features (such as a shared address book) and file sharing.

- Security—You don't want unauthorized people getting to your online storage or intercepting data enroute to or from your computer. Check the type of encryption and authentication used for account access and during data transfers, and find out whether the storage site itself uses encryption to help stop hackers.

Because even fee-based services sometimes offer a free trial period, you can try various services for little or no cost during your search for the best service for your needs.

Storing and Retrieving Online Files

The method you use for storing your files online and retrieving them varies with the provider and with the type of interface you choose. For example, both Xdrive Plus and Yahoo! Briefcase support Web-based access for uploading files as their default. This is tedious if you need to upload more than one or two files at a time; you must browse for each file individually using an interface similar to that used for selecting e-mail file attachments. A better bet is to download and install drag-and-drop support if you use 32-bit Windows; this will set up a drive icon within Windows Explorer and let you access your online storage as easily as you move files from one drive to another. Figure 10.4 shows files being copied to Xdrive Plus via drag-and-drop.

Xdrive Plus maps to Windows   Normal Windows copy
Explorer as a drive letter   progress window

FIGURE 10.4

After you install
the optional
Xdrive Plus
Desktop
Application, you
can use
Windows
Explorer to drag
and drop files
between your
online Xdrive
Plus storage (X:)
and your local
or network
drives.

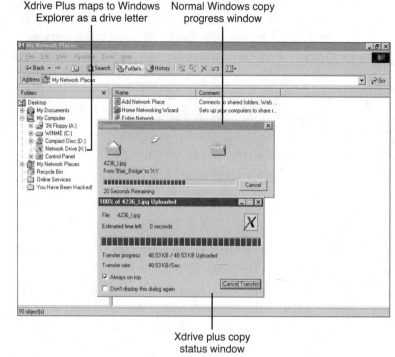

Xdrive plus copy
status window

Another concern with some online storage providers is the total file size you can transfer at a time. For example, Yahoo! Briefcase, whether you use the standard browser-based access or the optional Yahoo! Drive drag-and-drop interface, restricts a single file or the total of files transferred in a single upload to 5MB.

> If your online storage provider has a capacity limit per transfer, use the Details option in Windows Explorer to view the file sizes before selecting files, and use an archiving program to compress one or more files into an archive that's less than the maximum size per transfer. See "Overcoming File-Attachment Limits with Zipping Programs," **p. 82** in Chapter 6, for details.

Sharing Online Files with Others

By default, the files you store online are private, but they don't need to stay that way. Although some online storage providers have products specifically aimed at workgroups, most providers let you set up various levels of sharing for files or folders you specify.

For example, Xdrive Plus files and folders can be shared with other Xdrive Plus users, and you can specify read, create, edit, modify, share, and delete permissions (much like the permissions used with NT-based versions of Windows) on a group or user basis. Yahoo! Briefcase allows access to a wider range of users, including only you (Private), specified Yahoo! users (Friends), or everyone (Public) .

Summary

Online photo services can perform virtually every task that a normal retail or mail-order photofinisher can do for you, as well as make prints from digital scans you submit and create free online photo albums you can make available to family and friends.

You can use any popular Web browser to upload your digital scans, but drag-and-drop uploading, the fastest and most convenient way to transfer your own scans for display and printing, requires Microsoft Internet Explorer and a custom ActiveX control provided by the photofinisher.

Specify high-resolution scans from your film and make high-resolution (1,500 to 2,200 pixels wide) scans from your own pictures if you want to get high-quality 8×10-inch and larger prints.

You can use online file storage systems for backup, collaboration with other workers, and for the ultimate off-site backup. Some limited-space services are free, while others charge a monthly or annual fee. Many offer a limited-time free trial to get you started.

Evaluate online storage services on the basis of cost, speed, security, and ease of use. Be sure the service supports the special features (collaboration, automatic backup, CD-ROM archiving) you want and check the cost of additional storage beyond the minimum packages offered.

PLAYING INTERNET GAMES

CHAPTER HIGHLIGHTS:

- Learn about the major types of online games
- Discover how to fine-tune high-performance games to run well on any system

What You Need to Play an Online Game

After you install an online game, whether it's on a CD fresh out of the shrink-wrap or downloaded from an online site, you're ready to play. In most cases, you can play offline, too, and in either case, you won't need anything special to play. However, to play well, especially against the hordes of obsessed online game players in hyperspace, you need to bring a few things to the table, including the following:

- The fastest PC on which you can lay your hands—1GHz or faster processors are a good place to start, especially with today's lower system and motherboard/CPU prices.

- Fast 3D video cards—Insist on a video card featuring a GeForce 2 MX400/Pro/Ultra, GeForce 3, GeForce 3 Ti200/Ti500, ATI Radeon, or ATI Radeon 7500/8500 if you want to survive first-person shoot-em-ups such as *Quake III Arena* or *Tribes 2*.

- Lots of RAM—You need at least 128MB, and more is better. You can stuff up to 512MB into a system that is running Windows 9x/Me, and more if you have Windows 2000/XP.

- Fast, responsive controllers—Some games use the mouse and keyboard, whereas others work better with joysticks or steering wheels. Go with the USB port rather than the obsolete 15-pin gameport if you have a choice of connection types.

Ideally, you won't venture into online gaming unless you have a top-notch system. My son Jeremy, for example, now has a 1.4GHz AMD Athlon-based system and a GeForce 2 Ultra video card connected to our cable modem, and is so good at *Tribes 2* that he gets kicked off some servers. However, until recently, he was doing battle with a modest 500MHz AMD K6-2 based system. He still "fought" quite well against users with superior systems because he has mastered the art and science of tuning the game's settings to make the most of his system's speed and Internet connection speed.

Note

The tuning tips in this chapter primarily apply to first-person shooter games such as *Tribes 2*, *Quake III Arena*, and the original *Tribes* as well as sports games. Role-playing games (RPG) such as *Everquest*, *Diablo2*, *Warcraft*, and others are much less demanding of system performance, and play well even if you have a one-way cable modem connection and a modest 600MHz or slower system. If you get frustrated playing first-person shooters or sports games because your system isn't fast enough, try an RPG.

Tweaking Game Settings for Fast Performance

Even if you have the fastest gaming machine online, you should still fine-tune some game settings for even better performance. By contrast, if your system is well below the 1GHz mark or has a low-end 3D card (or built in motherboard video), tuning your system for speed instead of visual beauty could well mean the difference between playing several rounds or watching several rounds of your favorite death-match.

This chapter will focus on making adjustments to the menus in *Tribes 2* and *Quake III Arena*, but most first-person shooter and sports games have similar options.

Adjusting Video and Graphics

The first places to look for extra speed in online play, especially if you have a slow processor or an older video card, are the Video and Graphics menus (see Figures 11.1 through 11.3).

> **Note**
> Some games, such as *Tribes 2*, configure video resolutions and color depth on a separate menu from 3D graphics effects, while others, such as *Quake III Arena*, configure both types of settings on the same menu.

FIGURE 11.1

The *Tribes 2* video setup screen.

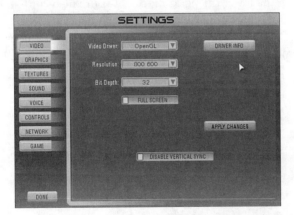

Some options to look at for extra speed include the following:

- Video Driver—If you have a late-model 3dfx video card, look for 3dfx proprietary Glide driver. Otherwise, choose OpenGL or Direct3D for other late-model 3D chipsets. Avoid the Software setting if possible. It will slow down your computer because it emulates advanced 3D features in software instead of activating the video card's 3D hardware features, and should not be used unless other settings don't work.

- Resolution—Although hardcore gamers shoot for a resolution in the 1024×768 or 1280×104 range, 800×600 is a good gaming resolution, especially on a 15-inch screen. Higher resolutions offer better visuals as they scale up, but also put extra strain on your system by forcing the system to draw more pixels per frame.

- Bit Depth (color depth)—32-bit color (more than 16.7 million colors) looks a lot better than 16-bit color, but some older 3D video cards slow way, way down in 32-bit mode. If speed is an issue, stick with 16-bit.

Note

Windows uses DirectX to control the function of 3D video cards, sound cards, and game controllers. Game developers can request DirectX functions, which DirectX software (incorporated into Windows) will translate into the appropriate hardware-specific command. If a particular device doesn't support a command in hardware, DirectX uses a slower emulation process to perform the command.

You should install the latest version of DirectX available for your version of Windows to improve gameplay. Download it from `www.microsoft.com/directx/homeuser/downloads/`.

Adjustments on the Graphics menu of a game such as *Tribes 2* (see Figure 11.2) or *Quake III Arena* (see Figure 11.3) start to test the 3D performance of your video card. Generally speaking, the lower the performance of your video card and system processor, the better the performance you will see if you move settings toward the low side. Note that because *Tribes 2* is primarily played in an outdoor virtual landscape, this player prefers high levels of visible distance and dynamic light visual distance, and medium to low values for most other settings.

FIGURE 11.2

You can make up for slow 3D card or processor performance by adjusting detail settings or turning off some advanced graphics features.

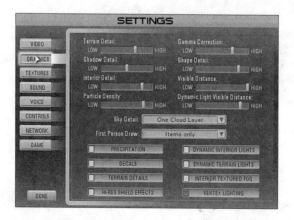

Unfortunately, *Tribes 2* doesn't provide a real-time preview of the changes made on any of these screens, although some other games do. If your game doesn't let you preview the results, try just one or two changes at a time before you apply them and go back to the game.

Quake III Arena doesn't offer as many graphics options as *Tribes 2*, but by adjusting its texture detail and geometric detail options you can coax extra speed from a slower system or less-capable video card (see Figure 11.3).

FIGURE 11.3

The *Quake III Arena* graphics setup screen controls resolution, color depth, and various 3D effects. Note the slider control for texture detail.

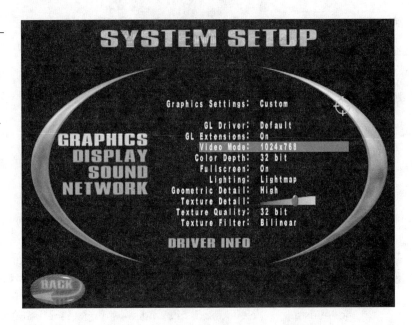

Because online gaming pits you mainly against tough real players, play offline during the fine-tuning process for your settings. If your game allows you to save a set configuration, you might want to develop several different settings to use for different lighting conditions or game settings.

Adjusting Textures

Texture quality and lighting (graphics) quality go hand-in-hand on most recent 3D video cards. Generally, more expensive and newer chipsets perform these tasks better than slower and older chipsets. As with graphics and video settings, you can speed up your gaming performance by simplifying the details of game elements. Some games use a single menu for all graphics settings (as in Figure 11.3), while others, such as *Tribes 2* (see Figure 11.4) provide a separate menu with many adjustments. In Figure 11.4, which illustrates the Textures settings used by my son when he plays *Tribes 2*, note that the highest-quality setting is used for shape texture detail. This setting provides the most realistic appearance for weapons, players, and vehicles. Note that medium-high detail settings are used for terrain and buildings, and fastest texture compression is used for speed.

FIGURE 11.4

You can make up for slow 3D card or processor performance by adjusting texture detail settings for the less-important objects in your game.

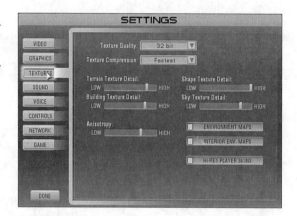

Depending on the game and your video card, you might have many additional texture and display options:

- Anisotropic filtering—Creates more realistic mapping of textures at an oblique angle to the viewer, such as the walls of a racetrack with advertising banners. Mid-range and high-end video cards offer this option.

- Antialiasing—When enabled, this smoothes rough edges of onscreen objects for a more realistic appearance. Some video cards can perform this on just foreground objects, while others can perform FSAA (full-screen antialiasing). FSAA can improve the appearance of the entire scene, but might slow down your computer.

- Bi-linear filtering—Used for texture maps, it helps eliminate the blocky look of stretching small texture maps across large polygons.

- MIP mapping—Mixes low-res and high-res versions of a texture used on objects that appear to recede into the distance.

- Tri-linear filtering—combines bi-linear filtering and MIP mapping for better-quality texture maps.

- Z-buffering—Renders only visible pixels in a scene; you can adjust the depth of the Z-buffer to favor speed (16-bit) or quality (24-bit or 32-bit). A setting of 16;24 provides a good balance of quality and speed.

■ Stencil buffering—Creates a virtual stencil for objects such as an airplane cockpit's window frame in a flying game and rerenders only the objects seen through the glass.

As Figures 11.5 and 11.6 show, you can also make many of these adjustments on the properties sheets of many recent 3D-optimized video cards. When you make the adjustments on the video card's properties sheet, they are used by all games that use the specified game API (application program interface). Settings within the game can override properties sheet settings for that game only.

FIGURE 11.5

The OpenGL properties sheet for the ATI Radeon VE video card with Performance presets selected. Disabled features such as full-scene anti-aliasing and anisotropic texture filtering improve video quality but can slow down gameplay if enabled.

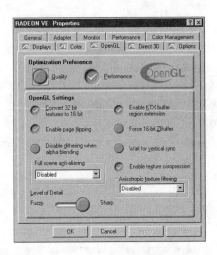

FIGURE 11.6

The Direct3D properties sheet for the ATI Radeon VE video card optimized for speed. To improve visual quality, enable antialiasing.

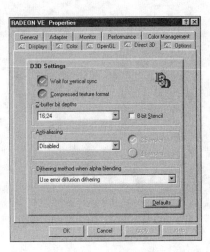

If your game lacks advanced 3D and texture settings, use the video card's properties sheets to adjust for best appearance, highest performance, or your preferred combination of settings.

3D Sound Settings

Realism in gaming comes from both the way the game looks and how it sounds. As with visual effects, 3D sound settings (see Figure 11.7) can affect the speed of gameplay.

Figure 11.7 illustrates the sound setup in *Tribes 2*. Typical adjustments shown in Figure 11.7 include

- Sound APIs—This affects the way sounds are rendered by the game; Creative Labs EAX 2 is supported by Creative's Sound Blaster cards; if you have a different brand, use Direct3D. Enabling the environment turns on 3D effects, even if you have only two speakers.

- Sound sampling frequency—44KHz is near CD-quality, but lower settings are also available.

- Sampling bitrate—16-bit is more realistic than 8-bit, but also takes extra time to perform.

- Channels—Select the number equal to the number of speakers you have.

FIGURE 11.7

Tribes 2's Sound settings menu allows you to adjust the volumes of different types of game sounds and fine-tune sound performance.

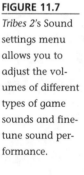
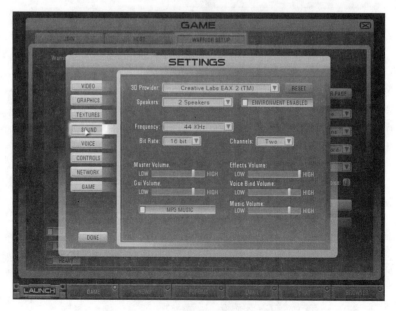

Tip

Sound cards that use the PCI slot are faster and support more-advanced features than ISA-based or motherboard-chipset based sound cards do. Because sound settings have less effect on gameplay than video, 3D, or texture settings, try using the best sound quality to start with if you have a PCI-based sound card. Adjust sound quality downward to improve game speed if your sound card uses the older ISA slot or is incorporated into the motherboard's chipset.

Adjusting Network Settings

The last major way you can adjust the performance of your online game is by tweaking the network connection options. Some games, such as *Tribes 2* (see Figure 11.8) and *Quake III Arena* (see Figure 11.9), make it easy with preset options, whereas others require you to adjust packet size and transmission speed manually.

FIGURE 11.8

If you have a very fast (1GHz or faster) PC and fast 3D video, the T1/LAN setting shown here in *Tribes 2* might be suitable for cable modem connections. Otherwise, choose cable/xDSL or equivalent from the menu.

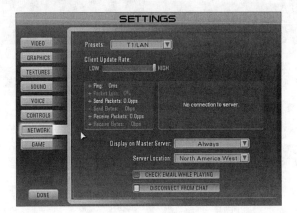

If you were an online game player before you switched to cable Internet service, it's essential that you recheck your network settings. Unless your game will automatically detect the optimal settings, your cable Internet connections will continue to use your dial-up settings, with horrible results for your online play.

Figure 11.8 shows a system using the fastest setting, T1/LAN available in *Tribes 2*. This is often the default setting for systems that are connected to a cable modem because most cable modems connect via a 10BaseT or 10/100 Ethernet network card. However, this setting is really too fast for systems around 700MHz or slower, or systems with low-end 3D video. Unless you have a very fast (1GHz or faster) system with a recent 3D video card, use the cable/xDSL setting instead.

FIGURE 11.9

Quake III Arena uses the same setting for LAN, cable modem, or xDSL connections, so you don't need to change it if you take your system to a LAN party one night and go back online the next.

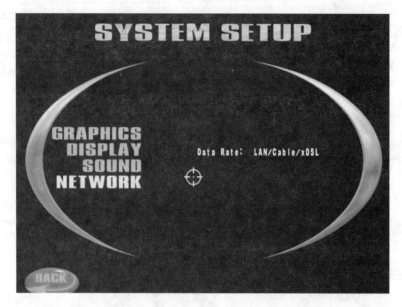

If you take your computer to a LAN party and play against other players on a network, you should use the T1/LAN setting for the greatest speed. However, if you prefer the cable/xDSL setting when you're online, don't forget to change back when you and your computer are back home and you prepare to go back online.

For more gaming help, I recommend GameSpy.com's PC Gaming site at www.gamespy.com/jump/genres.shtml. It's the place to go for action, RPG, sports, strategy, and other types of PC games, including your favorite online games.

Choosing the Best Game Server

Although some online games, such as *Diablo*, *Diablo 2*, and *Warcraft*, are played on software-assigned servers, most shooters such as *Quake III*, *Tribes*, and *Tribes 2* can be played on a wide variety of game servers. A game server hosts live players who connect online, and can support either individual or team play. Figure 11.10 shows a typical range of *Tribes 2*'s game servers.

FIGURE 11.10

Popular online games such as *Tribes 2* can be played on a wide variety of game servers.

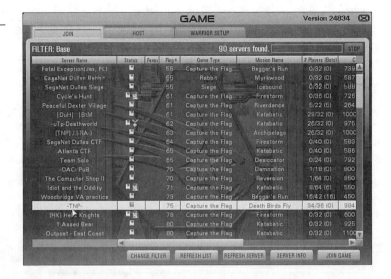

With so many game servers from which to choose, how can you get the best gaming experience? Look for these factors:

- Ping rate—This describes how long (in milliseconds) it takes for a data packet to go from your computer to the game server and back again. You want the fastest ping rate you can get among servers that meet your other requirements. If you use a server with a slow ping rate, the performance advantage of your cable modem will be greatly diminished.

- Game type—Many online games offer several different sets of rules; if you can't stand playing Capture the Flag, for example, it won't matter how fast the ping rate is. Look for a game type you prefer.

- Mission name—This identifies a particular map or level in a game. You need to have the map or level listed installed on your system before you can play it. Maps that vary from the stock maps/levels shipped with a game are called mods, and if you want to play against others using a given mod, you must find it online and download it before you can play it.

- Number of players and bots—The first number shown is the number of players currently playing the game, and the second number is the maximum capacity of the server. The number of bots (automated players) is listed in parentheses. Note that in Figure 11.10, Peaceful Dexter Village has five players playing, but all five are bots. The highlighted server (-TNP-) is just one player short of capacity, and real people control all 34 players.

Playing against bots is good practice, but it's likely to get boring after a while. For a challenge, choose a server in which human players are more prevalent than bots.

Setting Up Your Own Game Server

If you're tired of trying to find a game server with enough room for you and your friends, many online games let you create your own. For example, use the Multiplayer setting in *Quake III Arena* to start the process of creating a game server. You can create the server configuration manually, or download tools to make this process easier.

Complete directions and tips for creating a *Quake III Arena* game server are available at www.planetquake.com/quake3/q3aguide/server-setup_a.shtml.

For other game titles, check your manual or the publisher's Web site to see what multi-player options it supports.

If your computer is connected directly to your cable modem, you should have little difficulty in having your friends connect with you. Tell them the IP address of your system and they can go straight to it with their games.

However, if you're using Internet connection sharing software, a proxy server or a router, the firewall features of these sharing products can prevent your friends from finding your game server.

Use a site such as www.network-tools.com to determine what IP address is being used by your system while you're online. Give this IP address, not the IP address actually used on your network, to your friends.

You will also need to open the TCP ports needed for your game in your network configuration. The easiest way to do this is to enable the DMZ configuration in your router, but this disables all firewall functions. To maintain firewall protection for your system while allowing it to function as a game server, you need to know what TCP port(s) the game requires. For example, *Quake III Arena* uses TCP port 27960 to send and receive data. This port needs to be opened with your router, proxy server, or firewall configuration to allow your friends to access your *Quake III Arena* game server. See Chapter 15, "Using Microsoft Internet Connection Sharing," Chapter 16, "Using Other Computer-Based Internet Sharing Programs," and Chapter 17, "Router Your Way to Internet Sharing," for details.

GameAdmin.com offers a useful tutorial on setting up a Linksys router for use with a Quake III Arena game server at www.gameadmins.com/guides/linksys/linksys.htm.

You can find a list of TCP ports used by popular games at the Practically Networked ICS Configuration Mappings - Page 2 site. www.practicallynetworked.com/sharing/ics/icsconfig_maps_pg2.htm.

The configuration files listed are specifically designed for the ICS Configuration software available at the site, but you can open the file for your game in your browser to view the TCP port information you need.

Playing with Friends

Although the original online shooting games were strictly "me against the world" ("If it moves, shoot it!"), more recent shooters such as *Tribes 2* have made teamwork a virtue. One clever way to improve teamwork is to use IM (instant messaging services) such as AOL Instant Messenger or MSN Messenger to communicate with your fighting buddies. Instead of trying to figure out who's defending what in a game like *Tribes*, you can IM each other and coordinate your activities.

For more information about using IM services, see Chapter 8, "Using Internet Multimedia and Messaging."

The Microsoft SideWinder GameVoice combines voice-activated game control and real-time chat for even more online fun. Learn more about it at www.gamevoice.com.

Registry Tweaks and Online Gaming

Some online gamers who use Windows PCs aren't content with the many speed-tweaking options available in most online action games. Instead, they use Registry tweaks to speed up ping rate and other game-oriented factors. The trouble is, unless you use your PC for nothing but gaming, your Web-browsing and downloading speeds will be crippled.

System Maintenance for Best Performance

Because the display of other players and scenery happens on your computer in response to the data that the game server transmits, you want your computer to run as quickly as possible. Fortunately, the tweaks needed also improve all types of computer usage, not just gaming. Here are some simple ways to keep your system's performance at its best for gaming and general computer operations:

■ Use the latest video card and sound card drivers—Visit the card manufacturers' Web sites every few months for updated drivers.

> The Windows Device Manager sometimes shows the chipset identification instead of the actual hardware brand and model number for cards that use chipsets made by a third-party vendor. For example, many suppliers make GeForce3-based video cards. Because some video and sound card vendors modify the chipset makers' default drivers to add more features or support unique on-board hardware, go to the card vendor's site first for new drivers.

■ Adjust the disk-cache settings in Windows 9x/Me to improve read-ahead speeds—Open the System properties sheet in the Control Panel and click the Performance tab with Windows 9x/Me. Click File System, click Typical Role of This Computer, and change the setting to Network Server. Click OK and restart the system to apply.

■ Set Virtual Memory to a fixed size of about three times the size of your RAM—Open the System properties sheet in the Control Panel and click the Performance tab with Windows 9x/Me. Click Virtual Memory, click Let Me Specify My Own Virtual Memory Settings, and specify the same values for minimum and maximum. If you have 256MB of RAM, use 768MB for both values. Click OK and restart the system to apply. If you have more than one physical hard drive, choose the drive with the most space for the swapfile.

If you use Windows 2000 or Windows XP, you can spread your paging file (the name for the swapfile in Windows XP and Windows 2000) across multiple drives. In Windows XP, right-click My Computer, select Properties, click the Advanced tab, select Settings under Performance Options, and click Advanced to see the Virtual Memory settings. Click Change, then Custom size to change the size or location.

> Set both File System and Virtual Memory options at the same time before rebooting the system, to save time.

■ Defrag the drive containing your virtual memory file and temporary files—Unless you changed the location of virtual memory in the previous tip, this is the C: drive by default, and temporary files are stored by default in

C:\Windows\Temp. Use the Defrag option located on the C: drive's properties sheet, Tools tab, or a third-party product such as Norton Utilities/System Works' Speed Disk to put all files together and all empty disk space together.

Summary

No matter how fast your computer and cable Internet connection are, you can improve the speed of your system for online gaming by balancing visual and sound quality with performance. In general, the better-looking the screen display, the lower the performance of your system.

You can adjust the video and audio settings for a particular game through its setup screens, and for all games through the video card or sound card properties sheet. Because games might offer Open GL or Direct3D rendering options, you should adjust both types of 3D display for the performance and quality settings you prefer.

You can enhance your enjoyment of online gaming by choosing game servers that offer the options you prefer, or create your own game server to host your friends. If you have a firewall or router between you and the Internet, you must configure it to allow game players to access your computer. Use IM services such as MSN Messenger to cooperate with your friends.

Good system maintenance practices, such as installing up-to-date video and sound drivers, drive defragging, and swapfile setting adjustments, improve both gameplay and general computer operation.

SPEEDING UP YOUR CABLE INTERNET SERVICE

CHAPTER HIGHLIGHTS:

- How to adjust the Windows Registry for greater speed
- How to adjust MacOS Open Transport settings for greater speed
- Where to find alternative browsers
- How to use download managers to increase download speed even more
- How to use browser synchronization to pre-fetch favorite sites

Tweaking the Windows Registry

Cable Internet service is *much* faster than dial-up Internet service, but as with most computer services, you can achieve even faster speeds by making adjustments. If your computer runs Microsoft Windows, one of the most important—but potentially risky—ways to improve the speed of your cable Internet service is to adjust or add settings to the Windows Registry.

 How can you tell if these options are set correctly before you start fiddling around with your system? I recommend the SpeedGuide TCP/IP Analyzer feature available at www.speedguide.net. The analyzer displays the values for the settings listed in this section and recommends specific changes if needed.

What is the Windows Registry? The Windows Registry is the central repository for hardware, software, and system configuration information that Windows uses. Every time you install a new hardware device or new software or change settings, Registry settings are added or changed. The changes you make to the computer using the Control Panel are also reflected in the Registry. Unfortunately, the changes you need to make to the Registry for greater speed can't be done through the Control Panel or other software provided with Windows; you either need to make the changes yourself or use third-party software to make the changes for you.

Because the Registry tells Windows what to do, it should not be changed manually unless you back up its contents *first*.

 Whether you decide to install predefined Registry changes, use software to fine-tune your Registry, or edit the Registry manually, you need to back up your Registry before making changes; a damaged Registry will prevent your system from starting.

Making Backup Copies of the System Registry

As you learned in the previous section, Registry backups should always be made before making changes to the Registry. Because the Windows Registry's location and function varies from version to version, use the correct instructions for your version of Windows.

- Windows 95—Manual copy process: Use My Computer or File Explorer to open the \Windows folder, locate User.dat and System.dat, and make copies of these files. (I suggest adding the year-month-date to the name of each file, so that the backup User.dat becomes User_110101.dat.) By default, Windows 95 hides system files like these. To make them visible in Windows Explorer, do the following:

1. Click View, Folder Options.
2. Click the View tab.
3. Click Show All Files.
4. Click OK.

■ Windows 98—Back up with ScanReg. Run ScanReg from the Start menu, click Start, Run, type ScanReg in the dialog box that appears, and click OK. ScanReg checks the Registry for errors and automatically makes a backup copy of the Registry.

■ Windows Me and Windows XP—Back up with System Restore. Click Start, Help, use System Restore, and create a Restore Point (System Restore backs up the Registry and other system information). If you return to a Restore Point, Windows discards installed software and hardware changes made after the specified Restore Point.

■ Windows NT 4—Back up with Repair Disk. Click Start, Run, and type Rdisk. Click OK to start the Repair Disk utility program. Click Update Repair Info and follow prompts until the process is complete.

■ Windows 2000—Back up with the Backup program. Click Start, Programs, Accessories, System Tools, Backup to start the Backup program. Select Tools, and then Create an Emergency Repair Disk. During the process, provide a floppy disk when prompted and select Also Back Up the Registry to the Repair Directory.

Changing Windows Registry Settings for Greater Speed

Several settings in the Windows Registry affect the speed of your Internet connection, including the following:

■ MTU

■ MSS

■ RWIN

■ TCPWindow

If these values are set incorrectly, you're not getting the full benefit of your cable Internet connection.

Although you can manually edit your system's Registry or use an interactive Registry-tweaking program, many tweaking programs are designed for Windows 95 rather than for later versions of Windows. Instead, try installing the preconfigured

Registry patches available at the Speedguide.net Web site at `www.speedguide.net`. Click the link labeled Patches to find a list of patches and their uses.

If you use Windows 9x/Me, download the sguide_tweak_98_Me.zip patch to make changes for cable Internet and similar high-speed connections. Also download sguide_default_9x.zip, which resets the Registry to its default condition. Use sguide_default_9x.zip only after trying sguide_tweak_98_Me.zip, and only if your performance drops after trying the first patch.

Windows 2000 users should download sguide_tweak_2k.zip and sguide_default_2k.zip. Check the Speedguide.net Web site for Windows XP-specific tweaks.

These patches are all provided as .ZIP archives, so you will need to use WinZip or the built-in unzipping feature in Windows Me to access them.

After you extract the patch you need, right-click it in Windows Explorer and select Install to apply it. After you install the patch, save any open files, shut down your computer, and restart it so the patch can take effect.

> **Note**
> If you can't find predefined Windows XP-specific broadband tweaks at your favorite Web site, check out the powerful Tweak-XP utility from Totalidea Software. Available in English and several European languages, Tweak-XP offers predefined tweaks for popular cable modem and other broadband services, ad blockers, adjustments for Outlook e-mail security settings, and many more features useful for both Internet and general Windows operation. You can download it from `www.totalidea.de`; registration is about $30 US.

Before you apply changes to your system, you might want to test the speed of your system several times with the following Web sites:

- bandwidthplace.com/speedtest
- ww.zdnet.com/cc/bandwidth/speedtest.html
- www.dslreports.com/stest

Because of differences in the testing methods that each site uses, you're sure to get different results from each test. Just record the "before" results and the time you ran the test. To see if the Registry changes you made are truly helpful, run the same tests at a similar time of the day after you make the changes. Because of peaks and valleys in Internet traffic, you will see greater speeds at off-peak hours (like the early morning) than at peak hours (late afternoon). I recommend testing at off-peak hours because peak-hour test results are affected primarily by the speed of the Web server providing the test content rather than by the speed of your connection.

After applying the patches, you should see measurable to major improvements in your download performance from each test site if you test during off-hours.

If you previously applied patches or used tweaking software to optimize your dial-up analog modem Internet performance, you have an even bigger need to make changes for your broadband connection. Here's why: When you optimize a dial-up connection, you use different settings than broadband connections use. If you don't change the settings, you will slow down your cable Internet connection. If you changed your Registry settings once, you need to change them again.

Also, because speed test sites can be used by both dial-up and broadband users, the file size used for testing on some sites may be too small for accurate results. Try to use sites that use 1MB or larger test files.

Tweaking MacOS-Based Systems

While MacOS is a much different operating system than any version of Windows, it still uses TCP/IP to connect to the Internet, and the same TCP/IP settings (TCPWindow, MSS, and MaxMTU) still apply to a system running MacOS as they do to a system running Windows. If you don't set the values for these TCP/IP parameters to the best possible values, your MacOS-based cable Internet connection won't perform to its fastest potential.

MacOS uses Open Transport to provide TCP/IP connections to your Mac. Open Transport has predefined values for TCP/IP options that can be overridden with software for better performance. Sustainable Softworks (www.sustworks.com) offers IPNetTuner (formerly called OT Advanced Tuner) to make these changes for you.

You can use it interactively to determine the best settings for your cable Internet connection, and then use IPNetTuner to create settings documents you can automatically load at startup. IPNetTuner works with MacOS 7.5.3 or above and Open Transport 1.1.1 or later, so virtually any MacOS-based system used for Internet access is compatible. Register IPNetTuner for $25 per computer.

The same company sells IPNetMonitor ($30 per computer) to help you test, troubleshoot, and optimize your Internet connection. Its Monitor feature displays the current throughput of your system; test your system with Monitor before and after making changes with IPNetTuner to determine the best settings.

Get other MacOS-related broadband tweaking and usage tips from the DSLReports All Things Macintosh forum at www.dslreports.com/form/macdsl.

Alternatives to Internet Explorer and Netscape Navigator/Communicator

Even after you optimize the speed of your Internet connection at a Registry level, inefficiencies in your Web browser can still slow you down. Both Internet Explorer and Netscape Navigator/Communicator have become lumbering behemoths that take longer to view pages and download files than other browsers.

Fortunately, IE and Netscape aren't the only browsers in town. In a previous chapter, I mentioned Opera Software's Opera 5.x browser, which is considerably faster than IE and Netscape and supports multiple browser windows. You can now use Opera for free in an ad-supported version (register it to get the ads to go away and see a little more of the screen).

Opera is available from www.opera.com in two versions for Windows:

- With Java—About 10MB download
- Without Java—About 2.2MB download

Both support JavaScript, but only the version with Java will enable you to properly view Web sites that use Java for animations, interactive menus, or other content.

Opera browsers are also available for BeOS, Linux, Solaris, OS/2, QNX, Mac, and Symbian.

Tip

At more than 9MB, the Java-based version of Opera is a fairly hefty download, even for a cable Internet connection. For faster downloads, install a download manager first, as discussed in the "Download Managers" section of this chapter.

The free ad-supported version of the Opera browser is shown in Figure 12.1.

The multiple-window feature of Opera makes it easy to manage multiple downloads and searches. Other useful features include the following:

- Built-in Mirabilis ICQ-compatible instant messaging—Although it doesn't support voice or video chat, it allows basic keyboard chat to other ICQ users.
- Integrated search using AltaVista, Google, GoTo, and other tools—You can also search for images, video, MP3/Audio, and other items.
- Mouse gestures—Hold down the right mouse button and move the mouse left to go to the previous document, right to the next document, and other options.
- Automatic refresh—Opera can refresh the view of sites that change frequently at user-defined intervals.

■ Built-in e-mail and contact managers—You can stay in touch without leaving Opera.

■ Built-in download manager—This allows you to resume interrupted file transfers.

You don't need to stop using your favorite browser to try Opera; it can co-exist with both Navigator/Communicator and IE browsers.

FIGURE 12.1

The Opera 5.x browser, shown here, can display multiple windows. Click the buttons on the window bar at the bottom of the browser screen to switch between windows.

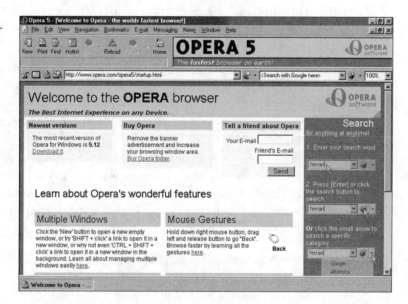

Download Managers

You will see a big boost in your download speed with cable Internet connections. As you learned in Chapter 6, "Ten Ways Cable Modems Make the Internet Better," this makes it easier than ever to keep your system up to date with automatic antivirus and operating system updates. However, what about patching up your Office or graphics suite? How about trying out the latest utility? And how about online music? The Internet has a huge amount of online content that's yours for the download, and even with a cable Internet connection, you can get it faster if you install a download manager first.

Download managers perform several tasks to make downloading faster and easier for you. Features vary by product, but typically include the following:

■ Letting you continue a download that's been interrupted—This is an absolute "must-have" if you have a one-way cable modem, because this type of cable

Internet service ties up your phone lines. A download manager lets you stop your download, make an emergency phone call, and continue the download later. Even if you have two-way cable Internet service, this features is still useful because Internet problems or a system lockup could stop your download prematurely.

■ Faster downloads from most sites—Instead of downloading the file in a single large (and relatively slow) chunk, download managers make multiple connections to a file whenever possible, enabling fast downloads. Each connection downloads part of the file, and the manager reassembles the file on your system when the process is complete.

■ Automatic location of the best source for a file—Most downloadable files are available on a wide variety of servers of different speeds and in different locations. Download managers can test the download speed of different sources for a given file and choose the server with the fastest response to provide additional download speed.

■ Download scheduling—Why download that hot new MP3 song or service pack in the early evening when everyone else is trying to get it? The scheduling feature found in some download managers lets you download late at night or early in the morning to bypass peak hour congestion on your local cable network or on the Internet (see Figure 12.2).

FIGURE 12.2

Scheduling a download session for early morning with Download Accelerator Plus.

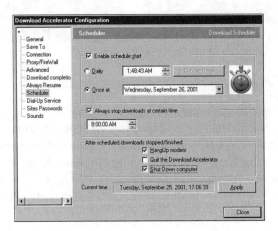

How much faster can a download be if you use a download manager? You might see speed improvements of three to five times, no improvement at all, or even a slight drop in performance depending on the location of the file and the type of server (http:// or ftp://) where the file is stored. Most download managers can be disabled and re-enabled on the fly, enabling you to choose the best download method for a particular file.

Major Download Managers

A number of download managers are available for use with major browsers, including these:

- Go!zilla—www.gozilla.com
- Download Accelerator Plus—www.dap.com
- FlashGet—www.amazesoft.com
- ReGet Deluxe and ReGet Junior—www.reget.com
- Net Vampire—www.netvampire.com
- GetRight—www.getright.com
- NetAnts—www.netants.com
- Netscape Smart Download—home.netscape.com

Most of these products are free, so what pays for their development? Advertising. Most download managers display ads during the download process, and the ad revenues fund distribution and development. If you're concerned about privacy, though, you should also be aware that many, but not all, download managers also install a feature called *spyware* into your system, which reports on your browsing habits to provide advertisers with more precise marketing information.

To find out which products might tattle on your surfing habits, check recent reviews of the products or look at the software's privacy policy before you click the Download or Install buttons.

Using Browser Synchronization

You probably fire up your Web browser at the beginning of each computing day and visit some business content-based Web sites. When you get home, you might sit down at your PC and check stocks and sports. The trouble is that everyone else in your cable Internet neighborhood might be doing the same thing, which slows down the connection. Just as you can use a full-featured download manager to set up big file downloads for off hours, you can prefetch your favorite Web sites to your system in off hours so they're ready for your perusal when you come to work or when you're ready to relax.

Internet Explorer 5.0 and above include this capability for pages you have selected as Offline Favorites. To start the setup process, do the following:

1. Navigate to the page you would like to view offline.

2. Click Favorites.

3. Click Make Available Offline.

4. Click OK.

5. The synchronization process starts to copy the site to your system; click Stop.

Repeat steps 1–5 for each site you would like to set for offline viewing.

After you have specified one or more sites you would like to view offline, click Tools, Synchronize to continue the setup process.

1. The list of current Web sites set for offline viewing is displayed; clear the checkmarks from any sites you don't want to synchronize, as in Figure 12.3.

FIGURE 12.3

Specifying sites for offline viewing.

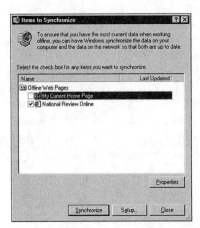

2. Select the first item you would like to schedule, and select Properties.

3. Click the Schedule tab, and then click Add.

4. Enter the frequency (number of days) and the time to perform the synchronization. Enter a different name than the default My Scheduled Update if desired.

5. Click the Download tab if you want to download additional pages other than the specified page (see Figure 12.4). You can specify the number of links, specify whether to download links outside the page's Web site, specify whether to limit disk usage to a specified amount, and specify advanced settings for content types to download. You also can specify a login name and password if required.

FIGURE 12.4

Setting site
options for
online viewing.

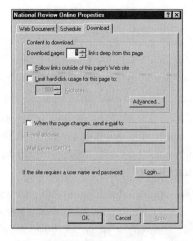

6. Click OK when the configuration is complete.

7. Repeat steps 2–6 for any additional sites you want to prefetch.

Leave your computer and Internet Explorer running, and your pages will be fetched automatically for you at the specified time.

Your offline-stored pages are displayed automatically—and quickly—when you browse to the specified URL or select the page from the Favorites list. Any additional levels you selected to be stored will also be displayed instantly.

 If your site changes periodically during the day, use the Refresh button to get the latest site contents.

Tweaking Your System for Better Gaming Performance

Cable modems provide much faster native performance for gaming than dial-up modems because of two factors:

- High download (and, for two-way users, upload) speed
- Low latency (ping rate)

However, you can still fine-tune system settings and individual game settings to achieve even faster speeds. To learn how to improve your gaming performance, see Chapter 11, "Playing Internet Games."

Summary

Microsoft Windows' Registry settings are not optimized for best cable modem performance. To obtain the best performance, you can download and install predefined Registry tweaks or use software specially made to perform the adjustments needed. The Registry settings for your version of Windows should be backed up before you perform any type of Registry changes.

MacOS also needs TCP/IP optimization to achieve best broadband performance. MacOS TCP/IP settings are made by adjusting Open Transport, and you can use software such as IPNetTuner to make the changes needed.

Changing to a faster browser such as Opera, which is available for most operating systems and most major languages, can improve your browsing speed. Opera also supports multiple windows, making complex searches for data easier to do.

Download managers enable you to download large files faster and to continue a download after an interruption. Most download managers are advertiser-supported.

Browser synchronization, a feature supported by Internet Explorer, allows you to download Web-based content to your PC during off hours and make it available for viewing later, whether you're online or offline. Browser synchronization allows you to bypass peak-hour Internet congestion and still have access to the Web sites you visit most often.

PART V

SECURING YOUR CABLE MODEM SERVICE

FIREWALLS AND YOUR PC

The Dangers of Always-On Internet Access

Especially if you have two-way cable Internet service, you're just a few moments (and a couple of mouse clicks) away from your favorite digital music, streaming video, e-mail, or Web site whenever your computer is on. However, that same "always-on" 24/7 access also makes your computer and the information you store on it a prime target for hackers.

Before the advent of high-speed, always-on Internet connections, it was theoretically possible for strangers to attack your computer, but it seldom happened to the ordinary user. Dial-up computers aren't online long enough to be targets, and because most dial-up connections are assigned a different IP address every time, it is difficult for hackers to locate a particular target. Now, cable modem and similar broadband connects make attacks a reality for many computer users. Attacks on your computer can come in many forms, including the following:

- Unauthorized access to your hard disk files
- Your computer being used as a way station to attack another PC
- Your passwords, credit card numbers, and other confidential data being transmitted to others

Even if you have up-to-date antivirus and script-blocking software as discussed in Chapter 14, "Stopping Computer Viruses," your cable Internet connection can present a wide-open front door to your valuable information because it's always on (if you have a two-way connection) and because increasing numbers of attacks come from worms that look for targets of opportunity.

Is your computer being used to attack other PCs without your knowledge? Are you wondering which regions are the most common sources of attacks on your system? Wondering how many attacks have happened today? Find out by surfing on over to the Distributed Intrusion Detection System Web site at www.dshield.org.

The Dshield Web site collects and displays data about computer intrusion attempts from all over the Internet. You can also submit reports of intrusions (attempted cracks) of your system to Dshield by signing up as a registered user and installing client software designed to work with your firewall software or router. By submitting reports to Dshield, you help yourself and other users battle intrusions.

Why Non-DOCSIS Internet Connections Are Vulnerable

As you learned in earlier chapters, your cable Internet connection is actually part of a neighborhood-wide network; you share bandwidth with other cable Internet users nearby. The earliest cable modems lacked any sort of encryption to protect one cable

Internet user from seeing another's traffic. Thus, if you used a home network to share your Internet connection with Internet Connection Sharing or a similar gateway program and the computer with the cable modem had shared drives, your information was wide open for other cable modem users in the neighborhood to view and copy. If the shared folder setting was for full access, your information was also available to alter or delete from a hacker's own Windows Explorer or similar file-management tool.

Unless your cable modem is a one-way model or an early two-way model that was produced before the DOCSIS standard, it's no longer possible for your neighbors across the street to invite themselves in for free hard disk viewing using just Windows Explorer. But, don't kid yourself: Plenty of bad guys (and gals) are out there who are looking for your PC and what it contains with powerful hacking tools.

Note

DOCSIS is the Data Over Cable Service Interface Specification, which provides common standards for how cable modems should operate. DOCSIS-compliant cable modems are now also known as CableLabs Certified Cable Modems. Different brands of cable modems that meet the DOCSIS standard can be interchanged on DOCSIS-compliant cable Internet networks. One of the major benefits of the DOCSIS standard is its use of encrypted signals between the cable Internet head-end and each cable modem, preventing casual snooping. Most DOCSIS-compliant cable modems are two-way models, but a few models capable of one-way service have also received certification.

Dangers in Shared Printer and Folder Access for All Cable Modem Users

Although encrypted traffic flowing to and from today's DOCSIS-compliant cable modems prevents the neighbors from firing up their Windows Explorer to spy on your system, that's not nearly enough to stop sophisticated hackers. Hackers use tools called port scanners to look for vulnerabilities in online computers that are configured to share folders and printers with other computers.

Note

A *port scanner* is a program that checks a particular IP address (such as your computer) for open TCP ports. A TCP port is a logical pathway between two computers that run the TCP/IP protocol, which every computer online must use. Ports are numbered from 0 through 65535, and they are used automatically by Internet services such as your Web browser (port 80), e-mail (port 110), and so forth. Computers that provide server features (such as file and print sharing) to other computers, even on a home network, can be attacked through TCP ports that must be left open to enable TCP/IP to provide file, print, and other services to function.

When a port scanner finds a computer online, the scanner starts sending open port commands to see if TCP ports can be opened, allowing the hacker to have access to your computer. If your online computer shares even a single drive, a single folder, or a printer, or has File and Printer Sharing installed (even if it's not in use) and is directly connected to your cable modem (not behind a router or on a network), you're vulnerable to port scanners.

Discovering How Vulnerable You Are

Former *InfoWorld* columnist Steve Gibson, creator of the terrific drive-testing program SpinRite, provides a free way for you to check your system for vulnerabilities when you're online. Set your browser to www.grc.com, click on the Shields Up icons on the home and following pages, and use the Test My Shields and Probe My Ports buttons to test your system. Figure 13.1 shows the results of a port test on a Windows 98 SE computer that is running File and Print Sharing, even though no printers or folders are set to be shared.

FIGURE 13.1

If you have Windows File and Print Sharing installed on a typical Windows computer, TCP Port 139 is wide open for exploitation by hackers, as shown here.

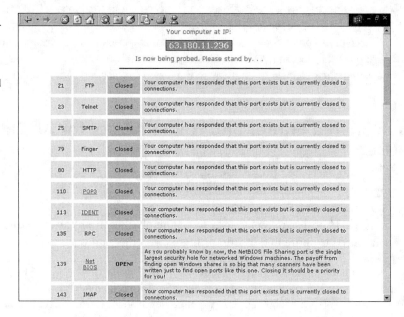

21	FTP	Closed	Your computer has responded that this port exists but is currently closed to connections.
23	Telnet	Closed	Your computer has responded that this port exists but is currently closed to connections.
25	SMTP	Closed	Your computer has responded that this port exists but is currently closed to connections.
79	Finger	Closed	Your computer has responded that this port exists but is currently closed to connections.
80	HTTP	Closed	Your computer has responded that this port exists but is currently closed to connections.
110	POP3	Closed	Your computer has responded that this port exists but is currently closed to connections.
113	IDENT	Closed	Your computer has responded that this port exists but is currently closed to connections.
135	RPC	Closed	Your computer has responded that this port exists but is currently closed to connections.
139	Net BIOS	OPEN!	As you probably know by now, the NetBIOS File Sharing port is the single largest security hole for networked Windows machines. The payoff from finding open Windows shares is so big that many scanners have been written just to find open ports like this one. Closing it should be a priority for you!
143	IMAP	Closed	Your computer has responded that this port exists but is currently closed to connections.

Your computer at IP:
63.180.11.236
Is now being probed. Please stand by...

Note

By default, older versions of Windows install all three major network protocols, TCP/IP, IPX/SPX (Novell), and NetBEUI (an enhanced version of NetBIOS, a simple network protocol designed for LAN use only). By default, Microsoft uses TCP/IP to carry NetBIOS traffic (which could be carried by NetBEUI) between computers.

Windows 2000 and Windows XP install only TCP/IP as their standard protocol, although you can also install other protocols.

Because Windows' File and Print Sharing uses NetBEUI, but TCP/IP ends up performing tasks that the NetBEUI protocol could perform, any Windows computer directly connected to the Internet with a cable modem or any other device can be attacked via TCP port 139. This port is used for NetBIOS services, as seen in Figure 13.1.

If you use a MacOS computer to get online, watch out for Macintosh Web sharing or AppleShare/IP, which leave TCP ports 80, 427, and 548 open to hackers.

To make matters worse, if you do share folders and don't have passwords set (or use really simple ones), your computer might as well be carrying a sign around saying "Kick me!"

Disabling Port 139 Access for Windows PCs

You can stop hackers from attacking your system via TCP Port 139 in a variety of ways. If Shields Up shows you're vulnerable and you don't need to share folders or printers on the PC connected to the cable modem, remove File and Print Sharing service from your Network configuration. With Windows 9x/Me, open the Network icon in the Control Panel, click the File and Print Sharing button, and clear the checkmarks next to both File and Print Sharing. Restart your computer, and you're protected. Of course, if the kids are looking longingly at your new high-performance inkjet printer and you're tired of getting off your PC so they can print pictures of their favorite singing groups, this might not be much of a solution.

If you're using Internet Connection Sharing or other types of proxy server/gateways products, only the computer that is being used as the gateway (and is thus connected directly to the Internet) is likely to be vulnerable.

Some broadband ISPs now block access to TCP ports 137 through 139 by default to prevent attacks on your system. If your cable ISP doesn't offer this option, ask them to add this setting to their network configuration.

If you need to maintain file or print sharing services on your PC but want to block hackers from attacking via TCP port 139, you need to undo Microsoft's default tying of NetBEUI and File and Print Sharing to the TCP/IP protocol.

You can do this by following these steps:

- Disabling NetBIOS over TCP/IP—This involves installing NetBEUI (if it's not already present); removing TCP/IP bindings to File and Print Sharing for Microsoft Networks, Client for Microsoft Networks, and logons; and disabling all references to Enabling NetBIOS over TCP/IP. See Figure 13.2 for an overview of the process.

- Unbinding TCP/IP from File and Print Sharing—This is similar to the preceding bullet, except that you can keep the Client for Microsoft Networks option checked. Use this option if you can't connect to your cable Internet service without using Client for Microsoft Networks as your login.

You must also perform these steps on the other computers on the network to enable them to access shared resources.

Figure 13.2 provides an overview of these processes.

FIGURE 13.2

After NetBEUI is installed, click on each reference to TCP/IP (left) and clear all bindings to logons, network clients, and file and print sharing (right) unless you need Client for Microsoft Networks. After rebooting, verify that NetBIOS is no longer enabled over TCP/IP (bottom).

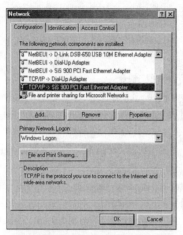
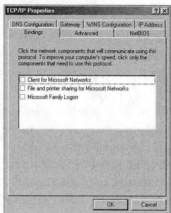
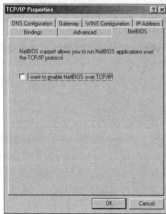

For a detailed step-by-step discussion of these processes, see the following Web sites:

- `Cable-dsl.home.att.net/#security`—Remove the #security from the URL to start at the top of the page for other topics of interest.

- `grc.com/su-bondage.htm`—This provides Windows 9x and Windows 2000 instructions and screen shots.

- `www.cablemodemhelp.com/winmesec.htm`—This provides Windows Me-specific instructions and screen shots.

Note

Windows XP doesn't install NetBEUI by default, and Microsoft no longer supports NetBEUI networks. However, you can install the NetBEUI protocol manually from the Windows XP CD-ROM for troubleshooting. It also works for network file/printer sharing as described here. See the Windows XP CD-ROM for installation details.

Disabling File Sharing Vulnerabilities on a Mac

If you're running a Mac on your cable Internet connection, you can block file sharing while you're connected by disabling it in the Control Panel. However, if other people on your home network need access to shared folders on your system, disabling file sharing isn't going to work. Instead, be sure you do the following:

- Disable Guest access—The Guest account can provide anyone on an AppleShare network (including outside intruders) full access to your system.

- Create login names for each user—If everyone on the home network needs access to the same folder, create a group with the File Sharing Control Panel.

- Set up passwords for each shared account—As with Windows File and Print Sharing, shared folders on a Mac with no password are easy pickings.

Tip

For much more detailed information on Mac security, I recommend the Macintosh Security site at www.securemac.com.

Whether you use Windows, MacOS, or some other operating system, securing file and print sharing services is only half the battle. Because unauthorized remote-control or file-transfer programs such as Nimda, SirCam, or others can send data from your computer, and so-called "spyware" programs can tattle on your browsing habits while displaying ads or providing you with a "free" utility program, you need a firewall to provide additional protection to your system.

Firewalls and What They Do

A *firewall* is a hardware device or software program that prevents unauthorized access to a computer or a network and unauthorized Internet traffic from traveling from a computer or network. Firewalls do this by examining each incoming data packet to determine whether it is going to a computer that has requested it and by examining each outgoing data packet to determine whether it has been sent. Corporate networks use firewalls along with routers (devices that route traffic between a network and the Internet) to allow network users to access the Internet safely, but prevent unauthorized access to the network from the Internet.

With the advent of high-speed, always-on Internet connections such as cable modems, firewalls have become important for both individual computers and networks of any size. Cable modem routers (discussed in Chapter 17, "Router Your Way to Internet Sharing") provide simple incoming firewall services to the computers connected to it, but firewall software (personal firewalls) are still useful for preventing unauthorized outbound traffic. What about a computer that's directly connected to the Internet? Firewall software can be used to provide a cost-effective safeguard against unauthorized traffic in both directions.

Hardware Versus Software Firewalls

The term "firewall" is often used interchangeably to describe both hardware and software firewalls, but in reality firewall products work in a variety of different ways.

The simplest firewall method is an inherent part of most Internet sharing software (such as Microsoft's Internet Connection Sharing and others) as well as broadband routers used for Internet sharing. They use a method called NAT (network address translation) to convert non-routable IP addresses used on a home or small-office network into public IP addresses used when the Internet is accessed from the network. Because the Internet never sees the actual IP address of a computer on a network that uses NAT, NAT acts as a firewall to block unauthorized inbound network traffic (traffic that wasn't requested by a computer on the network). However, NAT doesn't examine outbound data packets, so it provides no protection against unauthorized outbound traffic, and it can't check incoming traffic for undesirable contents.

Some vendors now sell firewall appliances that are connected to the cable modem or other broadband Internet device. Firewall appliances use packet inspection to determine what Internet traffic should be permitted to pass through the appliance to the network and what should be blocked. Some firewall appliances offer features such as optional anti-virus protection for all computers connected to the appliance, content filtering, blocking access to specified Web sites, and support for VPN (virtual private network) connections from remote users. While firewall appliances provide greater inbound-traffic protection than simple NAT-based firewalls found in routers and Internet sharing software, they aren't designed to block unauthorized outbound traffic from Trojan horse programs.

Major vendors of firewall appliances include

- SonicWALL—SonicWALL SOHO2; www.sonicwall.com
- WatchGuard—WatchGuard SOHO; www.watchguard.com
- Cisco—PIX 501; www.cisco.com
- Network Associates Technology—PGP e-appliance series (5, 10, 50 users); www.pgp.com

Many of these products can also be used as a router, and some also include a multi-port switch.

Personal firewall software adds a necessary layer of protection to your computer, even if it's behind a router, connection-sharing software, or a firewall appliance. Personal firewall software can block all outgoing Internet traffic, permit outgoing Internet traffic from authorized programs (such as Web browsers and e-mail clients) only, as well as block inbound traffic from crackers and intruders. Some broadband routers (which typically use NAT) can be configured to require clients to use a particular personal firewall program to provide enhanced protection.

Major Software Firewall Products

Because of the security risk of always-on Internet access and the increasing numbers of Internet-borne worms and Trojan horses that can take over your system and send confidential information to others, Internet security is one of the hottest topics today. Many vendors are providing solutions for home and small-office users. Some of the most popular and best software firewalls for PCs include the following:

- ZoneAlarm—This is a simple but effective firewall with the ability to block all Internet access automatically or with a single click. ZoneAlarm also allows you to establish rules for programs that access the Internet. It is intended for Windows 95 and above computers and is available at www.zonelabs.com.

- ZoneAlarm Pro—This is enhanced with e-mail script blocking, easy setup for Internet Connection Sharing and other types of home networking, and across-the-network management of protection. ZoneAlarm Pro is intended for Windows 95 and above computers and is available at www.zonelabs.com.

- Norton Internet Security 2002—This is a comprehensive suite containing Norton AntiVirus, Norton Personal Firewall, Norton Privacy Control (blocks private information from being sent through IM services and to unsecured Web sites), and Norton Parental Control (controls access to undesirable Web sites). Norton Internet Security 2002 is for Windows 95 and above computers and is available at www.Symantec.com.

- Norton Personal Firewall 2002—This supports home networks, automatically blocks port scanners, and features improved automatic determination of Internet-safe programs on your computer. Norton Personal Firewall 2002 is intended for Windows 95 and above computers and is available at www.Symantec.com.

- McAfee Personal Firewall—This supports home networks and provides color-coded alerts to tell you how severe the threat to your system is. McAfee Personal Firewall is intended for Windows 95B (Windows 95 OSR 2.x) and above and is available at www.mcafee.com.

Major MacOS-compatible firewall programs include the following:

- Norton Internet Security for Macintosh—The suite includes Norton AntiVirus, Norton Personal Firewall, and iCleans cookie/cache/Web history cleaner. It is available at www.Symantec.com.

- BrickHouse—This is a shareware GUI-based configuration utility for MacOS X's built-in firewall. BrickHouse includes preconfigured settings for typical home and office networks. Check out www.securemac.com/brickhouse.php for review and download.

- NetBarrier—This suite includes firewall, intrusion alarms, filtering for confidential information, Internet privacy features, and modem lock. NetBarrier is available at www.intego.com.

Note Windows XP has a built-in firewall that can prevent your computer from being detected by potential intruders (a feature often called stealth mode), but isn't designed to block outgoing traffic. You should still add a two-way firewall to your Windows XP operating system for maximum protection.

Finding Out Which Firewalls Work—And Which Don't

The list of software firewall products in the previous section is far from complete, but it is based on looking at the most critical issue of all: Does the firewall work? Most firewall programs on the market stop intrusions into your computer, but many don't stop data being sent from your computer.

Firewalls that allow Trojan horse programs to send data out of your computer are worse than useless because you think you're safe, even when you're not. If you're a Windows user, run Steve Gibson's LeakTest attack simulator program on your own PC. LeakTest simulates how typical Trojan horse and remote control programs behave: Such programs change the names of their executable files to masquerade as programs that are allowed Internet access (such as a Web browser or FTP program), and then send data from your computer to a remote server. You can download LeakTest from Grc.com/lt/leaktest.htm.

Use LeakTest to check out the security of your system, regardless of whether you have a firewall program installed. If you're in the market for a firewall, follow the link to the Personal Firewall Scoreboard to see how some of the major Windows players fared. Figure 13.3 shows the result of LeakTest when run on one of my systems that is located behind a router which provides NAT-based firewall capabilities.

FIGURE 13.3

Even with a
router (which
provides
inbound firewall
protection),
Gibson
Research's
LeakTest was
able to access
the GRC test
server. This com-
puter needs a
software fire-
wall!

If your Windows computer gets a result similar to the one in Figure 13.3, you need a
software firewall, even if you have a router, a firewall appliance, or connect through
a gateway PC. If your Windows computer already has a software firewall installed,
it's not providing adequate protection. You should look into an update, or consider
switching to a different product. Of the many firewalls on the market for Windows
users, the favorite of most reviewers is ZoneAlarm, which is free for personal and
non-commercial use.

If you're looking for MacOS firewall information, check the firewall ratings on the
Macintosh Security Site at www.securemac.com.

Using ZoneAlarm

ZoneAlarm is being covered in detail because it's free for home and non-commercial
use and can be updated to an even more powerful commercial package (ZoneAlarm
Pro).

ZoneAlarm can be downloaded free from its creator, Zone Labs, Inc.
(www.zonelabs.com). It uses a simple wizard to install, and automatically configures
itself to allow your Web browser to access the Internet. No other programs are
allowed to access the Internet unless you grant permission. Figure 13.4 shows a
ZoneAlarm alert triggered by Microsoft NetMeeting, which must act as a server to
permit two-way communication with other NetMeeting users. Figure 13.5 shows a
ZoneAlarm alert triggered by a program trying to access the Internet.

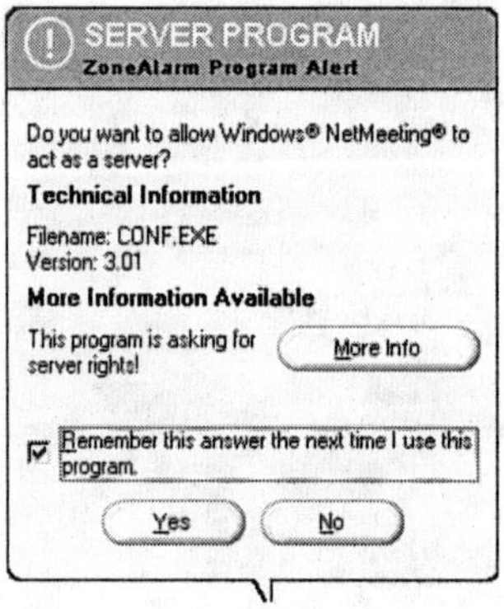

FIGURE 13.4

ZoneAlarm can permit NetMeeting to access the Internet just one time (click Yes) or every time it's run (click Remember), or ZoneAlarm can block NetMeeting's access (click No)—it's your choice!

FIGURE 13.5

ZoneAlarm isn't fooled by the use of a false name (LeakTest has been renamed Conf.exe to masquerade as the executable file-name used by NetMeeting, which has already accessed the Internet); ZoneAlarm detects that the program has been changed and won't allow Internet access unless you agree.

Figure 13.6 shows that ZoneAlarm blocks the GRC LeakTest program from connecting if you deny it permission.

FIGURE 13.6

ZoneAlarm prevents the GRC LeakTest program from connecting, indicating that it's providing true outbound firewall protection to your system.

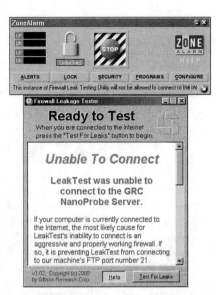

To see the current list of programs that ZoneAlarm has intercepted, click the Programs button. Programs with specific permission to access the Internet or a local network have a checkmark; others have a question mark. The Internet Lock button immediately shuts down Internet access to any program unless you have allowed it access with the Pass Lock option (see Figure 13.7).

FIGURE 13.7

The ZoneAlarm main menu (top) provides access to all functions including Internet Lock. The program menu (bottom) lists all programs that have accessed the Internet and their status.

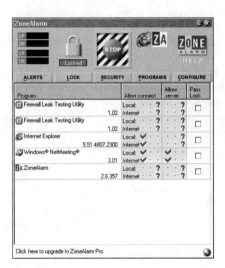

You can prevent unauthorized outgoing traffic from your e-mail client by using the Internet Lock or similar Internet shutdown features found on some cable modems or firewall programs after your e-mail client has retrieved your current e-mail. With the Internet Lock in place, you can open your e-mail without worrying about messages transmitting unwanted information back to the sender. Close your e-mail client and release the lock when you're finished and are ready to go back online.

Routers Versus Personal Firewalls

Virtually all routers (see Chapter 17) provide inbound firewall protection for the computers plugged into the router, and firewall appliances (which often also act as routers) add additional protection features for inbound traffic. Thus, it's a common misconception that router-based networks, or those that use a computer with a proxy server for sharing (see Chapter 16), have no need for a personal firewall program.

Unfortunately, this isn't true when you consider the threat from SirCam, Back Orifice, and other programs that send data out of your computer without your permission. You can use ZoneAlarm or any personal firewall programs that provide protection against unauthorized outbound traffic with your router without problems, and you should because the router or firewall appliance stops incoming attacks, whereas the personal firewall program stops outbound programs that run without your permission.

If you have never upgraded your firewall software, or haven't upgraded it since late 2000, your firewall probably is not as effective as it could be. Gibson Research's Personal Firewall Scoreboard at grc.com/lt/scoreboard.htm shows that older versions of so-called "leakproof" firewalls weren't effective until updates were performed. Some firewalls, such as Norton Personal Firewall, Norton Internet Security, ZoneAlarm, and others will automatically check for updates and might have fixed themselves. Check your vendor's Web site for the latest version information and update procedure.

In reality, personal firewall software and hardware products that have firewall features aren't competitors. They are both needed to provide protection against inbound and outbound threats. When you combine them with up-to-date antivirus software and protection against hostile e-mail scripts (see Chapter 14 for details), you have a highly secure computer.

Summary

Always-on Internet connections such as cable modems, provide a tempting target for would-be intruders. Port probe software can locate systems with open TCP ports and help intruders compromise your system.

While NAT-based Internet Connection Sharing software and routers provide a simple firewall with some measure of security against inbound attacks, they don't provide any way to control the contents of inbound Web traffic or provide network-wide antivirus support. Firewall appliances provide greater security against a wider variety of inbound threats, and can also control content, block access to undesirable Web sites, and provide network-wide antivirus protection, but can't block outbound traffic from Trojan horse programs.

Personal firewall software provides protection for both standalone and networked computers against both inbound and outbound threats. However, not all personal firewall software programs provide effective protection against outbound traffic.

Security Web sites such as Gibson Research's LeakTest and Shields Up! can help you detect problems with open TCP ports, firewall software, and firewall hardware and help you locate more suitable products for system protection.

14

STOPPING COMPUTER VIRUSES

CHAPTER HIGHLIGHTS:

- Learn how computer viruses threaten both your data and your PC
- Discover the different types of computer viruses.
- Learn to use popular products and services to stop viruses

How Viruses Threaten Your PC and Your Data

Computer viruses are some of the biggest threats to the well being of your computer and the information it contains. Current computer viruses can do any of the following:

■ Erase important files used by the Windows operating system

■ Erase the entire hard disk

■ Erase hardware setup information stored in the non-volatile RAM chip (CMOS chip) on the motherboard

■ Rename data and system files

■ Alter settings used by Office suite and e-mail programs

■ Take control of your computer and use it to attack other computers

■ Take control of your computer and send private information to other computers

■ Turn on your Web camera and sound card and spy on you

As you can see from this list of symptoms, computer viruses are no laughing matter. They have cost computer users billions of dollars in lost data and time, and they threaten the most important part of your computing experience: your personal information.

Types of Computer Viruses

The term *computer virus* is typically used to describe three different types of software threats to your system:

■ Trojan horses

■ Worms

■ True computer viruses

It pays to know the differences between these programs so you can take the appropriate steps to protect yourself.

■ Trojan horse programs—These pretend to be another type of program, but must be spread by the user; they lack the ability to spread to other systems unless you help them along by forwarding the e-mail containing the Trojan horse. The Picture.exe program, which pretends to be a compressed file called PICTURE.EXE but will actually attempt to e-mail AOL user information, is one of many examples of a Trojan horse program.

- Worms—These can spread themselves from computer to computer, either by copying themselves to another disk drive or by e-mailing themselves to other users. Sircam, one well-known example of a worm, can delete files or slow down your system, e-mail itself to others in your address book, attach a randomly selected document to its e-mail, and look for shared drives.

- True computer viruses—These can infect programs, document templates, e-mail systems, floppy and hard drives, and can even mutate into a slightly different form to evade detection. Chernobyl, which infects files and can overwrite the hard disk with random data or attack the motherboard flash BIOS chip, is a well-known example of a destructive computer virus.

Antivirus programs are designed to detect and stop all three types of behavior.

Why Cable Internet Users Must Be Extra Vigilant

Although cable Internet connections make it easier to protect yourself against computer viruses, they also make it easier to become infected and to spread viruses to others. Here's why:

- The "always-on" nature of two-way cable Internet connections enables e-mail clients to be running at all times. This makes it easier for worms to e-mail themselves to other users because the e-mail client might already be running.

- An "always on" system can be compromised without the user's knowledge by the use of Trojan horse remote-control software. Because the user is already connected to the Internet, a remote control program can be used to transmit information from the system or to implant destructive commands into the operating system for future execution.

- The widespread use of the free Microsoft Outlook Express e-mail client by cable Internet providers is another significant weakness. Because of its support of HTML-based e-mail (which can contain scripts and ActiveX/Java controls), Outlook Express is notoriously vulnerable to script-based worms and viruses, such as the infamous ILOVEYOU virus and many others.

Fortunately, a combination of effective antivirus software, changes in software configuration, and changes in your behavior can stop virus/worm/Trojan attacks in their tracks and prevent infections from even occurring.

You can learn more about the technical details of the vulnerabilities of Outlook Express by reading Symantec's report, "Prevent Current and Future E-Mail Worms," available online at www.symantec.com/avcenter/security/Content/2000_05_12.html.

Antivirus Software

The first line of defense against viruses/worms/Trojans is up-to-date and updated antivirus software. *Up-to-date* antivirus software is the latest software release published by a major vendor such as Symantec (Norton AntiVirus), McAfee (Virus Scan), Trend Micro (PC-cillin 2000) and others. Such products use the most advanced methods available for detecting viruses and preventing them from damaging or compromising your system. *Updated* antivirus software refers to the continuing process of installing updated information about known viruses and their behavior and, in some cases, updates to the antivirus software detection engine itself. In the past, many antivirus programs offered unlimited free updates, but because of the rapid changes in how viruses work and propagate themselves, and to help provide a stream of revenue to help pay for effective antivirus defenses against new viruses, most antivirus software now provides only one year of no-charge updates in the product price.

Outdated versions of antivirus programs are often sold at retail in "value" packaging (a CD-ROM jewelcase with minimal documentation) for much less than the current version sells for. I don't recommend this type of antivirus software because the software isn't capable of providing full protection against current threats, even if virus signature updates are available. If it were, it wouldn't be sold at such a big discount.

Similarly to the issues involved in using outdated software, it's false economy to continue to use antivirus software after your free update period has expired; doing so protects you against old viruses, not new ones. Although some users have loudly complained about having only a year of free updates when they purchase products such as Norton AntiVirus, the extremely fast nature of virus development means that you really do need a brand-new program every year anyway for maximum protection. The cost of a new program is modest (under $50 is typical), and you get another year of updates. Therefore, it is recommend that you buy a new version of your favorite antivirus program instead of buying updates.

For example, Norton AntiVirus 2002 has the following improvements over its predecessor, Norton AntiVirus 2001:

- 2002 automatically blocks both known and new script-based attacks such as IloveYou.

- 2002 scans and cleans outgoing e-mail, preventing the spread of viruses from one system to another via e-mail.

■ 2002 lets you check for viruses within Windows Explorer.

■ 2002 removes many common viruses automatically for you.

These changes make the upgrade a "no-brainer" decision, because Norton Antivirus 2002 will keep you much safer than the previous version.

Features to Look For in Antivirus Software

The first feature to demand in antivirus software is the ability to detect and stop viruses anywhere on your system. Originally, this meant that fast checking of hard and floppy drives (the favorite hiding places for early viruses) were the major considerations. Now, because most viruses are spread via e-mail, the checking of incoming e-mail is a high-priority task. For full protection, your antivirus program also needs to be present in memory at all times to provide full-time detection and prevention of e-mail, macro, and disk-based viruses/Trojans/worms. Most programs also let you schedule regular scans of your drives.

The second major feature to look for is the ability to easily download and install updates to the software. If you can't download and install antivirus updates without complex maneuvering, it doesn't matter how powerful the software is: You're not likely to use it or upgrade it. One of the reasons I like Norton AntiVirus is because of its LiveUpdate feature, which automates the download and installation process of both antivirus and other Norton software updates. A cable Internet connection allows you to downloaded and install updates in just a minute or two.

All current releases of antivirus software do a good job with these first two features. However, both of these options are basically reactive; they work after your system is attacked. Some of the latest antivirus software offers a third major feature: preventive measures to stop e-mail infections of other computers by checking outgoing e-mail messages. Some also offer a fourth major feature: preventing script-based viruses and worms such as the notorious "ILOVEYOU" and "Anna Kournikova" from running. Script-based viruses and worms use the popular Visual Basic programming language to damage and compromise your system.

Note

Although viruses are a problem for both Windows and Mac users, Windows users are far more likely to be attacked by viruses/Trojans/worms. This is because of the popularity of Windows and because of the permissive design of much of Microsoft's software. Macs are more secure than Windows because of the design of the operating system and MacOS, and can't be infected by Windows-dependent viruses. If you use a Mac, your system is still threatened by viruses, but your system is not as big a target as a Windows-based system is.

Using Norton AntiVirus

Although many high-quality antivirus programs are on the market, my personal favorite is Symantec's Norton AntiVirus, available in the following products for Windows and Macintosh:

- Norton AntiVirus—Complete antivirus protection.

- Norton Internet Security—Adds privacy controls and a personal firewall. The Mac version also has Aladdin iClean to remove Internet files. The Windows version also offers parental controls for family-friendly Web browsing.

- Norton System Works—Version 2002 for Windows adds Norton Utilities system diagnostic and repair tools, Norton CleanSweep Internet file removal, and Roxio's GoBack system recovery. The Mac version adds Norton Utilities, Aladdin Spring Cleaning program uninstaller and Internet file remover, and Dantz Restrospect Express backup.

- Norton System Works Professional (Windows only)—Adds all the features of System Works plus Norton Ghost system cloning and WinFax Basic fax sending and receiving.

Norton AntiVirus provides the following types of protection:

- Adjustable detection of unknown viruses—Norton's Bloodhound technology works by looking for virus-like behavior in applications.

- Optional auto-protect mode—This mode provides real-time detection of viruses/worms/Trojans.

- Rescue disk—This creates and configures a bootable set of disks that can be used to disinfect a system that has a virus.

- Scanning options—This controls whether system files are scanned at startup and what types of files will be scanned for viruses during full system scans.

- Optional e-mail and script protection—This prevents infected POP3 e-mail (normal server-based e-mail) from reaching your computer, but might not work with Web-based e-mail accounts such as Hotmail, even if you use a client such as Outlook Express to manage your e-mail. For maximum protection, be sure to use the auto-protect mode to catch viruses in real time.

Norton AntiVirus displays a status screen when you start it, providing immediate information about how your system is protected against viruses (see Figure 14.1).

FIGURE 14.1

NAV 2002 warns this user to run a full system scan and displays the system date and the date of the last virus definition update. Because the virus definitions are more than 90 days old, this user needs to run LiveUpdate to update the system's virus protection.

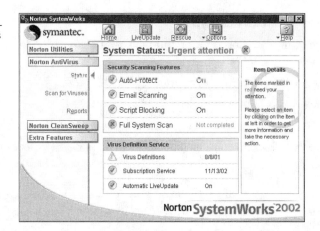

When LiveUpdate is run, it compares the configuration of your Norton AntiVirus program to the Symantec server and determines which updates you need. LiveUpdate can install both new virus definitions (see Figure 14.2) and updates to the program.

FIGURE 14.2

LiveUpdate will install new virus definitions for Norton AntiVirus 2002. The 530.9KB download takes little time with a cable Internet connection.

Tip

If you need to run updates manually, syndicated computer columnist James Derk (author of Scripps-Howard News Service's "Computer Central" column) recommends a daily update of your antivirus software. Seem crazy? Not really. Your cable Internet connection is so speedy that a daily update will take only a minute or two, and new viruses and similar threats are coming so fast that using last week's virus alerts might be too little, too late.

Major Antivirus Software Vendors

You can get more information about retail-packaged or downloadable antivirus programs from the following Web sites:

- www.Symantec.com—Norton AntiVirus

- www.McAfee.com—McAfee ViruScan

- www.pc-cillin.com—Trend Micro's PC-cillin 2000

- www.my-etrust.com—Computer Associates' eTrust EZ Antivirus and EZ Armor Suite

Many developers allow you to try their software for 30 days. Take advantage of these trial offers to help you find the best antivirus software for your needs.

 Note For additional choices, see the Antivirus Developer Index available at the Virus Bulletin Ltd Web site: www.virusbtn.com/AVLinks/.

Using Online Antivirus Services

There's no substitute for having full-time antivirus protection running on your system. However, if you have just added a new PC to your network after your favorite software store has closed, your antivirus software has expired, or you would just like a second opinion about a system that might be infected, online virus scanning provides a backup option that is useful in a pinch.

Online virus scanners come in two flavors:

- Free

- Subscription-based

Free services, such as Trend Micro's HouseCall and Central Command's Online Virus Scanner, can detect and remove viruses that are already present on your system, but can't prevent your system from becoming infected in the first place.

Subscription-based services such as McAfee.com's Virus Scan Online are designed to completely replace traditional self-contained antivirus programs. They provide a local client for real-time protection and a rescue disk feature, while storing virus scanning software and signatures on their own servers. You can usually try a free test scan of your system before purchasing the full package of services.

Most online antivirus services are optimized for use with Internet Explorer; if you use Netscape 4.x, you will need to download a supplemental file to allow the scanning program to run. Netscape 6.x isn't yet widely supported.

Web sites for online antivirus scanning include the following:

■ housecall.antivirus.com (HouseCall)

■ www.centralcommand.com/scan.htm (Central Command Online Virus Scanner)

■ www.McAfee.com (McAfee Virus Scan Online)

■ www.Symantec.com/securitycheck (click Security Check, then Scan for Viruses)

When you start an online virus scanner for the first time, you might be prompted to install an ActiveX control that the software developer provides. Accept the control, or you won't be able to run the scan. After the control is installed, select the drive(s) you want to scan, and start the process, as shown in Figure 14.3.

FIGURE 14.3

Trend Micro's HouseCall service provides free on-demand virus scanning via your Web browser.

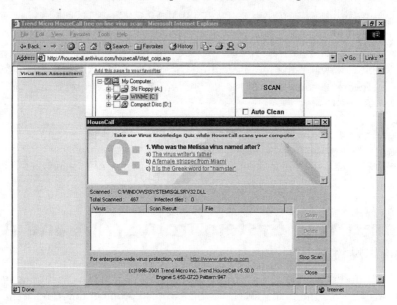

If viruses are detected and you didn't enable automatic repair, you will be prompted for steps to take to rectify the problem.

Safe Web-Based E-mail Services

If you prefer the "read-it-anywhere" nature of Web-based e-mail, but want protection against e-mail-borne viruses, consider these free e-mail services:

- Hotmail—www.hotmail.com
- ActivatorMail—www.activatormail.com

Both Hotmail and ActivatorMail use McAfee VirusScan to check for viruses on file attachments you download or upload. I know this feature works from personal experience: When the antivirus software on one of my computers expired, Hotmail's virus scanning feature prevented me from uploading a file attachment containing a Word macro virus. Hotmail not only alerted me to the presence of the virus, but it also prevented me from sending the infected file to other computer users.

ActivatorMail also offers automatic anti-spam filters (an optional feature with Hotmail). Both ActivatorMail and Hotmail provide 2MB mailboxes free of charge, and both offer optional extra capacity for a fee. You can use your standard e-mail client with both services when you're at your desk, or check your e-mail from any Web browser.

Some cable Internet ISPs also provide antivirus filtering; check with your ISP to find out. However, don't let this feature convince you to skip having up-to-date antivirus software. Because e-mail is only one way in which viruses can attack your system, it pays to be safe.

When you're away from home or the office and you're using a Web-based e-mail service, be sure to log in with the highest security setting available and clear the browser's cache when you're done to avoid leaving personal information on the computer.

Protecting Your System from Script and Active Content Attacks

Scripting languages, such as JavaScript and VBScript, as well as active content, such as ActiveX and Java, pose a double-barreled problem for your system. Allowing them their usual default of unlimited access to your system could clobber your system if you open a script or active content that contains a virus or worm. However, disabling these features prevents many Web sites and e-mails from being viewed properly.

Some of the latest antivirus programs contain integrated protection against hostile programs and scripts. If your preferred antivirus program doesn't, you can add protection to both your e-mail client and your Web browser by installing separate protection programs such as Finjan Software's SurfinGuard Pro, available from www.finjan.com/surfinguard/.

FIGURE 14.4

Finjan Software SurfinGuard Pro blocks a hostile downloaded program's payload.

SurfinGuard Pro allows you to monitor, block, or allow downloaded active content to run on your system. It runs automatically in the background as soon as you start your computer to intercept any attempt to write files to your system (as in Figure 14.4), change Registry settings, delete or alter files, and so forth.

Tip

SurfinGuard Pro also intercepts installation programs that you run manually after downloading patch or update files from the Internet. If you downloaded the program, be sure to allow the program to run.

Because many of today's e-mail clients are designed to display HTML just as your browser does, this type of protective software will stop hostile script and program threats entering your system through either pathway.

Changing Your Online Behavior

As this chapter has demonstrated, the threats to your system are greater than ever before, and thanks to the speed of cable Internet connections, viruses can enter your system faster than ever before. Although installing the latest antivirus and script blocking software will help prevent most attacks on your system, changing your online behavior will help just as much. Take the following steps to ensure your online safety:

- Check all the systems you use for up-to-date antivirus and script-blocking software.
- Use the speed of cable Internet connections to update your antivirus software daily.
- Don't open e-mail attachments from strangers, and be wary of unsolicited attachments, especially .EXE files.
- Don't pass along virus "alerts" you get from other users unless you check them at sources such as Symantec's Security Response page (www.sarc.com); check the Hoaxes and Jokes page first for the facts.
- Instead of sending short file attachments (which could harbor a virus), insert the text into your e-mail message.
- Use Windows Update to download and install all available patches for Internet Explorer and Outlook Express.
- Consider switching to another e-mail client instead of Outlook Express to improve online security.
- Before downloading utility software on the recommendation of a chatroom posting or spam e-mail, use reliable search engines such as Google, ZDNet, antivirus Web sites, and others to find out if the program offered is a legitimate one. For example, a program called Easyspeed.exe masquerades as a cable modem speedup utility, but is actually a Trojan that allows others to control your computer. As Internet security specialist Johannes B. Ullrich of DShield (www.dshield.org) puts it, "Don't take candy from strangers."

By practicing safe computing, you reduce the risk to your own systems and encourage safe behavior by others.

Summary

Computer viruses, Trojans, and worms can damage your data, prevent your computer from booting, and transmit sensitive information to unknown parties. Protect your computer with a comprehensive strategy that includes

- Up-to-date antivirus software that is updated frequently (even daily)
- E-mail protection through script blocking and scanning of incoming and outgoing e-mail messages and attachments

You can supplement your normal antivirus protection by using Web-based scanners to check your system, installing self-contained script-blocking software, and by using Web-based e-mail services that check messages and attachments for viruses.

The final line of defense is to change your online behavior in favor of safe computing and away from risky "taking candy from strangers" or "sky is falling" behaviors that put your computer and the computers of others at risk.

PART VI

SHARING YOUR CABLE MODEM SERVICE

USING MICROSOFT INTERNET CONNECTION SHARING

*C*HAPTER HIGHLIGHTS:

- What Internet Connection Sharing is (and isn't)
- Which versions of Windows support Connection Sharing
- Which systems can connect to an ICS-based network
- How to set up an ICS network with supported versions of Windows
- What your alternatives are for sharing your Internet connection

What Internet Connection Sharing Is—and Isn't

For years, people with one Internet connection but two or more PCs have sought to "share the wealth" by making it possible for multiple computers to use a single Internet connection. Although a number of products were developed for analog (dial-up) modem sharing, most of these were expensive, and their complex configuration was geared toward offices with IT technicians handy, not home users.

Microsoft's Internet Connection Sharing, or ICS, changed all of that. ICS first saw the light of day with Windows 98 Second Edition, and is also present under various names in Windows Me, Windows 2000, and Windows XP. What can ICS do for you, and is it the right solution for you?

Features of ICS

ICS, as the name makes clear, is designed to let you share your Internet connection with additional computers over a network. Like other types of software-based sharing discussed in Chapter 16, "Using Other Computer-Based Internet Sharing Programs," ICS isn't connection-specific. It can be used with all types of two-way broadband service such as cable modems, as well as with dial-up analog modem Internet services.

ICS has the following major features:

- Supports both Windows-based and non-Windows PCs on the same network
- Allows either dynamic IP addressing (no need for complex settings on systems sharing the connection) or manual IP addressing (for use when automatic IP addressing doesn't work)
- Supports most popular Internet uses (Web browsing, e-mail, IM chatting)

Limitations of ICS

Although ICS provides shared-connection users with basic Internet access, it also has limitations:

- ICS is a program that runs in the Windows system tray; if you start the computer which provides ICS services (also called the ICS gateway computer) in Safe Mode or have a crash that clears out the system tray, nobody can get online until the ICS gateway computer is restarted and ICS restarts.
- ICS has no provision for access control for network users. If you want to control where your kids can go online, you need to sign up with a filtered service or install software filtering on their systems.

- ICS lacks integrated network security. You must add your own firewall and anti-virus software to each system you want to secure; you must also make sure that your firewall software will work with ICS.

- ICS requires separate network connections to the cable modem or other broadband device and the rest of the network. This can prevent some types of advanced Internet features from working (see next point) and might use an additional PCI slot for the second network adapter.

ICS will work with USB Ethernet adapters, although this is slower than using a PCI Ethernet card.

- ICS will not work with one-way cable modem systems that use a separate analog (dial-up) modem. See Chapter 16 for alternative computer-based sharing solutions.

- ICS might not be able to play some online games or use advanced Internet messaging service features because its normal configuration doesn't support the mapping of logical ports needed by some Internet programs (except with the Windows 2000 and Windows XP versions of ICS).

To learn more about logical port mappings and to download a free utility program that will allow ICS to work with programs that need logical ports, go to the "Map Ports Through ICS with ICS Configuration" Web page at `www.practicallynetworked.com/sharing/ics/icsconfiguration.htm`.

Essentially, ICS provides you with bare-bones Internet sharing that's suitable for most users' basic needs. And, because the only additional cost is another network adapter for the computer with the shared connection, it's a low-cost solution as well. I've used ICS on both my home and office computers, and find it does a decent job at a price that's hard to beat.

The Hardware and Software You Need for ICS

Any of the following Windows versions can share their Internet connection with ICS:

- Windows 98 SE
- Windows Me
- Windows 2000
- Windows XP Home Edition
- Windows XP Professional

See the following sections for details.

The ICS gateway must have two separate network connections:

- A connection to the cable modem
- A connection to the network to allow other computers to share the cable modem

The most typical way (and the method that provides the fastest performance) is to use two 10/100 Ethernet cards, one connected to the cable modem, and the other connected to a 10/100-based Ethernet network.

Although you can also use ICS with USB Ethernet adapters, USB ports are slower than 10/100 Ethernet cards. If your cable Internet provider uses an Ethernet connection to the cable modem, or provides a choice of Ethernet or USB, go with 10/100 Ethernet whenever possible. However, if you have only one available PCI slot for networking, connect to the cable modem via the USB port and save the slot for your network card to avoid a performance bottleneck between the cable modem and computers on your network.

Overview of the Setup Process

Although the details of each ICS installation vary by Windows version, the overall process looks like this:

1. Make sure your cable Internet connection is working properly and that you have recorded the current settings. The computer with the connection is called the *ICS gateway computer*, and ICS will change the configuration of this computer.

2. Install a network adapter in each computer that will be sharing the connection. These computers are called ICS clients. To learn how to install a network adapter, see Chapter 17, "Router Your Way to Internet Sharing."

3. Install a network adapter in the ICS gateway to allow it to connect with other computers on the network.

4. Run the ICS setup program on the ICS gateway computer to configure it to share its connection with others.

5. Verify that the ICS gateway can access the Internet.

6. Configure other computers on the network to use the ICS gateway computer to access the Internet. While most versions of ICS have provision for a setup floppy disk, you can do this manually with non-Windows clients.

7. Verify that the ICS clients can also access the Internet.

Figure 15.1 shows you how a typical ICS-based network can be configured.

FIGURE 15.1

A typical home network using ICS to share a cable modem. Two network adapters are used in the ICS gateway: one to connect to the cable modem and the other to connect to the rest of the network.

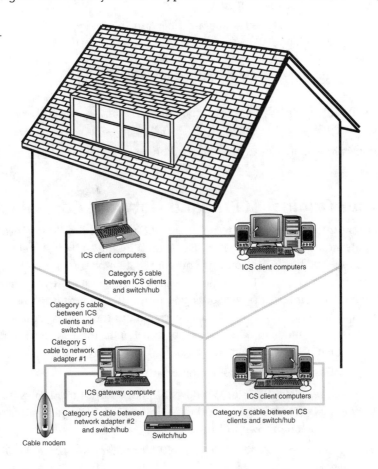

At the end of the ICS setup process, the settings originally used by the ICS gateway computer to connect directly with the cable modem have been transferred to Internet Connection Sharing's ISHARE entry in the Network components listing, a virtual network adapter to provide Internet services to both the ICS gateway and client computers.

The network adapter used to connect to the cable modem is now called the "Home" adapter, and the network adapter you installed to connect to the rest of the network is called the "Shared" adapter.

Warning

Before you install ICS on the computer with the cable Internet connection, which will become the ICS gateway computer, record your current network adapter settings using Table 15.1 as discussed in the next section.

If you decide to use another Internet sharing solution in the future, you will need to re-enter these settings to keep your computer working properly. You might be able to re-run your cable Internet connection software to reset your computer, or you might need to enter some or all of this information manually.

You will find excellent tutorials on the different variations of ICS at the Practically Networked ICS How-To Center: www.practicallynetworked.com/sharing/sharing.htm.

Windows XP-specific issues are discussed at: www.practicallynetworked.com/sharing/xp_ics/.

Recording Your Original TCP/IP and Network Configuration

Transport Control Protocol/Internet Protocol (TCP/IP) is the "language" used by all computers that access the Internet. Depending on the cable Internet service you use and the specific hardware you have on your system, you might need to record a lot of information, or just a few of the fields listed in this table. If you have a problem with your cable Internet service after you install ICS, referring to this information can help you get going again. And, if you find out that you can't use the automatic IP address setup mode for ICS clients, you must enter some of this information manually for each ICS client you connect to an ICS gateway.

To display this information, follow these instructions:

- With Windows 98 SE or Windows Me, click Start, Run. Type WINIPCFG in the dialog box that appears and press Enter. Click More Info to see a screen similar to the one shown in Figure 15.2.
- With Windows 2000 or Windows XP, click Start, Run, type IPCONFIG, and press Enter.

Figure 15.2 shows you how WINIPCFG displays information about a typical cable modem configuration before ICS is installed. Use the callouts in Figure 15.2 to help you complete Table 15.1 to record the settings for your own cable Internet connection.

FIGURE 15.2

Using
WINIPCFG on a
Windows Me
system to view
TCP/IP network
information.

Table 15.1   Internet Settings Before Installing ICS

Setting	Figure Key	Your System	Notes
Host Information			
Host Name	1		The first part of the name translates to the Host field in the DNS tab; the second part of the name translates to the Domain field. See Figure 15.14.
DNS Server #1	2		Click #3 to view the second server.
DNS Server #2	3		Click #3 to toggle between server #1 and server #2.
Node Type	4		
NetBIOS Scope ID	5		Not used.
IP Routing Enabled	6		Not used.
WINS Proxy Enabled	7		Not used.
NetBIOS Resolution uses DNS	8		uses DNS
Ethernet Adapter Information			
Ethernet Adapter Name	9		Will become the TCP/IP "Home" adapter after ICS is installed; click the down-arrow to view whether PPP or Dial-Up adapter is listed.
Adapter Address (same as MAC address)	10		Not important for ICS, but might be needed by routers used for sharing the connection (see Chapter 17).

Table 15.1 (continued)

Setting	Figure Key	Your System	Notes
IP Address	11		
Subnet Mask	12		
Default Gateway	13		
DHCP Server	14		Some cable modems provide an IP address automatically; if so, this field is filled in.
Primary WINS Server	15		Not used.
Secondary WINS Server	16		Not used.
Lease Obtained	17		Used only if #14 is in use.
Lease Expired	18		Used only if #14 is in use.

Note that IP address values (figure key#'s 2, 3, 11, 12, 13, 14, 15, and 16) are in the form xxx.xxx.xxx.xxx, where xxx is a number from 0–255.

The only other information you need to record is the workgroup name. Some cable Internet providers require you to use a particular workgroup name or you can't connect to the Internet. To see this information, follow these procedures:

In Windows 9x/Me:

1. Right-click Network Neighborhood(Windows 9x) or My Network Places and select Properties or open the Networks icon in the Control Panel. This displays your current network configuration.

2. Click the Identification tab.

3. Record the computer and workgroup names. You need to use a different name for each computer in your network, but all computers must use the same workgroup name.

4. Click Cancel to close without making any changes to your network configuration.

In Windows 2000:

1. Right-click My Computer and select Properties or open the System icon in Control Panel.

2. Click the Workgroup Identification tab.

3. Record the computer and workgroup names: you need to use a different name for each computer in your network, but all computers must use the same workgroup name.

4. Click Cancel to close without making any changes to your network configuration.

In Windows XP:

1. Click the Start button.

2. Right-click My Computer and select Properties.

3. Click the Computer Name tab.

4. Record the computer and workgroup names. You need to use a different name for each computer in your network, but all computers must use the same workgroup name.

5. Click Cancel to close without making any changes to your network configuration.

After you have recorded your current network adapter settings and workgroup name, you can go to the correct section for your version of Windows to start the ICS setup process.

Note

The setup processes for ICS Gateway applies only to the computer that has the cable Internet connection; for computers that will be connected to the ICS Gateway, see "ICS Client Setup," later in this chapter.

Refer to the ICS Client Setup section to see how you enter data into the TCP/IP configuration screens which is displayed by WINIPCFG or IPCONFIG.

Installing a Network Adapter

Unless your computer connects to the cable modem via the USB port, you used an Ethernet card or built-in Ethernet port to connect your computer and cable modem together. To enable Internet sharing to take place with ICS, you need to add another network adapter to your computer.

Add the same type of network adapter (10/100 Ethernet, HomeRF, HomePNA, Wi-Fi Wireless Ethernet) used by the other computers in your network to enable your cable modem-equipped PC to connect to the other computers in your network. See Chapter 18 for details of the following network types suitable for home use:

- 10/100 Ethernet
- Wi-Fi Wireless Ethernet
- HomePNA 2.0
- HomeRF

If you use an Ethernet card to connect to your cable modem and your network also uses 10/100 Ethernet, use WINIPCFG as discussed earlier to determine the brand and model of your installed network card. To make it easier to use ICS, buy a different brand and model of 10/100 Ethernet card to connect to your network.

After you install the second network adapter, your system might not be able to connect to the Internet because it can't tell which adapter to use.

If this happens to you, open the System Properties sheet (Click Start, Settings, Control Panel, System, [Hardware], Device Manager) and click the plus sign next to Network Adapters. Click the network adapter that connects to your PC network (not the cable modem), click Properties, and click Disable in this hardware profile. A red X will appear over the card's icon.

Open your Web browser and connect to a page to set your default network card. Then, open the Device Manager again and enable the new network card before proceeding with ICS installation.

Installing and Configuring ICS on the ICS Gateway Computer

While the details of installing and configuring ICS vary from Windows version to Windows version, the basic outline of the process is similar:

- ICS is installed only on the computer which connects to the cable modem; after installation, this computer is the ICS gateway, providing Internet Connection Sharing to the other PCs on the network.
- You need to add a network card, which can connect with the rest of your home network.
- You need to install the ICS software or select the option to enable ICS.
- After ICS is installed, you need to verify the ICS gateway can connect to the Internet. Once this is checked, you can configure other computers on the network to use ICS.

Remember, only one computer, the computer connected to the cable modem, needs to have ICS installed.

Installing and Configuring ICS with Windows 98SE

After you install a network adapter to enable your computer to connect to others, the process of turning a Windows 98 SE computer connected to a cable modem into an ICS gateway is a two-part process:

1. Install the ICS software on the computer with the cable modem.

2. Set up the ICS software to allow the connection to be shared.

The computer connected to the cable modem must have Windows 98 SE installed, not the original Windows 98, if you want to use it as an ICS gateway. To determine which Windows 98 release you have, follow this procedure:

1. Click Start.

2. Click Settings.

3. Click Control Panel.

4. Double-click System.

The General tab displays the Windows release information, as shown in Figure 15.3.

If your system displays 4.10.1998, it is running the original version of Windows 98 and doesn't include ICS. Use a third-party sharing program or a router to share your Internet connection.

> Third-party sharing programs are discussed in Chapter 16, "Using Other Computer-Based Internet Sharing Programs." Routers are discussed in Chapter 17, "Router Your Way to Internet Sharing."

FIGURE 15.3

The version number 4.10.2222A as well as the text indicates that this system is running Windows 98 SE and can be used as an ICS Gateway computer.

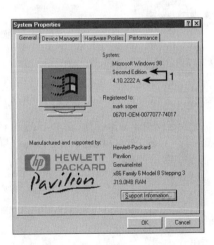

Windows 98 SE doesn't install ICS by default, even if you selected ICS as an option during the installation of Windows 98SE. To install and configure ICS, follow this procedure:

1. Click Start, Settings, Control Panel.

2. Double-click the Add/Remove Programs icon.

3. Click Windows Setup.

4. Double-click Internet Tools.

5. Click Internet Connection Sharing to checkmark it for installation.

6. Click OK.

7. Insert the Windows 98 Second Edition CD-ROM when prompted. During the file-copy process, you may be informed that some files being copied are older than files already on the system. Keep the file already on the system.

8. After the file-copy process concludes, the ICS Wizard starts. Click Next to continue.

9. Click Next to open the Internet Connection Wizard.

10. Select the network adapter you are using for your connection to the cable modem from the list of adapters shown (see Figure 15.4). The new adapter will be used for the connection to the other computers. Click Next.

FIGURE 15.4

Selecting the network adapter used by your cable modem.

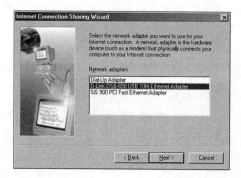

11. Provide a blank, formatted floppy disk when prompted for a client configuration disk (which can be used to configure other computers to connect to the ICS gateway). Click Next.

12. Click OK after inserting the disk, and Windows 98 SE prepares it for use with your other PCs.

13. Click OK when prompted and remove the disk.

14. Click Finish to complete the process.

15. Click Yes to restart your computer and complete the ICS gateway setup process.

Windows Me ICS Gateway Setup

Windows Me provides a much easier-to-use version of ICS as part of its Home Networking Wizard. To run the Home Networking Wizard on the ICS gateway computer, follow these steps:

1. Click Start, Programs, Accessories, Communications, Home Networking Wizard (HNW).

2. Click Next to continue from the beginning screen of the HNW.

3. If you've already run the HNW once, you will see an option screen with these choices: I Want to Edit My Home Networking Settings... or I Want to Create a Floppy Disk.... Choose Edit My Home Networking Settings. Click Next to continue.

4. On the Internet Connection screen, select the following options: Yes, This computer Uses the Following; InternetA Direct Connection to My ISP Using (select the network adapter connected to the cable modem). Click Next to continue (see Figure 15.5).

FIGURE 15.5

Selecting the network adapter that connects to your cable modem.

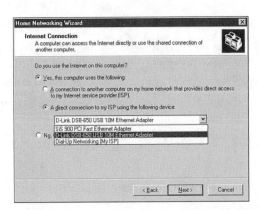

5. On the Internet Connection Sharing screen, select Yes (to share the Internet connection) and select the network card that connects to your home network (see Figure 15.6). Click Next to continue.

6. Provide a unique name for your computer and specify a workgroup name. The workgroup name will be used to identify the other computers to which you want to connect, but each computer on your home network will also need a unique name. The default is MSHOME, but if your computers are already networked together, Use this Workgroup Name will be selected, listing the name you have already chosen for your home network workgroup or the name required by your cable Internet provider for Internet access. All computers sharing the Internet connection must use the same workgroup name. Click Next to continue.

FIGURE 15.6

Selecting the network adapter that connects to your home network.

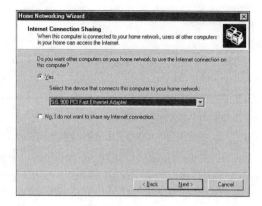

7. On the Share Files and Printers screen, you can choose to share the My Documents folder or printers on your ICS gateway, but sharing folders can pose a security risk. Click Next to continue.

For more information about the dangers of shared folders, see Chapter 13, "Firewalls and Your PC."

---

8. Choose to Make a Home Networking Setup Disk (used to configure Windows 9x computers on the network) when prompted. Insert a blank, formatted disk and select Yes. Click Next to continue, and Next again to create the disk.

9. Remove the disk and click Finish to complete the HNS setup on the ICS gateway. Click Yes to reboot your computer if prompted.

10. After you reboot, you will see a reminder about using the HNW setup disk on other computers. Click OK to close it.

Your ICS gateway is ready to provide sharing services to other computers.

Windows 2000 ICS Gateway Setup

Windows 2000 offers ICS capabilities as part of its normal Network and Dial-Up Connections folder. You need to log on as the Administrator or as a member of the Administrators group to perform these steps. After you install the correct network card needed to connect with your home network, follow this procedure to enable Internet sharing:

1. Click Start, Settings, Network and Dial-Up Connections.

2. Click the connection to your cable modem (normally Local Area Connection). To verify the correct connection, look at the details to the left of the folder (see Figure 15.7).

FIGURE 15.7

The network adapter detail is listed to the left of the icons in the Network and Dial-Up Connections folder.

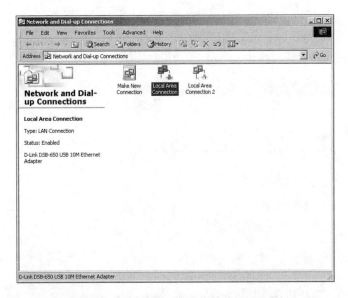

3. Right-click the connection icon and select Properties.

4. Click the Sharing tab and click the box labeled Enable Internet Connection Sharing for this connection.

5. Click OK. A warning box is displayed reminding you to set other computers to obtain their IP addresses automatically. Click Yes to enable ICS.

6. To configure the computers on the home network, see "Using Automatic IP Addressing" later in this chapter.

Windows XP ICS Gateway Setup

Windows XP (both Home Edition and Professional Edition) features a Network Setup Wizard (NSW) that incorporates ICS and an easy-to-use wizard. To set up a shared connection, you must log on as Administrator or as a member of the Administrators group. Then, follow these steps:

1. Click Start, All Programs, Accessories, Communications, Network Setup Wizard.

2. After reading the opening screen of the NSW, click Next.

3. Click Next to have the system detect network settings.

4. On the Select a Connection Method screen, select This Computer Connects Directly to the Internet. Click Next.

5. On the Select Your Internet Connection screen, Windows attempts to select the correct network adapter (see Figure 15.8). Verify or change the network adapter selected and click Next to continue.

FIGURE 15.8

Selecting the correct network adapter used by your cable modem.

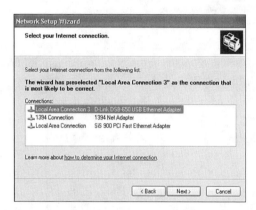

6. On the Computer Has Multiple Connections screen, click Let Me Choose the Connections. Click Next.

7. Make sure the network adapter that will connect to the other computers is checked; clear checkmarks from any other devices and click Next (see Figure 15.9).

FIGURE 15.9

Selecting the correct network adapter used by your home network. Note that an IEEE-1394 (FireWire/i.Link) card can also be used as a network device.

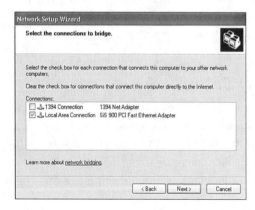

8. Describe your computer and enter a unique name for your computer. Click Next.

9. Enter the workgroup name; use the same workgroup name for all computers that are connected to your ICS gateway; use the name provided by your cable Internet vendor. Click Next.

10. Review the settings and click Next to apply them.

11. To create a network setup disk for use on other computers, supply a blank, formatted disk and click Next. You can also use the Windows XP CD-ROM or follow the instructions under "ICS Client Setup."

12. Click Next to write the network setup information, or click Format Disk if the disk needs to be formatted.

13. Remove the disk and store it. To use the disk to set up other computers on the home network, open the Netsetup program on the disk. Click Next to continue.

14. Click Finish.

After you configure the ICS clients, you will be able to share the Internet connection with them.

ICS Client Setup

You can set up an ICS client in three ways:

- Using the setup disk created by ICS to configure it for using a shared connection
- Self-configuring your client to use automatic IP addressing
- Self-configuring your client to use manual IP addressing (not available with Windows 2000 or Windows XP ICS)

The easiest configuration option if you use Windows 95 or above is to use the setup disk you created during the configuration of the ICS gateway. However, non-Windows computers running MacOS, Linux, or other operating systems can use the Internet as ICS clients if you configure them to obtain an IP address automatically.

If any of the clients previously connected to the Internet through a dial-up modem, you may need to disable automatic dialing of an Internet connection as described in Chapter 5, especially if you can't use a wizard to configure the setup.

Using the Network Setup Disk

The setup disk provided by the Home Networking/ICS wizards used by Windows Me and Windows XP provide a complete configuration solution for ICS client computers running Windows 98/98SE and Windows XP.

Opening the Netsetup.exe program found on the network setup disk starts the following procedure. (Click Start, Run, type a:\netsetup, and click OK to run.)

1. After network files are copied to your computer, you might be asked to reboot your computer.

2. After you reboot your computer, click Next to continue the wizard.

3. Click Next again after you read the network checklist and confirm that you have performed the necessary steps.

4. Select The Computer Connects to the Internet Through Another Computer and click Next.

5. Enter a unique name and description for the computer to identify it on the network. Click Next.

6. Enter the workgroup name. (This must be the same for all computers.) If your cable Internet ISP requires a particular workgroup name, be sure to use it. Click Next.

7. Review the list of changes to your system and click Next to apply them.

8. Click Finish.

9. Open your browser to connect to the Web.

The Windows 98 SE Client Configuration Disk works in a much different fashion. It contains two files:

- Icsclset.exe
- ReadMe.exe

The Icsclset.exe program can be used to configure the Web browser to use the shared connection, but doesn't configure TCP/IP. The ReadMe.txt file covers this process, which is also discussed in the next section.

If you have computers running Windows 95, older versions of Windows, or non-Windows computers on your network, or you used the Windows 98SE or Windows 2000 versions of ICS (which don't offer a setup disk for other computers), you will need to set up the ICS clients, as instructed in the following sections.

Using Automatic IP Addressing

If you use a computer that runs Windows 98 SE or Windows 2000 as your ICS gateway, or if you want to share the Internet connection with computers which can't use the Windows Me/XP setup disk, you will need to set up the ICS clients by configuring them to use automatic IP addressing.

As you might guess from the name, automatic IP addressing is much easier than manually setting the IP address. When you use the Windows Me or Windows XP setup disk to configure your clients, this is the method used to configure the clients.

Automatic IP addressing uses a feature called Dynamic Host Configuration Protocol (DHCP). DHCP enables ICS clients to get the settings you saw earlier in Figure 15.2 from the ICS gateway. DHCP also ensures that each computer is assigned a unique IP address to avoid conflicts. If two computers have the same IP address, the second computer's IP address (and its connection to the Internet) is disabled.

Manual IP addressing (see the next section) should be used only if automatic IP addressing doesn't work in your situation. Manual IP addressing can be used only with the Windows 98 SE or Windows Me versions of ICS.

To configure an ICS client to connect to the Internet using automatic IP addressing, follow these steps with Windows 9x or Me:

1. Click Start, Settings, Control Panel.

2. Double-click Networks to see a list of installed network components. (When you install a network card, several network components are installed during the process.)

3. Scroll down to the entry TCP/IP, *brand/model of your network card.*

4. Click this entry, and then click the Properties button to view the IP Address tab shown in Figure 15.10. Obtain an IP Address Automatically should already be selected; select it if an IP address is listed instead.

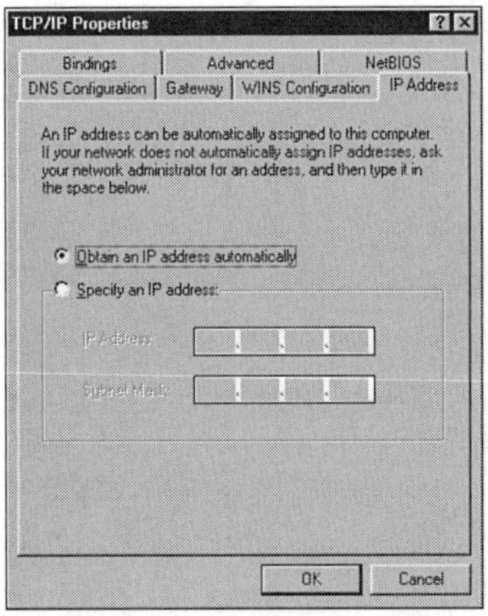

FIGURE 15.10

Setting the IP address as automatic. This enables this ICS client computer to get its IP address from the ICS Gateway.

5. Click the WINS Configuration tab shown in Figure 15.11. Select the Use DHCP for WINS Resolution option.

FIGURE 15.11

Enabling Use DHCP for WINS Resolution should also be set when you want to get an IP address automatically, even if you don't have Windows NT servers which are used for the Windows Internet Naming Service (WINS).

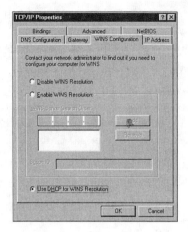

6. Click the Gateway tab and remove any entries listed (see Figure 15.12).

FIGURE 15.12

Verifying that no gateways are listed. DHCP will provide this information to your system.

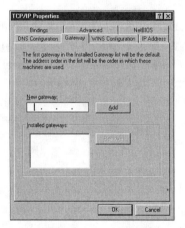

7. Click the DNS Configuration tab. Select Disable DNS if it is not already selected (see Figure 15.13).

8. Click OK, and then click OK again to exit the Network Properties sheet.

If you made any changes, Windows will need to reboot. After you reboot, you should be able to open your browser and go online immediately.

To configure a MacOS computer to use automatic IP addressing, use the TCP/IP Control Panel. Select User Mode. Click Basic, and then OK. Select Connect: Via Ethernet and Configure: Using DHCP Server. Save the settings when completed.

FIGURE 15.13

Disabling DNS.
DHCP will pro-
vide the DNS
entries needed to
connect to the
Internet.

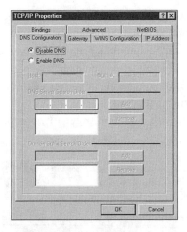

To configure other operating systems to use dynamic IP addresses, see the TCP/IP section of the operating systems' documentation.

Using Manual IP Addressing

Manual IP addressing can be used if automatic IP addressing doesn't work on your
ICS client computers. To enable it, you must make entries on the same TCP/IP
Properties sheet pages listed in the previous section for each computer. You will also
need some of the information you recorded in Table 15.1.

Using Manual IP Addressing can be tricky; a single mistyped value will keep your computer off the Internet, and using duplicate IP addresses will cause conflicts between
computers. Use Table 15.2 as a model to keep track of the IP addresses you assign to
computers.

You cannot use manual IP addressing with Windows XP or Windows 2000 ICS.

Because you must provide a unique IP address and name for each computer, you
should keep track of this information. Table 15.2 provides an example of how to do
this.

Table 15.2   Sample IP Address Worksheet

Computer Name (Add to Identification Tab in Network Properties)	IP Address	Method Assigned
ICS Gateway	192.168.0.1	Automatically by ICS setup
Den	192.168.0.2	Manual
Study Room	192.168.0.3	Manual
Master Bedroom	192.168.0.4	Manual

Note that each computer needs a unique IP address; use 255.255.255.0 for the subnet mask for all computers. Open the Network Properties sheet as discussed in the previous section to add the IP address and submask for each computer. WINS configuration should be disabled, and DHCP should *not* be used. Figure 15.14 shows you how to use the information you recorded earlier from WINIPCFG (refer to Table 15.1) to complete the other TCP/IP Properties sheet tabs for each computer. This information, unlike the IP address, is the same for each computer in your network.

FIGURE 15.14

Manually assigning gateway and DNS configuration data on each ICS client computer. This information is based on WINIPCFG information gathered from the ICS gateway computer before ICS was installed.

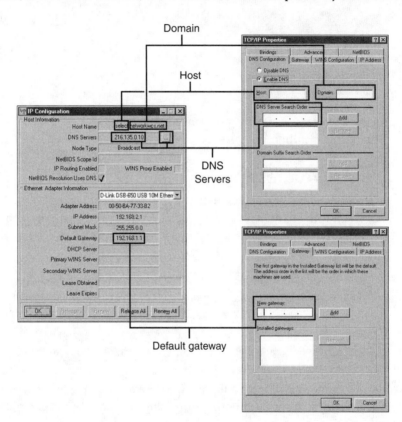

To configure manual IP addressing with a MacOS computer, open the TCP/IP Control Panel, select User Mode, choose Advanced, click OK. Then enter the data required. Use a unique IP address from the IP address worksheet, and enter the other data as recorded on the Network configuration worksheet (refer to Table 15.1). Save the settings when completed.

To configure other operating systems to use manually assigned IP addresses, see the TCP/IP section of the operating systems' documentation.

Alternatives to ICS

ICS isn't for everyone:

- You need to keep the ICS gateway computer turned on to provide Internet access for everyone.

- ICS doesn't support some advanced Internet activities.

- ICS uses up two PCI slots in most computers.

- ICS software isn't provided with Windows 95, original Windows 98, or other non-Windows operating systems. These computers can act as ICS clients, but cannot share their own Internet connections with other via ICS.

It's certain you will like sharing your cable Internet connection, but if you find that the limitations of ICS are bothering you, other alternatives are available:

- Third-party software solutions for sharing an Internet connection—These are more expensive than ICS, but they can allow you to control access for children's computers, provide a firewall, work with one-way cable modem services not supported by ICS, and might use only one network card in the gateway computer. See Chapter 16 for details.

- Hardware-based solutions—Routers and gateways cost more than ICS, but they can provide integrated firewall support, better support for advanced Internet features, and support for non-Windows computers. In addition, they don't require you to keep the gateway computer turned on to provide Internet access and don't require the use of two network cards. See Chapter 17 for details.

Summary

Internet Connection Sharing allows one computer running Windows 98 SE, Windows Me, Windows 2000, or Windows XP to share any type of Internet connection with other Windows and non-Windows PCs. ICS requires separate network connections to the cable modem and to the home network, which means in many cases that two network adapters must be installed. The ICS gateway must be left on at all times to allow other computers to access the Internet. Windows 98 SE and Windows Me versions of ICS don't permit TCP port mapping needed for specialized software unless third-party software is used.

Before you install ICS, you should use WINIPCFG or IPCONFIG to record the current TCP/IP configuration for your computer. You should also record the computer and workgroup name because Windows workgroup-based networks require each computer to have a unique name and use the same workgroup name.

The ICS setup process requires that the ICS gateway (computer with the Internet connection) have a network card installed to connect to other PCs first before the setup process starts. ICS must be manually installed with Windows 98 SE; other Windows versions enable ICS though wizards (Windows Me and Windows XP) or through the normal network setup process (Windows 2000). By default, all versions of ICS are designed to use DHCP, which assigns IP addresses to ICS clients. Windows 98 SE and Windows Me can also use manual IP addressing for clients, but Windows XP and Windows 2000 can't.

After the ICS gateway is configured and you've verified it connects to the Internet, you need to configure the other computers on the network to use its connection to go online. Windows 98 SE and Windows 2000 ICS require you to configure the Network properties for other computers yourself using automatic IP addressing. Windows Me and Windows XP create wizard floppy disks which can do this for you.

You can also add non-Windows computers to your network as long as they can be set to use automatic IP addressing, getting their addresses from a DHCP server, which is built in to ICS. The Windows 98 SE and Windows Me versions of ICS also allow you to assign IP addresses manually to each client PC; I recommend this only if automatic IP addressing doesn't work for some reason.

If you can't use ICS because your version of Windows doesn't support it, you don't use Windows, or you don't like the limitations of ICS, third-party sharing programs (Chapter 16) and routers (Chapter 17) are alternatives to consider.

USING OTHER COMPUTER-BASED INTERNET SHARING PROGRAMS

CHAPTER HIGHLIGHTS:

- What the differences are between Microsoft Internet Connection Sharing (ICS) and third-party sharing programs

- Where to get major third-party sharing programs such as WinProxy, WinGate, and Sygate Home Network

- How to remove ICS so you can install a third-party sharing program

- How to install and configure major third-party sharing programs

How Third-Party Sharing Programs Differ from ICS

At first glance, third-party Internet sharing programs look about the same as Microsoft's ICS software, except that ICS is free in Windows 98 SE, Windows Me, Windows 2000, and Windows XP, and third-party solutions cost money. Of course, if that were really true, this chapter wouldn't be necessary. Significant differences exist between ICS and third-party programs, and between the different third-party solutions themselves.

Following are some of the differences:

- Security—Microsoft's ICS lacks true firewall capabilities for the gateway computer (although Windows XP has a rudimentary firewall included that must be enabled manually). Most third-party programs offer firewall capabilities that protect both the computer connected directly to your cable modem and the rest of the network.

- Installation—As you learned in Chapter 15, "Using Microsoft Internet Connection Sharing," although ICS works in about the same way after it's installed on different versions of Windows, getting it installed can be mind-boggling, especially if you upgrade to another version of Windows. Every version of Windows has a different installation process for both the gateway server and the clients. Most third-party programs can be set up in about the same way on different versions of Windows.

- Features—ICS is a bare-bones sharing arrangement that can have problems with some advanced Internet features, such as game server hosting, whereas third-party solutions are more configurable.

- Access control—ICS has no provision for controlling Internet access unless you install third-party software, whereas some third-party solutions allow you to create a family-friendly home network that helps keep the kids away from the seedy side of the Internet.

- Network card usage—ICS requires separate connections to the cable modem and to your home network, whereas some third-party solutions let you use a single network card to connect to both networks.

Before installing any third-party Internet sharing program, you *must* remove Microsoft ICS from your gateway computer (the computer connected to your cable modem) and reconnect the computer directly to the cable modem. Use the Add/Remove Programs option in the Windows Control Panel to dump ICS. You might need to re-enter the IP address, gateway, and DNS information that ICS uses into your network card's TCP/IP configuration after removing ICS. Refer to the information you recorded in Table 15.1 (Chapter 15) to reconfigure your network card if necessary. Be sure your computer is working properly and can connect to the Internet after you remove ICS before you install the new sharing program.

If you didn't complete Table 15.1 before you installed ICS, you can view the TCP/IP properties for your Internet Connection Sharing, TCP/IP entry in the Network properties sheet. Record the information listed there in Table 15.1 before you remove ICS.

If your cable Internet service installation kit came with a setup CD, you might be able to use it to reconfigure your system after removing ICS. Be sure to check the paperwork supplied with it for any information you need to enter, such as the IP address of your gateway (cable modem) or network card.

Deerfield WinGate

WinGate was the first Internet sharing solution on the market, and continues to be a favorite with many users who want more powerful features than ICS. You can try WinGate free for 30 days by downloading a trial version from the WinGate Web site at www.Deerfield.com/products/wingate.

WinGate comes in three distinct versions:

- Home—Features automated setup for gateway and client PCs
- Standard—Allows access control by user, group, and Web sites
- Pro—Similar to Standard but designed for large networks

All three product levels have tiered pricing, which means that you need to buy a version that has enough licenses for the computers you want to network. For example, WinGate Home offers three- and six-user licenses; if you want to network four or five computers, buy the six-user license. If you need to network more than six users, you can buy additional three-user or six-user licenses.

This discussion focuses on WinGate Home. The same download can be used to evaluate Home, Standard, or Pro versions. The latest version of WinGate, 5.0, was in beta test as this book went to press.

Installing WinGate Home

WinGate uses a single setup program for both server (the computer with the Internet connection) and client. The opening screen of the installation process allows you to select either type of installation as well as view an installation guide and comprehensive help system.

If you're new to home networking, review the installation guide before you run the installation process.

If you select the WinGate server installation, the installer defaults to the evaluation option on the screen displayed in Figure 16.1. If you are installing a purchased version, select Install WinGate (first option) and enter the License Name and Key in the correct fields. You also can purchase online or install a two-station Lite version.

FIGURE 16.1

You can select to evaluate, purchase, or install an already purchased version of WinGate.

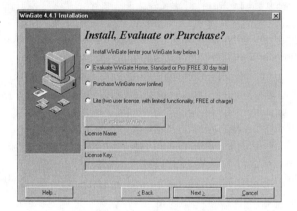

If you select the Evaluate option, the next screen allows you to select Pro, Standard, or Home and provides a simple explanation of each. You can change the default folder for installation, and the following screen allows you to disable Extended Network Support (ENS) if you would prefer.

ENS uses Network Address Translation (NAT) so you can add non-Windows PCs to your network and adds a firewall and bridging support. You should leave NAT enabled.

The next screen allows you to disable AutoUpdate, a program that automatically checks the Internet at specified intervals for product updates. Leave this option enabled because AutoUpdate will ensure your WinGate program is always the most current version.

The installation takes just a couple of minutes, and then you must restart your computer. Unlike ICS, WinGate Server does *not* change the TCP/IP settings of the network adapter connected to your cable modem. This feature of WinGate makes documenting your network very simple: When you run WINIPCFG or IPCONFIG on your gateway computer to see its settings, just select the network card used to connect to the cable modem and you'll see the actual settings it uses. By contrast, ICS creates a logical adapter called ICSHARE to take over the TCP/IP settings previously used by the network adapter connected to your cable modem.

The WinGate Server Gateway program, which controls WinGate, loads automatically into the system tray.

Note Unlike ICS, WinGate will not configure the IP address of the network adapter that connects with your home network. You will need to set it to an IP address not accessible from the outside world, such as 192.168.0.1, or your clients will not be able to access the WinGate server. For a step-by-step guide to WinGate setup for each Windows version supported, see the WinGate setup articles at `www.Deerfield.com/support/wingate/setup/`.

The WinGate client installation reminds you to make sure that Winsock2 (an update to the original Winsock program supplied with Windows 95; Winsock2 is included with more recent versions of Windows) is installed, copies the files, and finishes. If Winsock2 is not installed on your Windows 95 computer, the installer will quit. You can download Winsock2 from the downloads section of the Microsoft Windows 95 site: `www.Microsoft.com/windows95/download`.

The WinGate client is automatically enabled and will take advantage of the connection for Internet and networking. You need to be sure that each client is set to obtain an IP address automatically and use DHCP. See Chapter 15 for details.

Using the WinGate Client

After WinGate Server is installed on the computer with the cable modem and WinGate Client is installed on each computer sharing the Internet connection, you can connect online as long as your network hardware is set correctly. To verify that the network is configured correctly, click Start, Programs, WinGate Internet Client, WinGate Internet Client Applet. Click the WinGate Servers tab. Your WinGate server and its IP address should appear as in Figure 16.2.

FIGURE 16.2

Viewing servers in the WinGate Internet Client applet.

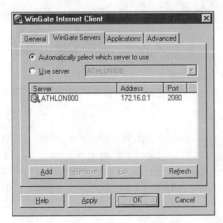

Note

> Although 192.168.0.1 is recommended as the IP address to use for the WinGate Internal network card (the one connected to your home network), you can also use 172.16.0.1, as in Figure 16.2. If your cable modem is using addresses in the 192.168.0.x range, this is recommended to avoid conflicts.

Use the Applications tab shown in Figure 16.3 to view the Internet-aware and network-aware programs that WinGate's firewall has configured. Three different levels exist:

- Local access—No Internet access for the listed program
- Mixed access—Outbound (to the Internet) access allowed; no inbound access
- Global access—Both outbound and inbound Internet access is allowed; few programs should ever be granted this level of access unless they are Web servers, FTP servers, or game servers

Use the Add button to add a program, the Remove button to take a program off the list, and the Edit button to change the settings for a program.

FIGURE 16.3

Viewing the access permissions for applications on a WinGate client.

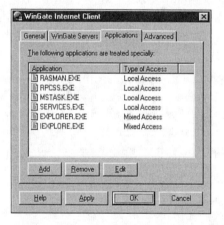

Use the Advanced tab to reset the WinGate client if you install AOL or other Internet software or install a new network card.

Using the WinGate GateKeeper

In WinGate Home, the WinGate GateKeeper, which runs on the WinGate Server, logs Internet activity, displays network configuration, and warns of system problems. You can open the GateKeeper from the System Tray or by clicking Start, Programs, WinGate. To view Internet activity, click the History tab near the bottom of the screen (see Figure 16.4).

FIGURE 16.4

Where are your home network users going online? The WinGate GateKeeper History shows you.

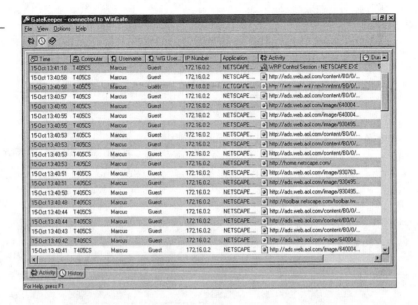

If you're evaluating WinGate version 5 and discover logons to undesirable Web sites, install the optional GateFilter plug-in to provide intelligent site blocking. This plug-in blocks access to offensive sex and gambling sites with accuracy more than 99%, thanks to its AI-based operation. The GateFilter plug-in was developed in conjunction with content-recognition vendor iCognito (www.icognito.com). Prices start at $39.95 for a three-user license.

If you have problems with your configuration, a System Messages tab will appear next to the Activity and History tabs shown in Figure 16.4. Each message will be logged, along with the reason for the message. The System Messages feature helped me determine that I had omitted setting up a private IP address for the network adapter connected to the home network.

Comparing WinGate Home to ICS

Using WinGate Home rather than ICS has several advantages, including the following:

- Configurable firewall
- Detailed network traffic monitoring
- Detailed network condition alerts
- Stability of IP address for network adapter connected to cable modem

- 30-day trial for all versions
- Support for plug-ins in Wingate 5

However, WinGate Home has several disadvantages compared to ICS:

- Doesn't configure IP addresses needed for network adapters
- Has very technical documentation
- Help file covers all three editions (Home, Standard, and Pro) without clear distinctions as to which features work with which edition of WinGate
- Tiered pricing means that you pay more as you add users to your network, and you may wind up paying for licenses you can't use

In addition to using the trial version of WinGate (which lets you evaluate Home, Standard, and Pro editions of WinGate with a single download), you also can search the online knowledge base to determine which WinGate edition best meets your needs. The knowledge base identifies which WinGate features require a particular edition of WinGate. Find the knowledge base at `www.deerfield.com/support/wingate/kb/index.htm`.

Ositis WinProxy

Ositis WinProxy, as the name implies, is a proxy server rather than a gateway program. Although both proxy servers and gateways use a computer to route Internet traffic from the Internet to other computers on a home network, the difference is significant: A proxy server can provide services such as content filtering and antivirus protection to the computers on the home network, while most gateways can't.

Installing Ositis WinProxy

The Ositis WinProxy program must be installed only on the server that is connected to the cable modem. The installation process runs from a compressed file. If you don't supply a serial number after rebooting the system, the program will run as an evaluation version for 30 days. A registration form is used during the installation, but only a few fields are required. You can download the program from `www.winproxy.com`.

If you're installing a local area network (LAN) at the same time as WinProxy, or if your LAN doesn't have the TCP/IP protocol configured for use, take a few minutes to read the "How to Set Up a Local Area Network" PDF file (available from `download.ositis.com/downloads/lanmanual.pdf`). This PDF file requires Adobe Acrobat Reader and is available online or after installing WinProxy. The Installation Wizard cannot add IP address information to your configuration, but this document makes it easy for you to understand the process. Reboot as directed and verify that your computers are connected before proceeding with the software installation.

After installation, WinProxy checks your system configuration. If a problem exists with IP address settings, an Installation Wizard runs to help fix the problem.

To help the wizard figure out the correct settings, be sure you have a live Internet connection running.

The wizard asks you for the following information:

- Whether you connect via a dial-up modem—Select No if you use a two-way cable modem, or select Yes if you have a one-way cable modem.

- The internal and external IP addresses of your computer—This information is used to create a firewall; use the Move buttons to move the IP address(es) listed to the correct column (see Figure 16.5).

FIGURE 16.5

Setting the IP addresses for your WinProxy server.

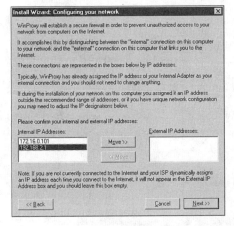

Use the information you recorded in Chapter 15, Table 15.1 to determine which IP address is External (to the cable modem) and which is Internal (to the network). The IP address used by the NIC that connects to your cable modem should be moved into the External position if necessary.

- E-mail address to send alerts—Verify or fill in this information.

After completing this information, WinProxy tests your connection. If the problem persists, the Installation Wizard is rerun to fix any additional problems. A successful installation produces a display similar to Figure 16.6.

FIGURE 16.6

The WinProxy setup on your server is successful when all applicable boxes are checked.

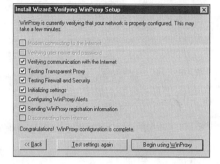

WinProxy generates a dynamic text document called Winproxy.cfg (displayable in Notepad) describing what to do next to connect client PCs to the WinProxy server. In most cases, you can configure client PCs to use dynamic IP addressing, although Winproxy.cfg also describes how to use manual IP addressing if you would prefer.

After setting up the WinProxy client PC's IP address as described in Winproxy.cfg, reboot the client PCs and they will be able to go online through the WinProxy server's Internet connection.

Using WinProxy

After WinProxy is running on the server PC, it provides Internet access for both server and client machines. Choose File, Install Wizard to fine-tune settings for protocols, the Administration password, and security settings. If you need to adjust default proxy settings, run the Properties Wizard from the File menu.

The default ConnectionView screen in WinProxy displays real-time network activity passing through your server to computers on the network (see Figure 16.7).

FIGURE 16.7

WinProxy's ConnectionView screen shows current proxy settings and activity from other computers on the network.

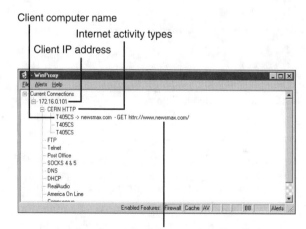

Internet resource being accessed by client

Choose File, Settings to display a multitabbed interface for detailed system configuration:

- The General tab is used to adjust IP address and overall system configuration settings.
- The Users tab allows you to control access by time of day or by user, and to allow users with different e-mail servers to access those servers.
- The Cache tab allows you to decide how often the WinProxy server should check for updated Web documents.
- The Logging tab enables an activity log that you can use to record Web activity and a detailed log for troubleshooting.
- The Site Restrictions tab lets you enable SmartFilter (an updatable list of blocked Web sites), configure blocked sites you select (blacklist), allow specific sites (whitelist), and block specified ad banners.

WinProxy will not block access to undesirable Web sites unless you enable the SmartFilter feature under the Site Restrictions tab. The SmartFilter service must be renewed after six months; contact Ositis for pricing.

- The Protocols tab enables or disables support for programs that require special TCP ports, such as NetMeeting, FTP, and others. Because port requirements can change, Protocols also allows you to edit port and other settings for most programs.
- The antivirus feature protects systems from e-mail and Web-borne viruses. However, it should be supplemented with scanning-type programs such as Norton AntiVirus at each workstation (to pick up viruses on floppy disks and removable media drives). Like SmartFilter, you must renew anti-virus protection after six months.

To get protection from viruses, be sure your clients connect to the WinProxy server using Transparent Proxy, not NAT Only or Classic Proxy. Transparent Proxy provides antivirus support, but NAT Only and Classic Proxy cannot. Also, Transparent Proxy provides a system-level firewall. This type of firewall provides better protection against unwanted network traffic than the application-level firewall used by Classic Proxy, which is a configuration option originally developed for older versions of WinProxy. NAT Only provides incoming firewall protection but no outgoing firewall protection.

Comparing WinProxy to ICS

The following are advantages of WinProxy compared to ICS:

- Integrated antivirus, system-level firewall and content control
- Logging of Internet traffic
- Extremely detailed and easy-to-understand documentation
- Clear instructions for handling a wide variety of network situations

The disadvantages of WinProxy compared to ICS are as follows:

- Long setup time might be needed on clients if DHCP is not used
- Tiered pricing may force you to buy more licenses than you need
- Might issue false warnings of configuration changes that need new IP address settings

Sygate Home Network

Sygate Home Network is designed to combine the ease-of-use of NAT-based network sharing programs such as ICS with features reminiscent of a proxy server, such as access control and a network firewall. Sygate Home Network will appeal to users who have limited internal space on their computers because it supports a unique feature called OneNIC. When the OneNIC configuration option is used, a single network card can be used to connect with both the cable modem and the network.

Sygate Home Network is sold in three-user, six-user, and larger-count versions, and a free trial can be downloaded from `www.sygate.com/free/sgdownload.com`.

Because Sygate is a gateway product, and the firewall feature protects only computers connected to the gateway, you should also download and install the free Sygate Personal Firewall on the computer that is connected to the cable modem.

Before You Install Sygate Home Network

It pays to stay at Sygate's Web site after you download Sygate Home Network but before you install it. For a QuickStart Guide called "Sygate Home Network 101—Installing Your Network," set your browser to `www.sygate.com/support/userguides/shn/`.

Step 1 provides an illustrated guide to how the OneNIC configuration process differs from normal two-NIC gateway configurations such as ICS, and step 2 provides step-by-step guides to configuring your server and your clients.

To be sure that your cable Internet connection works properly with OneNIC, start by connecting only the PC that will be used as the Sygate server to the hub or switch (which is connected to the cable modem) and install the Sygate Server software on that system. After you verify that you can still connect to the cable modem and the Internet, connect the other computers to the hub or switch and configure them as clients. If you have problems with the configuration, consider using a second network adapter.

Clients on a Sygate Home Network can be configured through Sygate software, Sygate's SGLAN program, DHCP service from the server (automatically assigned IP addresses—the easiest to do), or with manually assigned IP addresses.

The guides are laid out as long HTML pages. If you want to save them for reference in setting up your system while you're online but prefer not to print them, select the File menu in your Web browser and choose the Save option to store them on your hard drive. If you're using late releases of Internet Explorer, use the Save As Web Archive, Single File, option to create an .MHT file that has all the text and pictures. To view each guide in your browser while you're offline during the configuration process, click File, Open, and browse to the folder where the files are stored.

Alternatively, you can download the guide as an Adobe Acrobat .PDF file (requires Adobe Acrobat Reader) with this URL: `www.sygate.com/support/userguides/shn/`
`shn42_install_guide.pdf`.

Installing and Configuring Sygate Home Network on the Server

The Sygate Home Network program is a single self-extracting file that after opening some files, displays the screen shown in Figure 16.8. Select Server Mode for the computer that will share its Internet connection with others.

After performing some tests and checking to see whether any network devices need an IP address, the Sygate installer reboots the computer.

After restarting the computer, click Start, Programs, Sygate Home Network, Sygate Manager to continue the configuration process.

The basic interface shows some of the tools, but to get to configuration, click the Advanced button to change the display to what is shown in Figure 16.9.

FIGURE 16.8

Selecting Server Mode for the computer that shares its Internet connection.

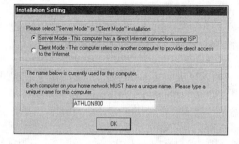

Basic menu (red highlights)   Advanced menu (blue highlights)

FIGURE 16.9

The basic (left) and advanced (right) menus of the Sygate Manager program.

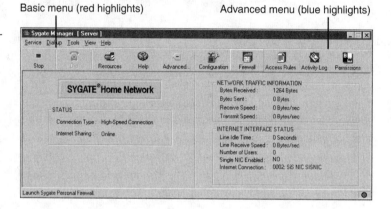

If you have only one network card, you will want to set up the system to use the OneNIC configuration. To do so:

1. Click the Configuration menu button.

2. Click Use Single NIC Mode; note the name of the network card.

3. Verify that Enable Internet Sharing at Startup, Enable Address Server (DHCP), and Enable DNS Forwarding are checked.

4. Unless you use a one-way cable modem, clear the checkmark next to Automatically Dial the Dialup Entry.

5. Click OK.

6. When prompted to reset the service, click No.

7. Close the Sygate Manager.

8. Shut down the computer.

9. Unplug the network cable running from the cable modem and plug it into your hub or switch using its Uplink port.

10. Run a network cable from your hub or switch to the network port for the network card from which you removed the other cable in step 9.

11. Restart the computer.

12. After the computer restarts and the Sygate Manager has started, be sure that client PCs are set to Obtain IP Address automatically, and then restart them.

13. Both your server and your clients should be able to access the Internet.

The Sygate Manager will load in its normal Basic mode every time you start the system. When you're satisfied the server and clients are working, click Tools, Minimize Manager When It Starts. The Manager will dock to the system tray.

Using Sygate Home Network

Beyond basic Web browsing, Sygate Home Network allows you to control additional features about your network. For example, click the Tools, Resources menu and you can share any drive on your server with other computers form the Local tab. Click the Network tab to see shared printers; you can get one-click access to other shared resources on other computers (see Figure 16.10).

FIGURE 16.10

Sharing a drive on a client PC with the Share Drive/Printer option.

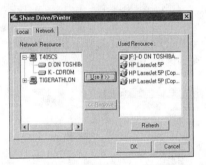

If you're having problems running an Internet-aware program on the clients, click the Access Rules tool (in the Advanced menu) and you can add configuration settings (called rules) to the server to let the program work. Sygate Server comes with many preset rules, as shown in Figure 16.11. Click Help to open a Web page on the Sygate site with many additional rules for streaming audio/video, popular online games, Microsoft NetMeeting, and many more.

To block access to certain Web sites, use the Permissions button to set up a BlackList of blocked sites. You can block sites completely or during a specified time period. Unfortunately, you must specify sites by IP address rather than by Web site URL.

FIGURE 16.11

FIGURE 16.11

Configuring the
Sygate Manager
to allow a client
PC to act as a
server for the
popular online
game *Tribes*.

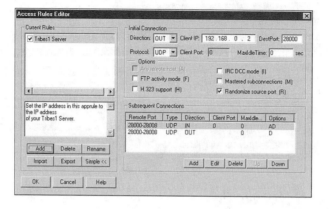

 Permissions prompt for a password, but the default setting is a blank password. To set
your own password, use the Change Password button when you open the Permissions
dialog box.

To make it easier to determine which sites to BlackList, enable the Activity Log in
Configuration to record client Internet access (see Figure 16.12). IP addresses and
Web site names (when reported) are listed. For example, if you wanted to block
access to www.garbagecan.com, you would enter its IP address (66.12.105.154) into
the BlackList section of the Permissions menu.

FIGURE 16.12

Click the
Activity Log but-
ton after you
enable this fea-
ture to see where
clients have
been online.

Activity Log

Date	Client	Opera...	Destination IP	Website	Sour...	Dest...	B
10/15/2001 23:56:40	192.168.0.3	PING	64.29.200.227		0	0	0
10/15/2001 23:56:41	192.168.0.3	PING	64.29.200.227		0	0	0
10/15/2001 23:56:42	192.168.0.3	PING	64.29.200.227		0	0	0
10/15/2001 23:56:43	192.168.0.3	PING	64.29.200.227		0	0	0
10/15/2001 23:57:42	192.168.0.2	HTTP	209.185.240.253	law3.oe.hotmail.com	3440	80	70
10/15/2001 23:57:43	192.168.0.2	HTTP	209.185.240.253	law3.oe.hotmail.com	3441	80	19
10/15/2001 23:57:43	192.168.0.3	HTTP	216.239.33.101	www.google.com	1102	80	30
10/15/2001 23:57:43	192.168.0.2	HTTP	209.185.240.253	law3.oe.hotmail.com	3442	80	19
10/15/2001 23:57:58	192.168.0.3	HTTP	66.12.105.154	www.garbagecan.com	1104	80	18
10/15/2001 23:57:58	192.168.0.3	HTTP	66.12.105.154	www.garbagecan.com	1105	80	22
10/15/2001 23:57:58	192.168.0.3	HTTP	66.12.105.154	www.garbagecan.com	1106	80	88
10/15/2001 23:57:58	192.168.0.3	HTTP	66.12.105.154	www.garbagecan.com	1107	80	10
10/15/2001 23:57:59	192.168.0.3	HTTP	216.136.145.152	apps5.oingo.com	1109	80	17
10/15/2001 23:58:03	192.168.0.2	HTTP	64.4.56.7		3445	80	83
10/15/2001 23:58:04	192.168.0.2	HTTP	64.4.56.7		3448	80	12
10/15/2001 23:58:09	192.168.0.2	HTTP	209.185.240.253	law3.oe.hotmail.com	3458	80	10

 To find out whether an IP address that doesn't list a Web site name is anything to worry
about, use a reverse IP lookup feature available on many Web site name registration
sites such as www.name-space.com/search/search.htm. A reverse IP lookup lets you enter
the IP address and find out which organization uses it.

For example, a reverse IP lookup on 64.29.200.227 reveals that this IP address is the
popular Internet news site Newsmax.com.

Because manual BlackListing is difficult to set up, you should consider purchasing a subscription to the SiteFilter service included with WinProxy after the initial six-month subscription expires. You can use BlackListing to supplement the filtering services provided by SiteFilter.

For even more control, you can use the WhiteListing feature to enable access to only the sites you specify.

If you close the Sygate Manager, the sharing service stays on. You must explicitly shut it down if you want to stop client access to the Internet.

Comparing Sygate Home Network to ICS

The following are advantages of Sygate compared to ICS:

- Single network card can be used to connect to both cable modem and network
- Detailed documentation is easy to understand
- Ability to log client Web activity
- Ability to restrict client Web activity
- Built-in configurable firewall for clients
- Easy configuration of firewall for special software needs

The only disadvantage of Sygate compared to ICS is tiered pricing.

Sharing for MacOS Users

Thanks to the multi-platform nature of TCP/IP, MacOS computers can share an Internet connection hosted by a Microsoft ICS server, a WinProxy server, or a Sygate Home Network server. However, WinProxy and Sygate support only 32-bit Windows (9x/Me/2000/XP) computers as servers; WinGate works only with Windows computers.

If you want to use your MacOS computer to share its cable Internet connection with other users, you need to use one of the following programs:

- IPNetRouter—www.sustworks.com; works with both old Macs (using 68030 processors or better) and current PowerPC-based Macs
- SurfDoubler—www.vicomsoft.com; supports up to three computers, parental access and site filtering controls (three-month subscription included)
- Internet Gateway—www.vicomsoft.com; supports up to 10 users (Standard, Plus, and Pro versions for more users also available), has business-level firewall, management, and monitoring features

The Practically Networked Web site offers configuration help for both SurfDoubler and Internet Gateway at www.practicallynetworked.com/sharing/vicom.htm.

As with most Internet sharing solutions used with Windows-based PCs, MacOS sharing programs require two network connections. G3 and G4 computers have little difficulty being used as servers because you can connect the cable modem to the built-in Ethernet port and add a NIC to connect to the home network for sharing.

However, if you're using an iMac, you have a problem: Although the iMAC has a built-in Ethernet port, it has no expansion slots for add-on cards; it uses the USB ports for add-on devices. Although USB Ethernet adapters abound for Windows-based PCs and work with Windows-based sharing products, MacOS doesn't support USB networking. Your iMac can share another computer's cable Internet connection, but can't share its cable Internet connection with others.

Alternatives to ICS—Which Is the Best?

Of the three Windows-based sharing programs covered in this chapter, I prefer Sygate Home Network for its ease of installation and reasonable feature set and WinProxy for its comprehensive approach to network control and family-friendly protection features. Both products are easy to install, but Sygate Home Network is a little more straightforward. WinGate Home is too limited in its features to be a compelling upgrade for an ICS user, and WinGate Standard looks too complicated for a non-expert to use. However, because all three products offer free trial periods, you can try them yourself to see which one you prefer.

MacOS users are likely to prefer Vicom's sharing solutions over IPNetRouter because of better company-based and third-party support. As with the Windows-based sharing products, you can download trial versions to compare them for yourself.

One disadvantage of all sharing programs is that if the common DHCP (dynamic IP addressing) feature is used, the gateway/proxy computer must be turned on and finish booting before any other users can access the Internet. If the gateway/proxy computer locks up or loses power, everyone is offline and must shut down and restart after the gateway/proxy computer is running again.

If you want network sharing that you can configure without having a computer on at all times, consider using a router. This is an option explored in much more detail in Chapter 17, "Router Your Way to Internet Sharing."

Summary

Windows users who want more control over Internet sharing than what ICS provides can choose from three different sharing products: WinGate, WinProxy, and Sygate Home Network. All of them support tracking of Internet use, but WinProxy and Sygate Home Network also provide built-in support for content filtering. WinProxy also supports network-wide antivirus features. WinGate is available in Home, Standard, and Pro versions.

Antivirus and content filtering features provided as a part of some sharing programs have a limited duration; you will need to pay an additional fee after the subscriptions run out.

MacOS users can share an Internet connection hosted by ICS, WinProxy, and Sygate Home Network servers, but need MacOS-specific software to share their connection with others. Only Macs with provision for a slot-based network adapter can be used as a sharing server with cable modems; iMacs cannot.

Trial versions are available for both Windows-based and MacOS-based products to help you determine which program is the best choice for your home or small-office network.

ROUTER YOUR WAY TO INTERNET SHARING

CHAPTER HIGHLIGHTS:

- What routers do and how they work
- How routers differ from using software connection sharing solutions
- What types of networks use routers
- How to add a router to an existing network
- How to include a router in your new network
- How to discover the security and other features you need

What Routers Do

A router, as the name implies, routes traffic between two different networks. Routers have been used for years in corporate networks to direct traffic between a network in one city and a network in another city. In more recent years, routers have become an essential part of the infrastructure of the world's largest network, the Internet. And, now, you can use low-cost routers made especially for use with cable modems and similar broadband devices to allow multiple computers to use your cable Internet connection.

How Routers Work

A router is easy to understand if you compare it to the connection-sharing software discussed in Chapters 15, "Using Microsoft Internet Connection Sharing," and 16, "Using Other Computer-Based Internet Sharing Programs." Most connection-sharing programs use two network adapters:

- One connected to a private network (other computers in your home or office)
- One connected to the cable modem or other broadband Internet connection

Each network adapter is assigned its own IP address in a different subnet.

 Note   A *subnet* is a series of IP addresses whose first three groups are the same. For example, the IP addresses 192.168.0.1 through 192.168.0.254 are part of the same subnet.

Normally, only computers on the same subnet can communicate with each other. But, connection-sharing software connects the subnets together to allow Internet traffic to flow to and from the computers on the home network.

Similarly, a router is configured with two IP addresses:

- The wide area network (WAN) address is the IP address used to connect to the cable modem; it's the same IP address originally assigned to your network card.
- The local area network (LAN) address is the IP address used to connect to the computers on your home network.

Note   *WAN*—Wide area network (the Internet)

LAN—Local area network (your home network)

And, just as connection sharing software does, a router connects the subnets together to provide Internet service to all the computers connected to it on the home network.

How Routers Differ from Connection Sharing Software

Most connection-sharing software uses a feature called network address translation (NAT) to convert the private IP addresses used on the home network into a public IP address. From the standpoint of an ISP, a NAT-based network is using just one IP address, regardless of the number of computers connected to the gateway. From a practical standpoint, proxy servers really work the same way, although the technical details differ. Figure 17.1 illustrates how NAT works.

FIGURE 17.1

NAT allows each computer on a home network to access the Internet with the same public IP address. NAT tracks which computer made the request, and routes the information requested back to the correct computer.

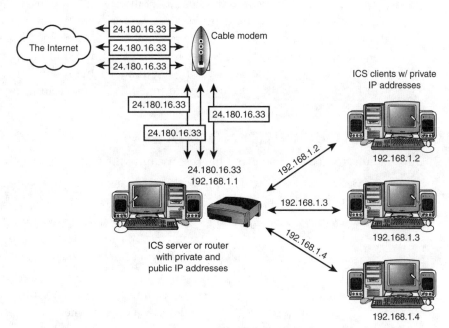

Because the gateway computer has a public IP address so it can access the Internet, it lacks the incoming firewall traffic-blocking feature inherent in a NAT-based network. Routers also use NAT, but because the router, not a PC, is connected to the Internet, all PCs on the network have the firewall protection for incoming traffic, which NAT provides.

Don't forget to protect the router's configuration from unauthorized changes. Changes to the router setup could prevent you from connecting to the Internet or disable the firewall features in the router, making your computers vulnerable to attacks. If your router uses a Web-based configuration setup, make sure you set a password to protect the settings. The configuration settings on some routers can be changed from the WAN side as well as the LAN side. If possible, disable WAN-side configuration (also called the administrative functions) in your router setup. See your router's instruction manual for details.

The second major difference is that of access rights. The computer that provides the gateway or proxy server function for others PCs has free access to Web services that require particular TCP ports to be opened (such as NetMeeting), whereas client PCs either can't open the ports needed or require the gateway or proxy to be configured to allow the traffic. With a router, you can provide the same level of access to Web services for all computers on the network, customize TCP port access for particular users, or turn off port blocking altogether for a particular user.

The third major difference is the stability of the network. Because computers that act as servers must balance handling network requests with the functions they perform for the person using the computer, they could be more prone to lockups and crashes, taking down the entire network. Because routers aren't running programs, printing files, displaying information, or doing anything else but routing, they're difficult to crash. The result is that as long as your router has power, your network works.

Types of Broadband Routers

Routers made for broadband Internet use have the following features in common:

- Support for the TCP/IP protocol—Corporate routers can route other types of network traffic, but all you need for the Internet is TCP/IP.

- Web-based configuration—Broadband routers usually have a Web server built in that you can access through your browser. Type the LAN IP address of the router, provide the password, and your browser doubles as the configuration tool for your browser.

- A port or antenna to connect to computers on the LAN—Some types of routers can connect to multiple network types, whereas others are designed for a particular network.

All major home network types can be connected to routers or gateways to provide Internet access to all network users.

10/100 Ethernet Broadband Routers

10/100 Ethernet broadband routers come in two major forms:

- Routers with a built-in 10/100 Ethernet switch and multiple ports—These routers, such as the one pictured in Figure 17.2, are the most cost-effective way to add router-based networking to a new network. The switch provides full-speed networking to the computers connected to it.

FIGURE 17.2

The front (top) and rear (bottom) of a typical 4-port broadband router/switch, the Linksys BEFSR41. Top photo courtesy of Linksys.

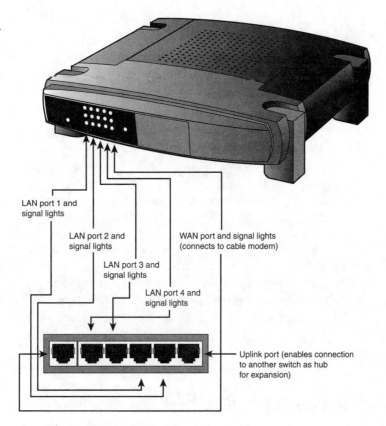

LAN port 1 and signal lights

LAN port 2 and signal lights

LAN port 3 and signal lights

LAN port 4 and signal lights

WAN port and signal lights (connects to cable modem)

Uplink port (enables connection to another switch as hub for expansion)

■ Routers with a single network port—These routers are designed to be added to an existing hub or switch, as shown in Figure 17.3.

Some routers also feature a USB port for direct connection to computers that have a USB port as an alternative to a 10/100 Ethernet adapter.

Note

If you need more ports than the router/switch contains, you can attach another switch or hub to the uplink port on most units. Make sure that you plug your cable into either port 1 or the uplink port; you cannot use both at the same time.

Other Types of Broadband Routers

Wireless Ethernet (IEEE-802.11b/Wi-Fi) routers connect to the cable modem through a Category 5 Ethernet cable, but use radio waves to communicate with clients that have compatible wireless network adapters. Some wireless Ethernet routers might also include a switch to allow 10/100 Ethernet-based systems to access the Internet or provide print-server functions.

FIGURE 17.3

Typical network
configuration for
a separate
10/100 Ethernet
router and
switch.

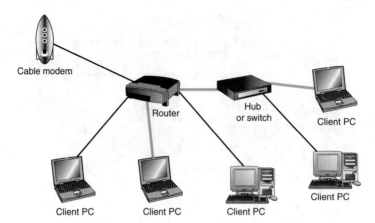

Phoneline-based networks (HomePNA 1.0 and 2.0) can also connect to a cable modem via an access point, which acts as a router. Some access points are designed to support multiple types of networks. HomeRF-based networks can use a wireless gateway to connect with a cable modem. These types of networks are diagrammed in Chapter 18, "Setting Up a Home Network for Sharing Your Internet Connection."

Many cable modems can act as routers, but each additional IP address will cost several dollars a month.

Router Features to Look For

Many broadband routers are on the market now, and more are arriving every day. Depending on the type of network you have, most of the following factors will be important to your choice:

- Integrated switch features
- Security features
- Configuration options
- Throughput speed
- Interoperability
- Manageability

Before you purchase a router, check the following sources to find the best products for your needs:

- *Manufacturers' Web sites*—Check the documentation, tech support, FAQs, and firmware update availability for the products you're considering.

■ *Networking Web sites*—One example is www.practicallynetworked.com; check its Sharing section for reviews, tips, and tricks.

■ *Product rating Web sites*—One example is Epinions.com. To find router reviews and ratings, go to Computers & Internet, Computer Hardware, Networking, Routers and Bridges, Routers.

Integrated Switch Features

If you want to buy a router for a new 10/100 Ethernet network, you can save money, power connections, and cable clutter by selecting a router with a built-in 10/100 Ethernet switch. You should select a switch with at least one more port than the number of computers you currently plan to have on your network.

For easy upgrading, look for a unit that also includes an uplink port, as shown in Figure 17.4. If you run out of ports on your router/switch, you can attach another switch to the uplink port using standard Category 5 network cable. If your router/switch lacks an uplink port, you will need to use a crossover cable, which is often more expensive and is sometimes hard to find.

FIGURE 17.4
When the capacity of a router/switch is used up (left), connect another switch (right) to the uplink port to expand the network.

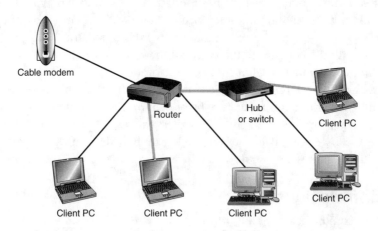

Most router/switch combinations support full-duplex networking. This doubles the rated speed of networking cards that support full-duplex networking.

If your cable modem uses a USB connector rather than a 10/100 Ethernet port, look for a router that supports a WAN device via the USB port. If you want to connect a computer via its USB port without installing a USB Ethernet adapter, look for a router that supports a LAN device via the USB port.

Security Features

A router provides a great deal of security to its clients because it handles the conversion of private IP addresses (which are hard to attack) to public IP addresses. However, you should ask yourself how secure the router is.

Routers with Web-based management interfaces should be password-protected. Find out how long the password can be, and what types of characters it accepts. And, because router configuration can be tricky, find out how to reset the router to its factory condition so you can start over. Some routers require you to connect a particular type of RS-232 serial cable and send commands to reset the router, whereas others have a recessed Reset button.

 If the router has a Web-based configuration utility, use the Save As feature in your browser to save your screens as you set up the router. Write in the password on your printout of the screens and save them for emergencies.

From the standpoint of user security, one of the newest features is the incorporation of router and software security. Chapter 13, "Firewalls and Your PC," discusses how firewall software can prevent unauthorized data from leaving your computer, and Chapter 14, "Stopping Computer Viruses," discusses the virtues of a full-time antivirus software defense. Linksys routers now have a free firmware upgrade that works along with the ZoneAlarm Pro personal firewall (see Chapter 13) and PC-Cillin 2000 antivirus software (see Chapter 14) to integrate these levels of protection with the incoming firewall provided by your router. The firmware upgrade allows you to require either or both products to be present on clients that access the Internet, and can exempt computers in given IP address ranges. See the Linksys Web site (www.linksys.com) for details of the models supported, firmware upgrades, and special multipack license pricing for ZoneAlarm Pro and PC-Cillin 2000 software.

Configuration Options

For maximum compatibility with the wide variety of broadband services and cable modem/network configurations on the market, make sure your router has these configuration features:

■ Automatic or fixed WAN IP addressing—Some cable modems provide a dynamic IP address to the network card connected to the cable modem. Because your router replaces the direct network card connection, it needs to provide the same option as well as supply a fixed IP address option (see Figure 17.5).

■ Flexible LAN IP address—Because you might not know what subnet your cable modem uses until you dig into your system to set up sharing software or a router, you need to have a choice of address ranges so you don't wind up using an address range with the cable modem. If your router did use the same address range, you might conflict with your neighbor's system down the street.

FIGURE 17.5

Configuring the WAN (cable modem) and LAN (network) IP address settings on a D-Link DI-704, a popular broadband router/switch.

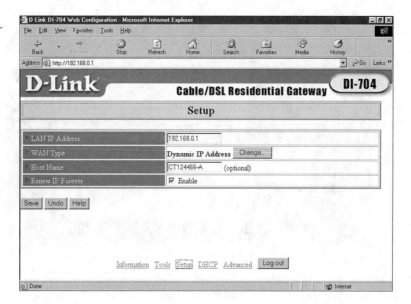

■ MAC address cloning—MAC addresses are unique to each network device, but different manufacturers and different types of devices use distinct ranges of MAC addresses. Some broadband providers frown on do-it-yourself home networking and will try to detect your router based on its MAC address. Cloning the MAC address of the network card you originally had used to connect to the cable modem keeps your network a secret.

■ DHCP server—If you don't want to worry about setting up IP address, gateway, and DNS servers on all the computers in your home network, look for this option, which assigns IP addresses to all the computers on the network. You should be able to set a starting IP address in the same subnet as the LAN side of your router, and be able to add the number of clients you want (see Figure 17.6).

■ Port configuration options—At a minimum, your router should be able to open several different ranges of TCP ports to allow various types of Internet services such as games and video conferencing programs to run with the router's firewall in place. Desirable options include the ability to place one or more PCs into a DMZ (demilitarized zone). This ability provides full two-way traffic without firewall protection, port filtering (which can block systems from any Internet access), and preset configurations for popular Internet programs that require server capabilities (see Figure 17.7).

FIGURE 17.6

Configuring the Linksys router to provide DHCP services for 10 users.

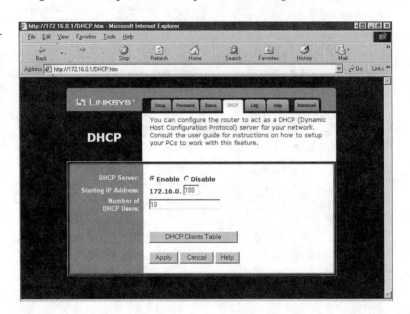

The DMZ feature permits programs that require too many port ranges for a router to open specifically or uses dynamic TCP port ranges (which change every time the program is run) to work correctly through the router. Because the router is set to pass all inbound traffic when the DMZ is enabled, use of a powerful firewall program such as ZoneAlarm Pro is highly recommended on systems that must use the DMZ feature. In addition, the DMZ feature should be disabled (returning the system to normal protection levels) as soon as the special program(s) needing DMZ access are stopped.

MacOS users can find an easy-to-understand list of TCP and UDP ports used by popular MacOS programs at www2.opendoor.com/doorstop/ports.html.

Both Windows and MacOS users will find LinNet's TCP/UDP Ports pages of ports and usages helpful in configuring routers and firewalls at www.ec11.dial.pipex.com/port-filter.shtml.

■ Throughput speed—Because of the overhead involved in managing packets and switching ports, different brands of routers with the same rated speed will perform at different actual speeds. The reviews available at the Practically Networked Web site test throughput and are reliable guides to router features in general.

FIGURE 17.7

The D-Link router has preset port options for several popular programs, or you can manually enter port requirements.

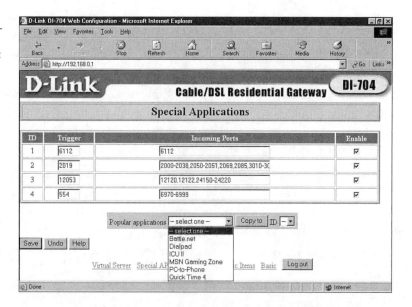

■ Interoperability—Because 10/100 Ethernet is a long-established standard, you can mix and match network adapters, switches, and routers without trouble. However, less mature networks—including wireless Ethernet (Wi-Fi), HomeRF, and HomePNA—might have problems mixing and matching network adapters and routers or gateways. For best results, avoid mixing and matching different brands of Wi-Fi wireless router/gateway devices and network adapters.

Tip

Some wireless routers (also called gateways or access points) support a wired Ethernet connection for setup and management; this is recommended because it bypasses interference and setup problems with initial configuration.

■ Versatility—If you plan to change home network types in the next year or two, a multinetwork router is a great idea. Some models on the market can handle all common network types, whereas some models handle just wired and wireless Ethernet. Some of these products include 2Wire's HomePortal 100 and 1000 series devices (www.2wire.com) and Compaq's iPAQ connection point (www.Compaq.com).

■ Manageability—The interface that the router uses for setup is important, as is the ease of firmware upgrades. Find out the procedure for firmware upgrades before you buy a router, and don't even think about buying a router that lacks this feature. If the router is a discontinued model, find out how long the manufacturer plans to continue technical support before you buy the unit.

Adding a Router to an Existing Network That Did Not Share the Internet

Adding a router to an existing network gives you the opportunity to put your entire network on the Internet, not just one computer. If you were *not* sharing your cable modem previously, the process follows the general outline given next.

 Note   Be sure to see your router manual for details.

1. Print or record the TCP/IP configuration used by your computer to connect to the cable modem. With Windows 9x/Me, use the WINIPCFG program described in Chapter 15 to display this information. Your router will use the settings used by your network adapter.

2. Make any changes needed in your computer's TCP/IP configuration to allow it to communicate with the router for configuration.

3. After connecting the computer to the router, enter the TCP/IP data you recorded for your computer into the router's configuration screens. Refer to Figure 17.4 for a typical example.

4. Store each screen into the router's non-volatile memory as you complete it. Look for an onscreen button such as OK or Apply or Save to perform this task.

5. For maximum ease of use, set the browser to supply dynamic IP addresses as in Figure 17.6.

6. Change the router's password after writing down the new password as a backup and after reviewing the procedure for resetting the router in case of errors in the configuration.

7. Connect the router to the cable modem and reset the cable modem so it detects the router.

8. Connect the router to the switch or hub you used previously by running a cable from the uplink port to the LAN port on your router, or unplug the cables from the hub or switch you previously used and connect them to the LAN ports on the router/switch.

 Note   If you don't have enough ports in your router/switch to handle all your PCs, run a cable from the old hub or switch's uplink port to one of the LAN ports on the router/switch. Then, plug some of the cables into the router/switch and the rest into the switch or hub. Switches provide faster performance, but if you're satisfied with the performance of your hub, keep it. You can always replace it later.

9. Reconfigure your computer to obtain an IP address automatically and reboot it if necessary.

10. Your computer should be able to go online after rebooting.

11. Install the TCP/IP protocol on the other computers on the network.

12. Set the other computers to obtain their IP addresses automatically and reboot them if necessary.

13. All computers should be able to go online; you might need to run the Internet Setup wizard to configure them to use a LAN connection first.

Adding a Router to an Existing Network That Was Used for Internet Sharing

The steps listed in the previous section for adding a router to an existing network are similar to those used when sharing software was used, but these additional steps must be taken first:

1. If you are using Internet Connection Sharing, the IP address settings used by the network adapter connected to the cable modem are not the settings you need to enter into the router configuration. Use WINIPCFG and select the ISHARE adapter to see the correct settings. Most other Internet sharing programs use the same IP address settings used before the program was installed.

2. After recording the IP address settings needed for the router, uninstall the Internet sharing program. Use the Add/Remove Programs icon in the Windows Control Panel. ICS will be listed as a Windows component, whereas the others will be listed as programs.

3. Remove the network card you used to connect to the cable modem (if you used a two-network card configuration). It is no longer necessary.

Continue from Step 2 in the previous section.

Making a Router Part of Your Network from Square One

If you are building a new network for the purpose of sharing an Internet connection, you should buy a combination router/switch (for 10/100 Ethernet) or router/access point (for Wi-Fi wireless Ethernet) and connect the computers to it.

Even though you are going to create a network for Internet sharing, verify that the cable modem works by setting up one computer to connect directly to the cable modem. After verifying that the cable modem and Internet connection work, transfer TCP/IP settings used by the network card connected to the cable modem to the router as described earlier in this chapter.

When working with a multistation network, get one computer working at a time before continuing to the next one. When you use a router that provides DHCP services for dynamic IP addresses, each computer uses these same settings:

■ Obtain an IP address automatically

■ Workgroup name (whatever the cable Internet operator dictates)

Each computer will require a unique name.

Most routers will come with operating system-specific instructions for setting up IP addresses.

If you are planning to use your router for VPN (virtual private networking) telecommuting back to your office, make sure your router supports the particular VPN standard used by your office network. Consult your office's network manager and the router manufacturers' Web sites to help determine what cable modem routers are compatible with your office's VPN.

Summary

Routers perform the same task as Internet sharing software; both enable multiple computers to share a single Internet connection. Both routers and Internet sharing computers use two IP addresses: a WAN (Internet) IP address and a LAN (network) private IP address. Routers provide incoming-traffic firewall protection for all PCs on the network and don't require a gateway computer to be left on at all times.

Routers are available for all major network types, including 10/100 Ethernet, Home PNA 1.0 and 2.0, and various wireless networks. 10/100 Ethernet routers can be purchased in two forms: with a switch or without a switch. Use the router/switch version to create an Internet-sharing network from scratch. The router without a switch connects to an existing network's switch or hub to provide Internet sharing to the network. Some routers can be used with multiple network types, enabling you to connect different networks to the same router or upgrade from one network to another in the future without replacing the router.

For easiest network configuration, use the DHCP feature provided by most routers to provide automatic IP addresses for network users.

Whether you create an Internet sharing network from scratch or add a router to an existing network, set up one computer at a time and check Internet connections before setting up the next computer.

SETTING UP A HOME NETWORK FOR SHARING YOUR INTERNET CONNECTION

CHAPTER HIGHLIGHTS:

How to install the most popular home network types:

- 10/100 Ethernet
- Home PNA
- Wireless networks
- How to use them to share a cable modem

Network Types—Overview

After your family or officemates have experienced the rush of cable Internet service, you will be faced with two alternatives:

- Creating a signup list so that you can have some time to yourself at the PC with the fast Internet connection
- Sharing the connection with others who are using multiple computers

It won't take long for you to decide that sharing the connection is better than waiting your turn at your own computer. In this chapter, you will learn how to build a home network that will make sharing your Internet connection possible, as discussed in Chapter 15, "Using Microsoft Internet Connection Sharing," Chapter 16, "Using Other Computer-Based Internet Sharing Programs," and Chapter 17, "Router Your Way to Internet Sharing."

Installing a home network makes more sense than ever today because, in addition to sharing your cable Internet connection, you can also share the following:

- Disk drives, including CD-ROM, CD-RW, and DVD drives as well as high-capacity hard drives
- Printers
- Documents

You can even send e-mail and use instant-messaging services to stay in touch at home, regardless of how far apart each computer is.

At one time, networking was extremely expensive and extremely difficult. Today, neither is true. Some types of networks can be built for less than $50 per user. However, to make an intelligent decision about home networking, you still need to consider how you will use your network, how much you are willing to spend per user, whether you want to run cable for the network, and whether you want to support roving users who might take their PCs from the kitchen table to the den or the study.

The following types of networks are the most popular for use at home or in a small office:

- 10/100 Ethernet—This is the fastest (100Mbps) and least expensive network to install, although it does require specialized cabling. Originally, Fast Ethernet ran at only 100Mbps speeds, but today's Fast Ethernet hardware is called 10/100 Ethernet because it also works with the older 10Mbps form of Ethernet known as 10BaseT.

- Home PNA 2.0—This is the second (10Mbps) version of the Home Phoneline Networking Alliance network standard. It uses your existing telephone cabling.
- Wi-Fi—Also called IEEE-802.11b, this is the most common form of Wireless Ethernet networking, running at a top speed of 11Mbps.
- HomeRF—This is a low-cost wireless network that's also less expensive than Wi-Fi or other types of Wireless Ethernet. The original version ran at just 1.6Mbps, but the new HomeRF 2.0 standard, running at 10Mbps, is now available. All network types require that your computer have one of the following:
    - Network card
    - USB network adapter
    - Built-in network port

Table 18.1 compares the major features of these networks.

Table 18.1   Major Home Networking Technologies

Network Type	Speed	Cabling Type	Network Topology	Connection Device Required	Relative Cost Per User
10/100 Ethernet	100Mbps or 10Mbps	Unshielded Twisted Pair, Category 5	Star	Hub or Switch (for 3 or more PCs)	Varies (low unless in-wall cable installation by professionals is required)
HomeRF 2.0	10Mbps	None	Peer-to-peer	N/A	Moderate
HomePNA 2.0	10Mbps	Telephone cable	Bus	N/A	Moderate
Wi-Fi (IEEE 802.11b)	11Mbps maximum (varies with transmission conditions)	None	Star	Access point (required for Internet access, optional for LAN access)	High

Understanding Network Topologies

If you're planning to network your home, you need to understand the practical effects of the Network Topology entry in Table 18.1. Networks that have a star topology require additional hardware to connect computers to each other. In the case of a wired network such as 10/100 Ethernet, you need to run a cable between each computer and a central hub or switch, as shown in Figure 18.1 if you want to network three or more computers.

Tip

If you want the speed and low cost of 10/100 Ethernet but only have a two-computer network, you don't need a switch or a hub. Just install a 10/100 Ethernet card in each computer and use a Category 5 crossover cable to connect them.

If you decide to add more computers to the network later, you will need a hub or a switch and standard straight-through Category 5 cable between each computer and the hub or switch.

If you want planning to network your home, you need to understand the inconspicuous network cables for use in your home, use light gray Category 5 cabling. Other typical cabling colors (red, yellow, and blue) don't blend very well with typical home decor. Therefore, if you decide to install a 10/100 Fast Ethernet network, be prepared to hide the cabling or run it through walls if you don't want to spoil the look of your den, living room, or bedroom. Fast Ethernet computers can be as far as 328 feet (100 meters) from the hub or switch, so you don't need to worry about running out of range as you run cables wherever it's necessary to put them out of sight.

FIGURE 18.1

A star topology Ethernet network as it might be installed in a typical home with cable modem service.

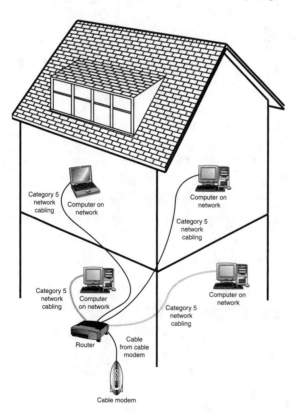

Tip

You can buy pre-built Category 5 cables in lengths from 7ft to 100ft at most computer and office-product stores. For longer cable runs, check with online dealers or build your own.

If you want to build your own Category 5 network cables, check out the illustrated DUX Computer Digest guide at www.duxcw.com/digest/Howto/network/cable/index.htm.

The HomePCNetwork Web site has an excellent illustrated tutorial on running wires through walls at www.homepcnetwork.com/index.htm?wireintro.htm.

Although a Wi-Fi wireless Ethernet network also uses a central access point to permit Internet access, it needs no wires, and each computer can be hundreds of feet away from the access point; the exact range varies with the network hardware used and the speed of the connection. As with 10/100 Ethernet, if you decide to use a router to share the Internet connection, the router can be incorporated with the access point, or be a separate device. See Figure 18.2 for a typical example.

FIGURE 18.2

A Wi-Fi wireless network also has a star topology because data is routed via the access point, which can also serve as a router, as shown here.

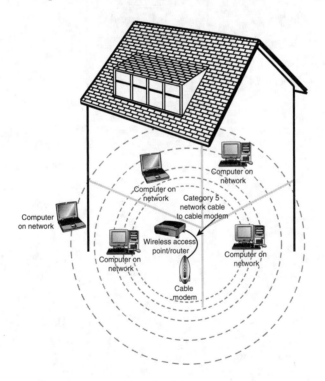

You may run into interference problems with your Wi-Fi network if you have 2.4GHz cordless phones or satellite dishes because Wi-Fi also uses the same 2.4GHz frequency. As an alternative, consider the HomeRF 2.0 wireless network, which has similar speed and uses a different frequency.

The other major wired network standard, HomePNA 2.0, piggybacks on your existing phone lines and requires little if any new wiring. Because each computer passes information to the next one on the network, you don't need a central access point for networking, although a router can still be used, as shown in Figure 18.3.

FIGURE 18.3

A typical home network using HomePNA 2.0. Existing telephone wiring carries data between computers and allows for simultaneous use of the phone for voice calls.

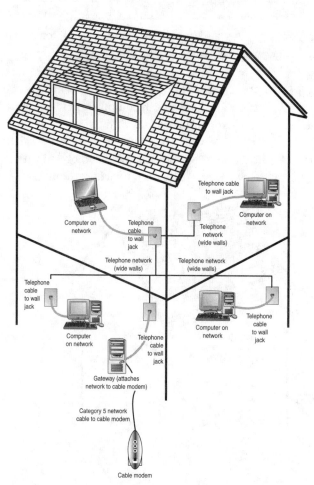

The HomeRF network (see Figure 18.4) doesn't require a central access point, either; sending stations on the network relays information directly to the receiving stations. It also supports Internet sharing with a separate or integrated wireless router/gateway device.

FIGURE 18.4

A typical home network using HomeRF. The wireless gateway is used only for Internet traffic; all PC-to-PC data transfers are sent directly between computers.

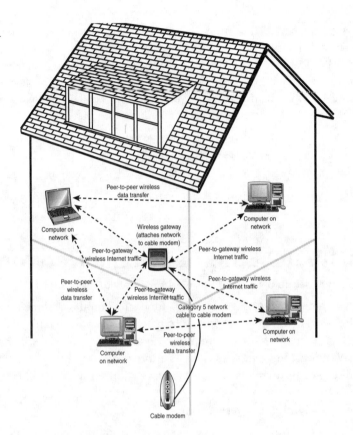

Selecting the Best Network for You

From the standpoint of low cost and high performance, 10/100 Fast Ethernet is the best network to choose. Unfortunately, cabling can be a major hidden expense, and a big headache in many homes.

If you're looking for complete flexibility in equipment location, freedom from wires, and don't mind the highest average cost per computer, Wi-Fi is your best choice.

If your home or small office is well equipped with telephone jacks, you can have speed just a bit lower than Wi-Fi for much less per station by selecting HomePNA 2.0-compliant equipment. Watch out for the original HomePNA 1.0 standard that might still be on the market. At just 1Mbps, it's just too slow.

HomeRF gives you the wireless flexibility of Wi-Fi at a much lower cost, but you need to specify HomeRF 2.0 to have acceptable speed; HomeRF 1.0 products (which run at just 1.6Mbps) are still available from some sources. HomeRF is also limited to ten users per network, but this shouldn't be a major concern for most home users.

Unlike other types of networking, HomeRF-compliant network hardware often doesn't mention the HomeRF name. Look for the speed of the device: A wireless adapter that runs at 1.6Mbps is compatible with HomeRF 1.0, while a wireless adapter which runs at 10Mbps is compatible with HomeRF 2.0. You can mix and match different brands of HomeRF-compliant hardware; check the HomeRF Working Group, Inc. Web site (www.homerf.org) for a list of compatible products.

Major vendors of HomeRF products include:

- Proxim Symphony HomeRF—www.proxim.com
- Intel AnyPoint Wireless Home Network—www.intel.com/anypoint
- Motorola/General Instruments BB160 series—www.gi.com/homenetworking.html

Installing a 10/100 Ethernet Home Network

If you want to set up a 10/100 Ethernet home network, you need the following:

- One network interface card (NIC) for each computer—Some recent computers have on-board network ports, but most require you to add a card or a USB Ethernet adapter. If you are planning to use computer-based sharing (Windows Internet Connection Sharing or a third-party sharing product as discussed in Chapters 15 and 16), you will need two 10/100 Ethernet cards, or one 10/100 Ethernet card and a USB Ethernet adapter for the computer that will be sharing its Internet connection with others.

- Category 5 cabling to run between each computer and the hub or switch—This type of cable connects to an RJ-45 port (which resembles the RJ-11 telephone cable port used on modems, but is larger and has connectors for eight wires).

- A hub (slower and cheaper) or switch (faster and more expensive) to which all computers connect (refer to Figure 18.1)—AC power must be available for the hub or switch. If you plan to use a router for Internet sharing, use a router/switch combination in place of a normal hub or switch.

- Network client software—Included with all major operating systems, including 32-bit Windows and MacOS.

Before you purchase your 10/100 Ethernet hardware, take a look at the chapters on sharing your Internet connection. Although you can share the connection with a hub or switch-based network by adding a second NIC to your computer to handle the incoming signal from the cable modem, you can also buy a combination router and switch to allow networking and sharing. Buying the combination router and switch is less expensive than buying a router later, even though you need to buy your network cards and cables separately. See Chapters 15 and 16 for the details of dual-NIC sharing, and Chapter 17 for the details of router-based sharing.

Computers can be up to 328 feet (100 meters) from a hub or switch; you can use a hub or switch to boost the signal if you have computers that are farther away than this.

Although hubs are less expensive than switches with the same number of ports, the lower cost can come at a significant sacrifice in speed. A 10/100 Ethernet hub connected to 10/100 Ethernet cards must split the 100Mbps Fast Ethernet signal among all of its ports because it does not identify unique computers connected to each port. Thus, a five-port hub provides only 20Mbps of speed to each 10/100 card (100÷5=20). However, a 10/100 Ethernet switch, which is able to recognize and channel data to a specific computer connected to a specific port, provides up to full 100Mbps speed to each port. In addition, because most 10/100 switches and 10/100 Ethernet cards support a feature called *full duplex*, which enables devices to send and receive data at the same time, your 10/100 Ethernet network will actually run as fast as 200Mbps! And, if you mix and match 10/100 and 10BaseT Ethernet, hubs slow everyone down to the lower speed, while switches support 100Mbps connections between 10/100 cards, and 10Mbps connections between 10/100 and 10Mbps cards.

While some low-cost router/switch devices support connections between only two ports at a time, they switch rapidly enough between ports that you won't notice any drop in performance on a home network.

Figure 18.5 illustrates a typical 10/100 Ethernet network kit ready to network two desktop computers; three more computers can be added by purchasing additional network adapters.

Boxed 10/100 Ethernet network kits, such as the one shown in Figure 18.5, are the fastest, easiest, and often the least expensive way to set up a small home or home-office network. However, you should avoid models that contain a hub instead of a switch because switches provide faster network performance. Also, if you are planning to use a router to share your Internet connection (see Chapter 17), your best move is to buy a combination router/switch and the network adapters you need as separate components.

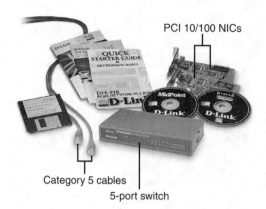

PCI 10/100 NICs

Category 5 cables

5-port switch

If you want to add a notebook computer to your network, you need a PC Card-based
10/100 Ethernet network adapter, shown in Figure 18.6, or a USB Ethernet adapter
(see Figure 18.7). Desktop computers that lack free expansion slots can also use a
USB Ethernet adapter, but USB Ethernet adapters are slower than internal 10/100
Ethernet cards.

10/100 Ethernet PC Card

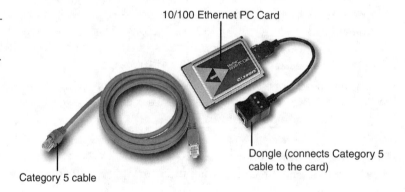

Dongle (connects Category 5
cable to the card)

Category 5 cable

Warning

Many different options are available to you for PC Card 10/100 Ethernet adapters.
Some models integrate a 56Kbps modem to save a slot, whereas others fit only into
BusCard versions of the PC Card slot. If your notebook computer has BusCard slots, this
type of PC Card adapter is preferable because BusCard PC Cards are faster than normal
PC Cards. If you travel a great deal, you might also want to consider a PC Card or
BusCard adapter that doesn't require a dongle; dongles are easily damaged or lost.

FIGURE 18.7

A typical USB Ethernet adapter. Photo courtesy of Linksys.

Setting Up the 10/100 Ethernet Network

Follow these steps to install the network:

1. Decide where to place the hub, switch or router/switch. AC power must be present, and you need to choose a location that is easy to access and enables you to run the cables to it. You will need to run a Category 5 cable to the router/switch from the cable modem if you decide to use that form of Internet sharing.

2. Install the network card or adapter (if required). Some late-model PCs and most recent Macs have built-in Ethernet, but others require you to install cards.

3. Install network support software, including operating system and hardware drivers.

4. Run the Category 5 cable between the hub/switch/router-switch and each PC on the network. Stores sell cables up to 100 feet long. If you need longer cables, you can either use Category 5 connectors to bridge short cables together, or buy bulk cable, connectors, and tools in a cabling kit to build your own.

5. Configure your network for Internet sharing. See Chapters 15–17 for details of your preferred method.

Windows 98, Me, and XP all feature various Internet Connection Sharing or Home Networking wizards to make setting up your network easier. As part of the process, they can create a disk you can use on older Windows 95 machines to automate the setup process.

If you prefer (or require) manual setup, your network hardware provider will supply detailed instructions with their hardware at their Web sites, or you can use the links available for both PC/Windows and Mac networking at www.practicallynetworked.com/ linksnw.htm.

Installing a HomePNA 2.0 Phoneline Network

If you want to install a HomePNA 2.0 home network, you need the following:

- One network interface card (NIC) for each computer—A few recent computers have on-board HomePNA 2.0-compliant network ports, but most require you to add a HomePNA 2.0 network adapter card or USB adapter.

If you are planning to use computer-based sharing (Windows Internet Connection Sharing or a third-party sharing product, as discussed in Chapters 15 and 16), the computer that will share its Internet connection will need a HomePNA 2.0 card or USB HomePNA 2.0 adapter to connect with the network. That computer might also need one 10/100 Ethernet card or a USB Ethernet adapter to connect with the cable modem.

If you prefer to use hardware-based Internet sharing, you can purchase a gateway that is compliant with the HomePNA 2.0 standard from a variety of vendors. See Chapter 17 for details.

- Network client software—This is a part of all major operating systems, including 32-bit Windows and Mac OS.

If you compare this list with the list of requirements for 10/100 Ethernet networking, you can see that HomePNA 2.0 networking is much simpler. You don't need to worry about a hub or a switch, and you don't need to rewire your home (assuming that every room that needs a network connection has a phone jack already). You pay for that simplicity, though, in two ways:

- Speed—Home PNA 2.0 runs at 10Mbps, whereas 10/100 Fast Ethernet running in full-duplex mode runs as high as 200Mbps.
- Cost per computer—A two-station starter kit for HomePNA 2.0 networking costs about 50% more than a two-station 10/100 Ethernet starter kit that contains a switch, and HomePNA 2.0-compliant network cards can cost up to twice as much as 10/100 Ethernet cards.

However, both the purchase and installation process are simpler for HomePNA 2.0, so the extra cost might not be a major issue for you.

Figure 18.8 compares a PCI-based HomePNA 2.0 network card to a 10/100 Ethernet card.

If you want to add a notebook computer to your HomePNA 2.0 network, you need a PC Card-based HomePNA 2.0 adapter or a USB HomePNA 2.0 adapter. Computers that lack free expansion slots can also use a USB HomePNA 2.0 adapter Ethernet adapter, but USB HomePNA 2.0 adapters are slower than internal HomePNA 2.0 network cards.

FIGURE 18.8

A typical
HomePNA 2.0-
compliant net-
work card (top)
and a typical
10/100 Ethernet
card (bottom),
both designed
for the standard
PCI expansion
slot.

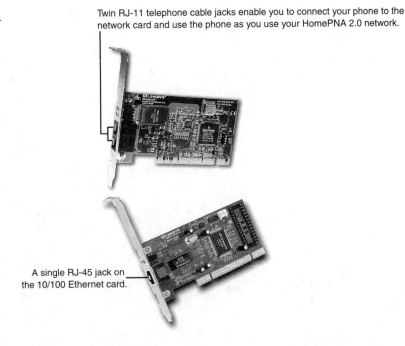

Twin RJ-11 telephone cable jacks enable you to connect your phone to the
network card and use the phone as you use your HomePNA 2.0 network.

A single RJ-45 jack on
the 10/100 Ethernet card.

Warning

Make sure the HomePNA-compliant network cards and adapters you buy are HomePNA
2.0-compliant. Some HomePNA 1.0-compliant network hardware (1Mbps speed) is still
on the market. Running at only 1Mbps is too slow for use with today's systems.

If you take a notebook computer home from work and want to attach it to a network at both locations (even though your home uses HomePNA 2.0 and your office
uses 10/100 Ethernet), you can buy a single PC Card or USB adapter that will support both types of networks. See Figure 18.9 for an example.

FIGURE 18.9

Dual-purpose
10/100 Ethernet/
HomePNA 2.0
PC Card (top)
and USB
adapters (bot-
tom).

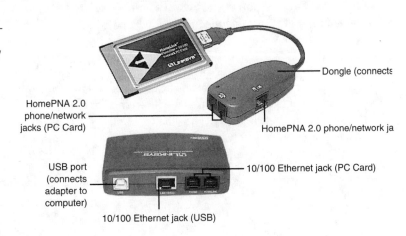

Dongle (connects

HomePNA 2.0
phone/network
jacks (PC Card)

HomePNA 2.0 phone/network ja

USB port
(connects
adapter to
computer)

10/100 Ethernet jack (PC Card)

10/100 Ethernet jack (USB)

Setting Up the HomePNA 2.0 Network

Follow these steps to install the network:

1. Install the network card or adapter (if required). A few late-model PCs have built-in HomePNA 2.0 ports, but most require you to install cards or adapters.

2. If the phone jack you want to use for your network card already has a telephone connected to it, unplug the phone from the jack and plug the phone into the port labeled Phone on the network adapter. Attach a cable from the phone jack to the port labeled Network or Homelink on the network adapter. You can use the network and your phone at the same time.

3. Repeat step 2 for other computers you want to network.

4. Configure your network for Internet sharing. See Chapters 15 through 17 for details of your preferred method.

Installing a Wireless Ethernet (Wi-Fi) Network

If you want to set up a Wireless Ethernet (Wi-Fi) home network, you need the following:

- One network interface card (NIC) for each computer—A few recent notebook computers have built-in Wi-Fi network hardware, but most computers require you to add a card or a USB Wi-Fi adapter. Wi-Fi network cards are available for desktop computers (PCI card), notebook computers (PC Card), and computers that have only USB port for expansion (see Figure 18.10).

- Network client software—Included with all major operating systems, including 32-bit Windows and MacOS.

Most vendors' PCI versions of their Wi-Fi adapter cards actually act as a docking station for the PC Card version of the adapter. Some vendors sell their PCI adapters with the required PC Card included in the package (see Figure 18.11), whereas others require you to buy both the PCI adapter and the PC Card to build a complete PCI wireless solution.

Even though most Wireless Ethernet hardware is compliant with the Wi-Fi standard, which specifies interoperability between different brands as part of the standard (see www.wi-fi.org for details), you will have an easier time getting your network working correctly if you buy your network cards and access point or access point/router from the same vendor. If you mix and match hardware, you could be caught in a finger-pointing game if you have problems.

FIGURE 18.10

A typical family of Wi-Fi wireless products, including a wireless access point, USB, PC Card, and PCI wireless network adapters. The PC Card is used in notebook computers that lack Wi-Fi support and also acts as the transceiver for the PCI card used in desktop computers. Photo courtesy of Linksys.

Access point (can also include a router)

USB network adapter

PC Card network adapt

PCI network adapter (requires PC Card adapter)

FIGURE 18.11

D-Link's DWP-500 Wi-Fi wireless PCI adapter includes the DWP-650 wireless PC Card. Photo courtesy of D-Link Systems, Inc.

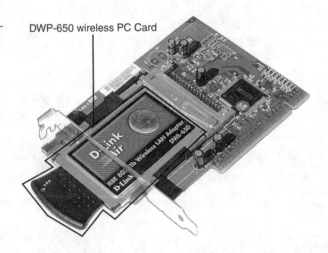

DWP-650 wireless PC Card

Note

If you are planning to use computer-based sharing (Windows Internet Connection Sharing or a third-party sharing product as discussed in Chapters 15 and 16), you might need a 10/100 Ethernet card for the computer. That card would connect with the cable modem, unless you can connect to the cable modem via a USB port.

Depending on the size of the area where you want wireless access to be possible and the range of your access point, you might need just one access point, or additional access points might be needed.

> If you plan to share your Internet connection via a router, as discussed in Chapter 17, buy a combination wireless access point/router device. Some of these devices might also enable you to connect with an existing wired network or set up a print server.

Unless you have a large home, a brick home, or plan to work outside at a considerable distance from the access point, you probably need only one access point. Note that the connection speed of Wi-Fi devices drops below 11Mbps if a reliable connection cannot be achieved at that speed because of distance or obstructions.

Regardless of the number of access points you need, you need only one router. So, the first access point should also include a router; if necessary, additional access points can be used to transfer Internet traffic to the access point/router.

Setting Up the Wi-Fi Wireless Ethernet Network

The process of installing the network follows these steps:

1. Decide where to place the access point. AC power must be present, and you need to choose a location that is easy to access and enables you to run the cables to it. If you are planning to use a combination access point/router, select a location that enables you to run Category 5 cable from the access point/router to your cable modem.

2. Install the network card or adapter (if required). Some notebook computers have built-in Wi-Fi support or might come with a separate Wi-Fi wireless PC Card, but most notebook computers and virtually all desktop computers will require you to install adapters.

3. Install operating system network features and hardware drivers.

4. Configure your network for Internet sharing. See Chapters 15–17 for details of your preferred method.

Installing a Wireless HomeRF Network

If you want to install a HomeRF-based wireless network, you need the following:

- One network interface card (NIC) or adapter for each computer—Current HomeRF-compliant adapters are available in PC Card and USB forms from various companies (see Figure 18.12).

■ Network client software—Included with all major operating systems, including 32-bit Windows and MacOS.

FIGURE 18.12

Proxim's Symphony-HRF family of HomeRF-compatible network products includes a USB adapter (center), a PC Card adapter (left), and a cordless base station to share the cable modem (right).

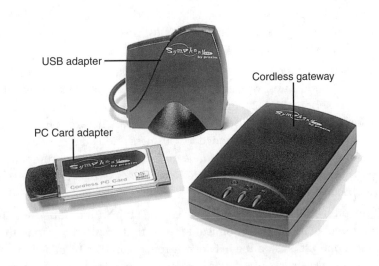

If you are planning to use computer-based sharing (Windows Internet Connection Sharing or a third-party sharing product, as discussed in Chapters 15 and 16), you might need a 10/100 Ethernet card for the computer to connect with the cable modem. The alternative is connecting to the cable modem via a USB port.

If you plan to share your Internet connection via a hardware device (router), as discussed in Chapter 17, buy a wireless gateway (also called a base station by some vendors). Some of these devices might also enable you to connect with an existing wired network.

Setting Up the HomeRF Wireless Ethernet Network

The process of installing the network follows these steps:

1. Check the distances between computers. HomeRF supports distances between PCs of up to 150 feet. If you need longer distances, consider Wi-Fi or a wired network solution.

2. Install the network card or adapter.

3. Install support software for your operating system and network hardware.

4. Configure your network for Internet sharing. See Chapters 15–17 for details of your preferred method.

Summary

You can network your home or small office with any of a number of technologies, including 10/100 Ethernet, HomePNA 2.0, HomeRF 2.0, and Wi-Fi. A few computers have built-in network adapters, but in most cases you will need to install the appropriate network adapter.

10/100 Ethernet requires Category 5 cabling, which can be expensive to install, although cards, hubs, switches, and routers are the least expensive of the major network types. HomePNA 2.0 and HomeRF 2.0 have comparable 10Mbps speeds, and neither requires special wiring; hardware for these networks is more expensive than 10/100 Ethernet. Wi-Fi is designed for business and is the most expensive home network to buy, but offers a wider range and can handle more computers than HomeRF 2.0 can. Users should avoid obsolete HomePNA 1.0 and HomeRF 1.0 network hardware because of their low speeds.

Although a 10/100 Ethernet network can be built with a hub, a switch or a router/switch, it's most economical to use a router/switch to connect with the cable modem and the PCs on the network. A router can also be added to an existing network. Other networks use router-like devices sometimes referred to as gateways or base stations to connect to a cable modem.

The process of installing any home network requires you to install a network adapter and networking software. The configuration of the TCP/IP protocol varies with the type of Internet sharing you decide to use.

PART VII

TROUBLESHOOTING YOUR CABLE MODEM

TROUBLESHOOTING YOUR CONNECTION TO THE INTERNET

CHAPTER HIGHLIGHTS:

- Learn how to interpret the signal lights on the front of your cable modem

- Discover the correct way to find wiring problems

- Detect problems with your Ethernet network adapter or USB ports

- Learn what TCP/IP is and how to make sure it's configured correctly

- Find out why you should keep your setup software CD handy and when you should reuse it

- Track down problems that are beyond your doorstep so you won't waste time trying to fix Internet or ISP problems

Understanding the Signal Lights on Your External Cable Modem

If your browser can't connect to the Internet some fine day, the signal lights on your external cable modem are the first place to look for clues as to what's wrong. Although numerous models of modems on the market, this chapter will use the Toshiba PCX1100/PCX1100U and the US Robotics 6000 two-way external cable modems as examples.

Figure 19.1 illustrates the front panels of the Toshiba cable modems, while Figure 19.2 illustrates the front panel of the US Robotics cable modem.

FIGURE 19.1

The front panel lights of a typical vertical-style two-way cable modem, the Toshiba PCX1100/ PCX1100U.

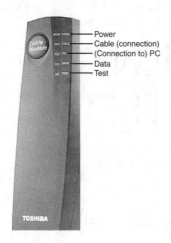

FIGURE 19.2

The front panel lights of a typical horizontal-style two-way cable modem, the US Robotics 6000. US Robotics' history as a dial-up modem maker shows in the large number of signal lights used and the fairly cryptic names for each light.

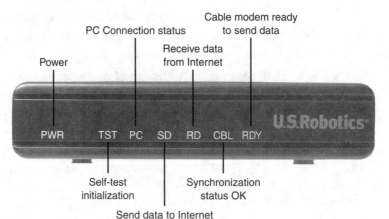

Tables 19.1 and 19.2 provide examples of how to use the signal lights to troubleshoot a problem with the cable modem. While your cable modem may vary, one of these examples should be similar to the way your modem works; check your documentation for details.

Table 19.1 Signal Lights on the Toshiba PCX1100 Series Cable Modem

Signal Light	Color	Off	Blinking	On	Items to Check
Power	Green	No power	N/A	Power on	AC adapter, AC cord plugged into unit
Cable	Green	No cable signal from CATV network if power on	Synchronizing and registering with network	Cable modem ready	Coaxial cable to cable modem; coaxial cable into splitter
PC	Green	No Ethernet or USB connection to computer if power on	N/A	Ethernet or USB connection to computer is present	Verify USB or Ethernet cable properly plugged into cable modem and PC; correct type of Ethernet cable used; check USB or Ethernet port on PC for proper operation
Data	Green	No data transfer in progress if power on	Data transfer in progress	N/A	No problem apparent unless light stays off during Web page opening, e-mail sending/receiving, or file downloads/uploads
Test	Amber	Self-test OK if power on	Self-test in progress	Self-test failed	Reset cable modem

Table 19.2 Signal Lights on the US Robotics 6000 Cable Modem

Signal Light	Off	On	Items to Check
PWR	No power	Power on	AC adapter, AC cord to unit
TST	Power-on self-test completed normally	Power-on self-test did not complete	Check CBL and RDY lights for possible causes; contact cable modem vendor for repair or replacement if CBL and RDY lights don't indicate a problem

Table 19.2 (continued)

Signal Light	Off	On	Items to Check
PC	No Ethernet or USB connection to computer if power on	Ethernet or USB connection to computer is present	Verify that USB or Ethernet cable is properly plugged into cable modem and PC; verify correct type of Ethernet cable used; check Ethernet or USB port on computer for proper operation
SD	Data is not being sent	Data is being sent	
RD	Data is not being received	Data is being received	
CBL	No signal being received from cable network	Signal being received from cable network	Check coaxial cable; turn on TV connected to cable to verify cable TV service is working
RDY	Cable modem may not have completed initialization or does not have a valid connection	Cable modem ready for use	Unplug cable modem, wait 30 seconds, plug back in to re-initialize: check with provider to make sure service to your location has not been shut off or suspended.

The shaded boxes in Tables 19.1 and 19.2 indicate potential problem areas to check. As you can see from Tables 19.1 and 19.2, when signal lights are off, it's usually bad news. However, if the Test/TST signal light stays on, this also indicates a problem with the cable modem.

Because the process of synchronizing the cable modem with the CATV network can take as long as 30 minutes if the cable modem is turned off, it should be left on at all times.

Checking Your Wiring Connections

Tables 19.1 and 19.2 indicate that the first place to check problems is with the power cord or power switch. If no power reaches the cable modem, no connection can take place. The next area to check, particularly if the cable, PC, or data lights are out, is to check the wiring going to and from the cable modem. Figure 19.3 compares loose and properly connected coaxial cables on the rear of a 3Com "sharkfin" cable modem. Figure 19.4 compares loose and properly-connected Cat 5 Ethernet cables attached to a typical Ethernet card.

FIGURE 19.3

Loose (left) and properly connected (right) coaxial cables.

Loose coaxial cable; note large amount of screw thread visible.

Coaxial cable correctly screwed into place

FIGURE 19.4

Loose (top) and properly connected (bottom) Cat 5 Ethernet cables. Note the link light is lit only when the cable is properly connected and both ends of the cable are attached to devices which are turned on.

Loose cable; lock is not engaged.

Link light; it is visible only when the cable is properly attached and both ends of the cable are energized.

Fully inserted cable; lock is engaged.

If you need to replace the Cat 5 cable running from your cable modem to your computer or router, be sure to choose a cable that's at least as long or longer than the cable included with the cable modem; using a shorter cable will reduce the power level in the cable and could cause signal loss. Also, be sure to check the cable type. While most cable modems use a standard Cat 5 cable, some might use a crossover cable (which reverses the order of some wire pairs). Both types are available at most computer stores and departments. Installing the wrong type of cable will prevent data transfer between the cable modem and your computer or router.

Coaxial Cable Troubleshooting

If your coaxial cable connections to the cable modem appear sound, look at the cable itself. If there are several splices in the cable, this can cause a loss of signal quality from the CATV network to your cable modem. If the cable has cracks or tears in the outer jacket, it should be replaced.

To determine whether the cable running to the cable modem is at fault, disconnect the splitter from the CATV cable coming into your location and connect the cable modem directly to the CATV cable. If you can now synchronize with the network and make a connection, the splitter or the cable running from the splitter is defective and should be replaced.

Properly connected CATV cables should be immune to weather problems, but if you find that you're having loss of connection problems with your cable modem (or cable TV, for that matter) when it rains or snows, you may have unprotected connections between cable segments or bad splices on your cable. Ask the cable provider to check your outside cable and its connection to the fiber-optic cable for problems. Rubber boots and tape can be used to secure splices and connections against weather problems.

Correcting Cable Modem Problems

Loose cables, or using the wrong cable between the cable modem and the Ethernet card in the computer or the router's WAN port, will cause loss of signal. Loss of signal will result in most of the problems listed in Tables 19.1 and 19.2. If the cables are the correct type, appear in good condition, and are attached correctly to the cable modem and the PC, check the Ethernet adapter or USB port on the PC as discussed in the following sections. A self-test failure can sometimes be cured by resetting the cable modem by either pressing the reset switch on the cable modem (if available) or by turning off or unplugging the cable modem, waiting for 30 seconds, and turning it on/plugging it back in again. If the self-test continues to fail, contact your ISP or cable modem vendor for repair or replacement.

If your modem spontaneously reboots, which will cause it to go through the POST and force it to resynchronize to the cable network, look for interference sources nearby, such as power spikes coming from refrigerators, vacuum cleaners, air conditioners, or EMI (electromagnetic interference) such as cordless phones.

Troubleshooting Your PC's Ethernet and USB Connections

If your computer's connections to the cable modem malfunction, your ability to get online with any cable modem is non-existent. Problems with your Ethernet and USB connections can come from any of the following sources:

- Hardware and device driver failure
- Incorrect port configurations
- Resource conflicts with another device

Here's how to solve these problems.

Troubleshooting Ethernet Port/Card Problems

If the Ethernet port, card, or adapter has failed, you may be able to determine this from one of the following symptoms:

- The signal lights on the back of the Ethernet card aren't lit up when the computer is on and a cable from a working cable modem, switch, or router is plugged into the card (see Figure 19.5).
- The Windows Device Manager doesn't list the card, or displays the card with a red X across the card listing.
- The card is not displayed as a PCI/PnP device when you turn on your system.
- The Mac TCP/IP Control Panel doesn't display a MAC address for your Ethernet card or port.

If your Ethernet card fits into a PCI, ISA, or PC Card (notebook computer) slot, you can replace it. In Windows, be sure to remove it from the Device Manager before you physically remove the card from your system. Be sure to install the correct drivers for your new card.

If you replace your Ethernet card or port with a new Ethernet card or new motherboard with a built-in Ethernet port and your system can't connect afterwards, you may need to call your cable Internet provider and provide them with the MAC address of your new Ethernet port. Some providers tie their service to the MAC address, which is unique to each Ethernet device. Windows users can display the MAC address with WINIPCFG or IPCONFIG; MacOS users can open the TCP/IP Control Panel to view the MAC address.

If your Ethernet port is built into your system and you have an open PCI expansion slot, you may be able to install a replacement 10BaseT or 10/100 Ethernet card as an alternative to repairing your system or replacing your motherboard. If you use a notebook computer with a built-in Ethernet port, you can use a PC Card-based 10BaseT or 10/100 Ethernet adapter as a replacement. Windows-compatible network cards are widely available; MacOS-compatible cards can be purchased from dealers specializing in Mac hardware.

Tip

If you use an iMAC, your Ethernet port is built in and you have no expansion slots. If your Ethernet port fails, you must get your computer fixed or use your USB port to connect to the cable modem if this configuration is supported by your cable modem.

While hardware failures can take place, it is more likely, especially with Windows-based systems, that problems with your Ethernet port or adapter come from a resource conflict with another card or from a problem with your drivers. The Windows Device Manager, shown earlier in Figure 19.4, can help you determine which of these is the problem.

To open the Windows Device Manager:

1. Click Start, Settings, Control Panel.

2. Click the System icon. The General tab (listing Windows version and RAM) is displayed.

3. Click the Device Manager tab if you use Windows 9x/Me; if you use Windows 2000/XP, click the Hardware tab, then the Device Manager button.

4. You will see a listing of hardware similar to Figure 19.5. A circled ! (exclamation mark) symbol next to a device indicates a conflict with other devices or a driver problem. A red X indicates the device has failed or has been disabled.

FIGURE 19.5

The Linksys EtherPCI LAN Card has a configuration problem, as shown by the yellow ! symbol.

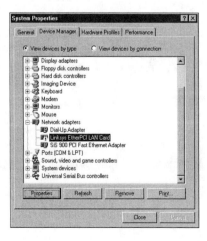

5. Click the Properties button to check the Device Status. If the message indicates a driver problem, use the Update Driver button shown in Figure 19.6 to install new drivers for the card; some versions of Windows call this button the Reinstall Driver button. If a conflict with another device is indicated, click the Resources tab to see the details. You may be able to change the settings of either the Ethernet card or the other device to resolve the conflict.

6. After installing new drivers or changing settings, you may need to restart the system.

Windows' plug-and-play hardware detection and configuration make resource conflicts unlikely, unless you have installed a non-plug-and-play card or have made other manual changes to hardware settings. Windows 95 is more likely to have hardware conflicts than Windows 98 or newer versions of Windows.

FIGURE 19.6

Using the Update Driver button to resolve a problem with a Linksys EtherPCI LAN Card.

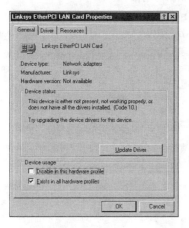

Macintosh users should reinstall the extensions used for their built-in Ethernet port or Ethernet card if a software problem is suspected.

Troubleshooting USB Port Problems

Many late-model cable modems don't require you to install or use an Ethernet port because they can connect to the built-in USB port found on virtually all recent PCs. Although connecting the cable modem to the USB port is more convenient than opening up your system to install a 10BaseT or 10/100 Ethernet card, there are some disadvantages:

- The current version of USB, USB 1.1, is slower than an Ethernet card
- The high amount of traffic going to and from your cable modem may cause other USB devices connected to your system to slow down
- Some versions of Windows may not support a particular USB device

Some of the problems you may encounter with USB include:

■ USB port not enabled in system BIOS

■ USB drivers not loaded

■ Not enough power to USB port

If you don't get a connection light showing on your cable modem when you plug it into a USB port, your USB port may not be enabled or working. Check the following:

■ Windows version—You must be using Windows 98 or greater. See the section "Learning What Operating System Your Computer Is Using" in Chapter 3 **(p. 33)**, "Making Sure You're Ready for Cable Internet Service," to learn how to determine what version of Windows you are using.

■ USB port status—Open the Windows Device Manager as discussed in the section on Ethernet troubleshooting earlier in this chapter and scroll down to the bottom of the hardware listing. You should see a category called Universal Serial Bus controllers. Click the plus (+) sign next to this category to display its contents (see Figure 19.7). A red X indicates the device has been disabled; check its Properties sheet for an option to re-enable it. A yellow ! sign indicates a driver or conflict problem.

FIGURE 19.7

This system has properly-working USB ports and a generic USB hub (an external device which allows you to plug multiple USB devices into a single port on your system).

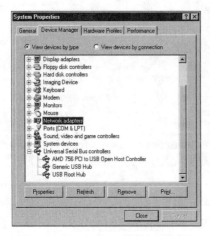

■ USB hub power issues—Because many external devices connect to the USB port, and most systems have only two, four, or six USB ports, many users prefer to attach multiple devices to a USB hub. Most standalone USB hubs come with a small AC adapter to make sure that all USB devices have plenty of power; such hubs are called self-powered hubs. USB hubs built into monitors, keyboards, and other devices are usually bus-powered, drawing power from your system's USB ports. Bus-powered hubs may not provide adequate power for some devices. If your cable modem won't work when you plug it in through a bus-powered hub, connect it directly to a USB port on your system, or purchase a self-powered hub and use it for your cable modem and other USB devices.

Tip

If the Universal Serial Bus category is not displayed in the Windows Device Manager but your system has USB ports present, they have been disabled in the system BIOS. See your system documentation for details on how to access your system BIOS (you normally press a particular key such as Del to access the setup program) and enable these ports. If your system originally used Windows 95 and was later upgraded to Windows 98 or another Windows version which supports USB ports, the ports may have been disabled during system assembly at the factory.

Troubleshooting Firewall Problems

As discussed in Chapter 13, "Firewalls and Your PC," firewalls provide a vital level of protection against intruders. However, an improperly configured firewall could stop all traffic or not allow programs you want to use with the Internet to connect. Here are typical problems and solutions:

- You can't connect to any sites—Your firewall's traffic-blocking feature may be enabled. For example, ZoneAlarm can be configured to block all Internet traffic when the screen saver is on, or on demand; this feature is called the Internet Lock. Turn off the traffic-blocking feature and try again. If your firewall doesn't offer automatic traffic blocking, it may have crashed or be incorrectly configured. Disable it completely and try the connection again. Reload or reconfigure your firewall software if you can connect only when the firewall is disabled.

- Your new Internet-ready program can't connect, but existing browsers and other programs will connect—Your firewall may need to be "taught" about your program. Some firewall programs detect attempted connections to the Internet from new programs and will not let them make a connection until you allow the connection. Others need to be manually configured to allow the program to access the Internet.

- A program that could previously connect to the Internet is now being blocked by the firewall—Some firewall programs let you grant multiple levels of Internet access to a program. For example, Zone Alarm lets you grant one-time permission to connect or every-time permission to connect to any given program, but if that program tries to act as a server (sometimes required when a program is receiving updates from the Internet), you need to grant that level of access specific permission. This is normal behavior. Just be sure to grant the level of permission that's appropriate to the program and what it normally does. This could also happen if you updated the program to a new version. Because many firewalls carefully check a program's file size, date, and other characteristics to prevent a Trojan Horse program from masquerading as a program that has been granted Internet access, an updated program may appear to be "new." Set the firewall to allow the updated program appropriate permission to access the Internet.

If none of the issues brought up here resemble your problem or just fail to fix it, you should contact technical support the developer of your firewall.

What If It's Not Your Fault? Provider and General Internet Problems

The connection problems listed in Tables 19.1 and 19.2 aren't always traceable to your equipment. Here's how to tell if the problems are beyond your control.

- ▩ Your cable TV is also out—A problem with the CATV signal feed to your neighborhood will take out both your cable TV and your cable modem because the same fiber-optic cable services both.

Note | Before you assume the entire network has gone down, check the condition of your CATV/cable modem splitter. If the coaxial cables going into the splitter are loose or damaged, this could disrupt either or both of your cable-based networks.

- ▩ Your cable modem is unable to synchronize with the CATV network, and you have verified that the cables are secure—If the cable modem side of the CATV network has failed, this is a typical result. Reset the cable modem and try again to be sure the problem is outside your home.

- ▩ Some Web sites respond properly, but others are slow or time out—This indicates a problem with either the Internet as a whole or particular sites. Major disasters, such as the Baltimore railroad tunnel fire in the summer of 2001, can affect Internet backbones. (Major service provider UUNet ran much of its traffic through the fiber-optic lines in that tunnel.) The rerouting around failed backbones that is a basic feature of the Internet can slow down access in general or to some sites. Similarly, the destruction of the World Trade Center by terrorists in September 2001 caused some Web sites to be completely down for a day or longer.

To help you determine if the problems are with your system or exist outside your home or office, it pays to understand the role that Transport Control Protocol/Internet Protocol (TCP/IP) plays in the transmission of data around the Internet.

What TCP/IP Is and How You Use It

Every computer on the Internet, whether it's a PC running Windows, a Mac, a Linux box, or whatever, must use the protocol suite (a collection of software) called TCP/IP to connect to the Internet, send data, and receive data from Web sites and e-mail servers. You can compare TCP/IP to a universal language for computer networking. TCP/IP has many elements, but you don't need to understand all of them to use TCP/IP.

IP Addresses

How much do you need to understand? The first part of TCP/IP that you need to understand is the IP address, which is used to identify your computer online.

IP addresses are of two types:

- Private
- Public

Private IP addresses are used on networks, such as the ones you create with Internet Connection Sharing, other proxy server/gateway software, or routers. These addresses are converted into a public IP address whenever you access the Internet. Private IP addresses make your computer less vulnerable to hacking and attacks, but require special configuration to allow some online games and programs—such as NetMeeting—to work. Public IP addresses need no conversion, but make your computer more vulnerable to attack.

Whereas some cable Internet vendors provide a fixed IP address for your computer, others configure the cable modem with a fixed IP address and use the cable modem to assign your computer a dynamic (changing) IP address. Regardless of the type of IP address you have, your computer must be configured correctly if you want to go online.

Configuring Your System

In most cases, your cable ISP will provide you with a setup CD-ROM that will install the correct software and settings for your system. If you use Windows 9x or Me, you can use the WINIPCFG program described in Chapter 18, "Setting Up a Home

Network for Sharing Your Internet Connection," to view and record these settings as a backup. Use IPCONFIG with Windows NT/2000/XP to view and record these settings. With MacOS, open the Apple menu, select Control Panels, select TCP/IP, and note the setting for IP Address.

If your cable ISP requires you to configure your connection manually, follow the sequence given in the "ICS Client Setup" section of Chapter 15 (**p. 237**) and substitute the settings that your ISP provided for either manual or automatic IP addressing.

Note

After you change TCP/IP or other network settings, you must reboot your computer if prompted before the settings will take effect.

Reinstalling your setup software is often the fastest and best way to reconfigure your system in the event that original settings are lost.

Tip

Be sure to have your operating system CD-ROM handy if you need to reinstall your cable Internet setup software because some of the files needed are operating-system specific. If you use automatic update features such as Windows Update, some of the operating system files on your computer may be newer than the ones coming from the CD-ROM. Keep the newer files if you get a warning during installation that you're about to replace a newer file with an older one.

Troubleshooting Problems with WINIPCFG, Ping, and Tracert

If you have problems with your cable Internet connection, programs that display your current TCP/IP configuration, check your connection with the Internet, and check the routing of your connection with a given Web site or server are very valuable. Windows 9x and Me include the following diagnostic programs:

- WINIPCFG—Previously discussed; Windows 2000 and Windows XP users can use IPCONFIG to perform the same tasks
- Ping—Included in all Windows versions and in MacOS X; users of older MacOS versions must download a third-party utility

Tip

For a wide range of Ping and other useful Mac utilities, see the following Web site: www.macosarchives.com.

Using WINIPCFG to Troubleshoot IP Address Problems

Every computer needs a valid IP address to go online. If your computer is set to obtain an IP address from the cable modem (or from a gateway computer or router), you could see any one of a wide number of IP addresses. However, if you see any of the following addresses, you have a problem:

- 169.254.xxx.xxx—Addresses in this series are used only when your computer is configured to obtain an IP address from a DHCP server (such as the cable modem, gateway PC, or router) and the DHCP server couldn't be reached. Because this address wasn't received from the DHCP server in your network, you can't get online until you get a valid IP address. Solution: Turn off your PC; make sure the cable modem, gateway computer, or router is on and running properly; check your cables between your PC and the cable modem, gateway PC, or router; and then restart your computer.

- 0.0.0.0—Don't worry about seeing this unless you can't access the Internet. Some older versions of Windows—such as Windows NT 4.0—use this setting to enable DHCP addressing. Solution: Make sure that your network adapter is connected and working and that you have installed the correct drivers for the card.

- 192.168.100.xxx—The cable modem is working, but it has lost connection with the cable network. Solution: See the Tips earlier in this chapter to re-establish contact with the cable network.

- No IP address—Solution: Make sure that your network adapter is connected and working and that you have installed the correct drivers for the card. If you need to reinstall TCP/IP, do so after reinstalling the card.

Using Ping to Troubleshoot IP Connection and Driver Problems

Ping is used to send a signal to a specified IP address or Web site and receive a response back from that address or Web site. You can ping your own computer, your router or gateway, your cable modem, or your ISP.

Note | Some Web sites won't respond to Ping for security reasons.

The Ping command is run from the command line in Windows; MacOS users should check the instructions for MacOS X or for their preferred third-party Ping utility.

To open a command-line window in Windows 9x/Me:

1. Click Start, Run.

2. Type command and click OK.

To ping a particular address, type Ping *xxx.xxx.xxx.xxx* and press Enter. (Replace *xxx.xxx.xxx.xxx* with the actual IP address.) To ping a particular Web site, type Ping *Websitename* and press Enter. (Replace *Websitename* with the actual Web site.)

Here's how to use Ping to check your cable Internet connection:

1. To make sure your system has TCP/IP installed, Ping 127.0.0.1 (also called the local loopback)—Regardless of the IP address assigned your computer by your ISP or DHCP server, your system uses this IP address for testing. If your system responds as seen in Figure 19.8, you have the TCP/IP protocol installedb. If you get an "unknown host" message, reinstall TCP/IP and configure it as directed by your cable ISP, your gateway/proxy server program, or your router vendor.

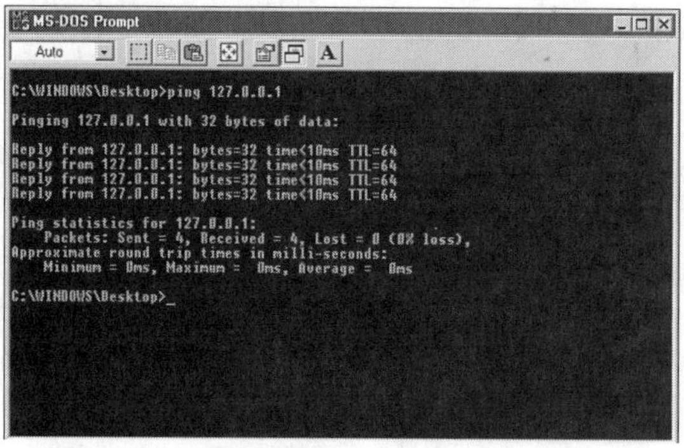

FIGURE 19.8

Using Ping to test your own system's TCP/IP software.

2. To see if you can connect with your cable modem, ping its IP address—If you connect via a gateway or proxy server computer or a router, ping its IP address first, then your cable modem's IP address. If you are unable to ping a particular device, check cabling, and then check your IP address setup.

3. To see if you can connect with the Internet, ping a favorite Web site as in Figure 19.9.

Error messages you might see include the following:

■ Unknown host—You might have misspelled the IP address or Web site, but if you spelled them correctly, this error indicates that you can't reach the address or Web site specified. Check cabling, and then IP configuration.

■ Host timed out—A normal message for some sites that don't respond to pings for security reasons; if all IP addresses you ping display this information, your Internet connection has a speed problem beyond your control.

FIGURE 19.9

Using Ping to
test your connec-
tion to the
Internet; note
that Ping speci-
fied the Web
site, but the out-
put also lists the
site's IP address.

To troubleshoot problems with Internet Connection Sharing, third-party gateway and proxy-server programs, and routers, see Chapter 20, "Troubleshooting Internet Sharing."

To troubleshoot Webcams, Internet media players, and instant messaging programs, see Chapter 21, "Troubleshooting Internet Multimedia and Instant Messenger Software."

Summary

Connection problems can be caused by loose or damaged cables, Ethernet or USB port failures, cable modem failures, power problems, TCP/IP network configuration problems, firewall configuration or operation problems, and suspension/shutoff of your cable modem service.

Use the signal lights on your cable modem to determine the most likely causes of connection problems to the Internet, your computer, or your router.

The Windows Device Manager helps you track down possible problems with USB and Ethernet ports in your PC.

Firewalls may not allow new or updated programs to access the Internet until you specifically authorize them to do so.

You can use software utilities such as WINIPCFG, other IP configuration programs, and PING to check your TCP/IP configuration and check your Internet connection.

TROUBLESHOOTING
INTERNET SHARING

*C*HAPTER HIGHLIGHTS:

- Solving problems with Internet Connection Sharing
- Fixing problems with third-party connection programs
- Getting the glitches out of your router

Troubleshooting Computer-Based Sharing

Broadband addiction is a "disease" for which no computer user wants to find a cure. Going "cold turkey" when the sharing method you use has stopped working isn't good for anybody's nerves. This chapter helps you discover solutions for the most common problems with both software and router-based solutions.

Troubleshooting Internet Connection Sharing

Internet Connection Sharing (ICS), the free sharing software that's part of Windows 98 Second Edition (SE) and above, can be difficult to troubleshoot because of the extensive changes it makes to the computer that shares its Internet connection.

Problems with ICS can result from the following:

- Incorrect or incomplete installation of ICS components
- Problems with DHCP services that ICS supplies to client computers
- Damaged software files or Windows Registry keys

Microsoft does an excellent job of covering the major sources of problems on the ICS host computer under Windows 98 in the following knowledge-based articles:

- Description of Internet Connection Sharing Q234815
- How to Troubleshoot Internet Connection Sharing Problems Q238135

Search support.Microsoft.com by knowledge base article number to locate these articles.

Before installing ICS, print or save this and cross-referenced articles for reference.

Most descriptions of troubleshooting ICS deal with setting up the ICS host (server), which can be difficult, but there's a lot less coverage about client issues with ICS. This section takes a look at the neglectedparts of ICS troubleshooting.

A comprehensive checklist for both ICS host and ICS client configuration is available at www.dewassoc.com/support/networking/ics_4.htm.

You Can't Really Choose ICS as an Option During Windows 98 SE Installation

Although ICS is shown as an option during some types of installation, this is misleading. You must still run the ICS setup wizard from the Internet Connections tab or install ICS from scratch before it will work. For more details, see Microsoft Knowledge Base article #Q229829.

Why the Client PC Might Report a 169.254.0.x Number As Its IP Address

As you know from Chapter 15, "Using Microsoft Internet Connection Sharing," when ICS is set up in its default configuration, the DHCP server built into ICS automatically assigns client PCs IP addresses in the 192.168.0.x range (1–254). 192.168.0.1 is the IP address of the network adapter connected to the home network in the ICS host computer, and the rest of the network is assigned 192.168.0.2 and upward. A 169.254.0.x-series number is assigned by Windows 98 and Windows Me (and by MacOS 8.5 and 8.6) if the operating system can't find a real DHCP server on the network.

Although WINIPCFG can be used to release (give up the old address) and renew (get a new address) a dynamic IP address, this works only if the system can find a DHCP server on the network. This is seldom the case. It's usually necessary to shut down the system and restart it *after* you discover what the problem is.

Why can't an ICS client find a DHCP server on the network when the ICS host performs DHCP services? The simplest answer is usually that the ICS client was booted *before* the ICS host. Because ICS is a program that loads and runs in the system tray of Windows, it's not present until the computer has finished booting. If you shut down the ICS host, allow it to boot completely before starting up your ICS clients. In most cases, that solves the problem.

It's also possible for physical problems, such as loose or damaged cables or a bad network adapter, to cause a problem with receiving DHCP assignments of IP addresses. However, as with any computer problem, check the simple stuff first.

Microsoft has included a patch for Windows 98 on the Windows 98 CD-ROM. The patch enables you to release a 169.254.0.x address and renew to get a usable IP address without rebooting. The file is called IPAC_OFF.INF and it's located in the \Tools\MTSUTIL folder. Right-click it and select Install to change the appropriate value in the Windows 98 Registry.

For more information about this patch, see the following Web site (which also has a copy of the file in case you're using a Windows 98 installation that lacks this folder): www.jmu.edu/computing/helpdesk/patches/win98_dhcp.html.

ICS Fails on the Host After You Change a Network Card

ICS and the network cards in the host are intimately involved with each other. In fact, in Windows 98 SE, if you change a network card in your ICS host computer, ICS will usually fail and can't work again until you reinstall Windows 98 SE.

You can prevent this time-consuming problem from happening by following this procedure:

1. Uninstall ICS with the Windows Add/Remove Programs dialog box.
2. Remove your old network adapter from the Device Manager.
3. Remove the old adapter physically from the computer.
4. Install the new network adapter and its drivers.
5. Reinstall ICS with the Windows Add/Remove Programs dialog box.

As a rather painful alternative, you can edit the Registry and manually install some settings and some network components. See the following page at the Practically Networked Web site for details: `www.practicallynetworked.com/support/ics_avoid_98se_reinstall.htm`.

Other useful tips for getting ICS to work on both the host and client PCs are available at `www.practicallynetworked.com/sharing/ics/ics_troubleshoot.htm`.

ICS Won't Work with Internet Software that Requires Specific TCP Ports to Be Opened

ICS wasn't designed for sharing Internet services that require opening specific TCP ports. I never had a problem when I used ICS in my office because I used typical Web services such as Web browsing, FTP, and e-mail, which ICS is designed to support. However, game hosting, NetMeeting, and some other programs discussed in earlier chapters do require non-standard ports to be opened. This is difficult in ICS.

In fact, the process for mapping ports requires that you create an .INF file unless you are using the Windows 2000/Windows XP versions of ICS, which have built-in port mappings. If you don't think that creating an .INF file is much of a challenge, examine any .INF file on your system (they're used for installing hardware and software in Windows) and you will change your mind. Microsoft has a knowledge base article #Q231162 on the process; it comes with a extensively commented sample .INF file that you can use to get started, but if you're like me, you will take one look and be ready for an alternative.

A good free alternative is available online at the Practically Networked site: Harley Acheson's ICS Configuration. Use it to create custom port mappings for ICS after you get the required port information from the software vendor. Get it from `www.practicallynetworked.com/sharing/ics/icsconfiguration.htm`.

Follow the links on the page to find preconfigured .ICS configuration files for popular programs.

A Portable Computer Used with ICS at Home Won't Connect to the Network at the Office, or Vice-Versa

Chances are you have a notebook computer with a network port or card that you have tried to use at home and at the office. If you configure it for one environment, it won't work in the other. What's wrong?

Nothing, really, but it sure *looks* like a problem. Three different possibilities exist when you move your trusty portable PC between networks:

- You can't connect at all.
- You can access the Internet but not other shared resources (printers, shared folders, and so on).
- You have full access to the Internet and shared resources.

The first option is the most likely if you use ICS with a DHCP server at home (the default), but your office network uses a fixed IP address. The second option is the most likely if both your ICS network and the office network use a DHCP server. Because the workgroup name doesn't match, you can't access workgroup network resources, only the Internet. About the only way that you can have full access in both places is if both your home and your office are running versions of ICS that use the Home Networking Wizard, which sets the default workgroup name as MSHOME! That isn't likely.

The usual solution is to grumble loudly and reset your network configuration (which might mean peeking at another computer at home or the office for the correct settings or looking at a dog-eared cheat sheet you prepared after the first time this happened). With Windows 9x/Me, you must reboot after making any changes to your network configuration before they take effect, which wastes even more time.

An alternative is available: Globesoft makes the MultiNetwork Manager to provide an easy tabbed interface for changing network settings as needed for different home and office networks, including wireless networks. Try it at `www.globesoft.com/Common/frm_products.html` before you buy it.

Troubleshooting Third-Party Sharing Programs

As Chapter 16, "Using Other Computer-Based Internet Sharing Programs," demonstrates, the major third-party sharing programs are quite a bit different from ICS and also from each other. Thus, the troubleshooting tips in this section are symptomatic in nature: Contact the software vendor for more details about the solutions for each problem.

Clients Can't Locate the DHCP Server (169.254.0.x IP Addresses)

This behavior has three possible causes. Two of these are familiar if you read the ICS discussion earlier in this chapter:

- The server (which provides DHCP services) was booted after the workstations, so that DHCP services were not available at the right time. Make sure the server boots first.

- A hardware (cable or network adapter) failure prevented DHCP information from reaching the DHCP server. Tighten loose cables or replace defective hardware, and then reboot the server and the clients.

Some third-party sharing programs have additional possibilities:

- The sharing program wasn't configured to run at startup. Unless you don't want to offer Internet sharing at all times, you should configure the sharing program to run at startup. If you choose to run it only on demand, set the clients to have manually assigned IP addresses in the same subnet as the server PC.

- The client didn't load the proprietary client. If you configure the clients to use a proprietary program for connection to the server, the program should be configured to load automatically at client startup.

Clients Can't Access Some Web Resources, Although Web Browsing Works

Proxy-based programs might require you to manually enable newsgroups and e-mail. If you choose manual IP addressing, you might also need to provide detailed software configuration for common programs to every computer on the network.

This is an easy step to overlook, because ICS and some of the simpler third-party sharing programs don't require this amount of configuration. You might also need to configure TCP ports for Web applications that require the computer to work as a server (such as NetMeeting and some games).

Clients Can't Connect to the New Server After You Changed Sharing Software

The most likely reason for this is that clients still have the old IP address stored for their network adapter. Run WINIPCFG (Windows 9x/Me) or the equivalent program and release, and then renew the IP address.

Clients Can't Log On to Some Sites or at Particular Times of the Day

The most likely reason for this condition is if the server is set to enforce access limitations. If you have done this at home, you should enforce access limitations only after explaining the reasons to the family.

Unless you go a step further and set up startup passwords on different computers, a minor child could bypass restrictions on the "kids' PC" and use the adult's PC, because the restrictions are by IP address. You might also want to use manual IP addressing in such cases. If you use dynamic IP addressing, a computer where you want to restrict access might receive a different IP address that's unrestricted because other computers on the network aren't turned on (and therefore won't claim their normal IP addresses).

Troubleshooting Routers

Because routers work in a fashion similar to sharing software (they usually provide dynamic IP addresses to computers on the network), the symptoms of common problems are familiar if you have read earlier parts of this chapter, although the causes might vary.

Can't Connect to Web Server in Router to Configure It

If you previously used a proxy server sharing program or other program that used special scripts or settings in the Web browser, reset your browser to connect directly with the Internet. With Microsoft Internet Explorer, click Tools, Internet Options, Connections, LAN Settings. Clear all checkmarks and fields, and then click OK. Retry the connection.

If your browser is configured correctly, make sure you have connected your PC to the router correctly and you are using the correct type of IP address settings for the router.

Can't Connect to a Particular Cable Internet Service

Even though cable Internet service is provided by a relative handful of companies (@Home and RoadRunner are the two titans), variations in cable modem hardware, cable network configuration, and local partner preference make for a bewildering array of possible issues in using a router to connect to a cable modem.

Part of the problem is caused by the fact that routers aren't PCs, and many cable Internet service providers use a setup CD to configure the system. Here are general suggestions to get you through difficulties:

- If possible, before you buy a particular router, see if the vendor's Web site addresses the problems you might have in connecting it to your cable Internet service. For example, the FAQ page for my D-Link DI-704 router/switch has clear step-by-step instructions for both @Home and RoadRunner cable modem services.

- Firmware updates for your router and cable modem might be necessary; check with the vendors to see what the latest firmware releases are and what they do.

- MAC address cloning (telling your router to use the same MAC address as your network adapter) is a good idea, even if you aren't sure the cable Internet provider is tracking this information.

Clients Connected to the Router Have DHCP Addresses in the 169.254.0.x Range

If the router, cable and network hardware, and client PCs are all working, this should never happen. If it does, check the following:

- The router's power connection and power switch—If the router has lost power, it can't assign anybody IP addresses. Make sure the router is in a secure location.

- Loose or damaged network cables and network adapters—As with other networks that have DHCP addressing errors, failures here will also cause problems.

Duplicate IP Address Errors on Network

If you used a fixed IP address on your network card that is connected to your cable modem, you need to change it to a dynamic IP address after you configure the router with the IP address information. If you forget, both the router and your computer will have the same IP address.

After you configure your PC to use a server-assigned IP address, reboot your computer so it can get a working IP address from the DHCP server in the router.

If you decided to assign your own IP addresses to each computer, you probably have duplicated the address on the network. Check the configuration on each PC until you find the problem and then correct it.

Can't Connect with the Internet from Any PC After the Router Is Installed

If you properly configured the router, check your cabling. Make sure the cable modem is connected to the WAN or Network port on the router, and that the client PCs are connected to the LAN ports (usually numbered 1, 2, 3, and so forth).

What if you're not sure you configured the router correctly? Connect only one PC to the router, fire up your browser, and double-check your settings for host, domain, gateway, IP address, and so on. As with any other issue in computers, mistyping doesn't work. Every item of data must be exactly right or it won't work.

If you're not sure you have the router configured correctly and want to start over, check the documentation for information on resetting the router to its factory setting.

Some Web Programs Won't Work After the Router Is Installed

The router acts as a firewall for incoming traffic. Programs such as NetMeeting and others that require you to open TCP ports require that you use your router's port-mapping features. You will need to know the TCP ports used by your software before you can start.

If your program requires more open port ranges than your browser can allocate (usually 10 is the limit) or if you want to use a program such as NetMeeting which uses dynamic port allocation), you will need to use the router's DMZ feature. DMZ turns off the firewall feature completely for the specified system, so you should use a personal firewall program so that computer has some protection. I prefer ZoneAlarm or ZoneAlarm Pro.

Check with your router vendor for specific instructions to configure the router for popular programs such as NetMeeting.

Troubleshooting Router Hardware and Cabling Problems

As discussed in Chapter 17, "Router Your Way to Internet Sharing," and 18, "Setting Up a Home Network for Sharing Your Internet Connection," routers are an increasingly popular way to share a single cable Internet connection with several users. Normally, the router's operation is transparent: Each computer behaves as if it's the only computer connected to the cable modem. If the connection fails, though, check the following:

- Power to router—Most low-cost routers use a small AC adapter which could be dislodged from the wall socket or surge protector; check the surge protector's on-off switch if the AC adapter appears to be connected to both the router and the surge protector.

- Router configuration—If the router has been reset to its factory configuration, the settings needed to go online have been lost; open the router's configuration screens and check the settings against the settings required by your cable Internet provider. Reset the router's configuration to the settings needed to get online. Be sure to record the settings for re-use, and use a password to prevent tampering with the router's configuration.

If the router can't retain custom settings, its non-volatile RAM may be defective; contact the manufacturer for return and repair information.

- Incorrect cable connections—If you have a failure with just one computer connected to a router with a built-in Ethernet switch, you may have plugged its cable into the uplink port instead of a normal LAN port. The uplink port is used to connect an additional hub or switch to the router/switch device, and can't be used for additional computers. Unplug the cable from the computer from the uplink port and connect it to a LAN port. If you're out of ports, buy a switch, connect a standard port on the switch to the uplink port on the router/switch, plug some of the computers into the new switch, and leave the rest connected to the router/switch.

The uplink port often shares its internal wiring with one of the LAN ports on a router/switch, switch, or hub. For example, if the uplink port is next to LAN port #1, you can use either the uplink port or LAN port #1. If you use the uplink port to add a switch for more capacity, unplug the cable from port #1 on the router/switch and plug it into a port on the new switch.

■ Incorrect cable type—Crossover Category 5 cables (which reverse some of the wire pairs at one end of the cable) are used only in special circumstances, such as for connecting two computers without using a hub or switch, or between some cable modems and a PC. If you use the wrong cable type between a computer and the hub, switch or router, the computer with the wrong type of cable can't connect to the network. If you use the wrong cable type between the cable modem and the router, no one can access the Internet. If you have a cable modem that uses a crossover cable, make sure you mark that cable carefully to avoid confusing it with normal network cables.

Troubleshooting Special Connectivity Problems

If you have a one-way cable modem or a MacOS-based network, you have special network issues not already addressed. Here are some answers.

Can't Connect with Your One-Way Cable Modem

One-way cable modems that use a separate dial-up modem can't be used with a router. Check the Telco Return page at Practically Networked for tips on sharing and proxy server programs that will work with your one-way cable modem:

`www.practicallynetworked.com/sharing/telcoreturn.htm`.

AppleTalk Problems with Cable Modems

It's common for AppleTalk-based networks to have problems co-existing with cable modems, especially with DOCSIS-compliant cable modems now being used by many cable Internet service providers. Installing a broadband router will allow AppleTalk to work reliably, prevent it from stopping your cable modem, and allow all your users to access the Internet. For details see `www.macfixit.com/extras/appletalkaccess.shtml`.

As an alternative to AppleTalk, consider changing your Apple-based network to TCP/IP Open Transport. You will need to use TCP/IP to connect your Mac to ICS and other sharing programs which run on a Windows-based server.

Summary

Computer-based sharing can fail for a variety of reasons. When ICS or other computer-based sharing programs are used, the computer with the shared Internet connection must be turned on and have the sharing software loaded before others can connect to the Internet.

Microsoft ICS needs third-party software to map specific TCP ports for use with NetMeeting or other specialized software. Other types of sharing software and routers can map specific TCP ports for certain programs. If the correct TCP ports aren't available, the program will stop working.

The IP address release/renew feature can sometimes be used to restore a lost connection to a DHCP server, but in many cases you need to reboot the clients after the DHCP server has finished booting.

Incorrect router configuration or lost settings can cause all users on a home network to fail to connect. However, if sharing software fails, in some cases the computer with the Internet connection may still be able to reach the Internet. Incorrect cabling between PCs and the router or between the router and the cable modem can also cause connection failures.

One-way cable modems can't use routers and should use connection-sharing software instead. MacOS systems which use AppleTalk should use a router instead of using sharing software.

21

TROUBLESHOOTING INTERNET MULTIMEDIA AND INSTANT MESSENGER SOFTWARE

CHAPTER HIGHLIGHTS:

- How to fix common problems with Webcams, media players, and IM clients
- How to tell whether you have a hardware or software problem
- Where to get updates and replacement drivers for your Webcam
- How to make sure the automatic update features of your software are enabled

Troubleshooting Webcams

Webcams are a marvel of simplicity when they work. When they don't, well, let's just say that they can be extremely annoying if you're just dying to say "hi!" to a distant loved one or send out a video e-mail for a birthday or holiday and can't.

Some of the common problems with Webcams include the following:

- Webcam is not detected.
- Webcam can't capture video.
- Webcam picture is fuzzy.
- Webcam can't save video clip.
- Webcam can't e-mail video clip.
- Webcam can't deliver video e-mail.
- Webcam can't open video e-mail.
- Webcam can't be viewed by the other user in a video conference using NetMeeting or other software.

Webcam Is Not Detected

Most Webcams plug in via the USB port. If your Webcam was working, and now it has stopped, check the following:

- The USB connector—Make sure it's plugged all the way into the USB port.
- The USB hub—If you plug your Webcam into a hub, make sure its powerpack is connected to a working AC adapter and that the hub is plugged securely into a USB port on the computer.

If the Webcam is the first USB device you have used on your Windows PC and it isn't recognized, you need to make sure that your PC meets the following requirements:

- Windows 98/Me or Windows 2000/XP
- Drivers are available for your Webcam and Windows version
- USB ports are enabled

If you can't find drivers tailored specifically to Windows Me or XP, keep in mind that Windows Me can use most Windows 98 drivers, and Windows XP can use most Windows 2000 drivers.

To determine the version of Windows in use, do the following:

1. Open the Control Panel (click Start, Settings, Control Panel).

2. Open the System icon by double-clicking it.

3. The General tab (the default tab) displays the version of Windows in use, as in Figure 21.1.

FIGURE 21.1

This system is using Windows 98 Second Edition, which supports USB devices.

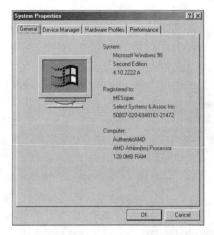

Although some late versions of Windows 95 support some USB devices, most USB devices require Windows 98 and above. Upgrading your Windows 95 system to Windows 98 SE, Windows Me, or Windows XP is recommended if you plan to use USB devices extensively.

If you have verified that your system is using the correct version of Windows, the next step is to determine if the USB ports are enabled and working correctly. After opening the System properties sheet as described earlier in this section, click the Device Manager tab (Windows 98/Me) or Hardware, Device Manager (Windows 2000/XP) to view the devices installed in the system. Click the plus (+) sign next to Imaging Device to see your Webcam, and click the plus (+) sign next to USB devices to see your USB devices, as in Figure 21.2.

If a USB port or Webcam has a red X next to its icon, it has been disabled. Check the properties for the device and re-enable it. You might need to restart your computer. If a USB port or Webcam has a yellow exclamation mark (!) next to it, it's not working because of a driver problem or hardware conflict. Check the properties for the device and solve the problem listed.

Imaging device category   Webcam

FIGURE 21.2

The Windows
Device Manager
displays a prop-
erly installed
Webcam and
USB controllers.

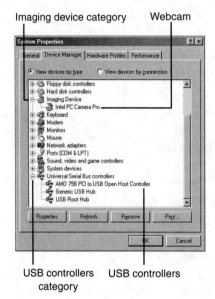

USB controllers   USB controllers
    category

Webcam Can't Capture Video

If the Webcam appears to be installed correctly in Device Manager but won't capture
video, check the following:

- Another program might already be using the Webcam—Close any other program that can use the Webcam, such as video capture programs, IM clients,
  NetMeeting, and so on, and try again.

- Turn the Webcam on—You might need to press a Power button on the
  Webcam to turn it on with some programs.

- Open the lens cover—Make sure you haven't left a lens cap on or closed the
  shutter. If so, simply remove the cap or open the shutter and check to see if
  the preview window now displays video.

- Check the battery power—If your Webcam doubles as a digital camera, it
  might need a new set of batteries.

- Check for a software error—A software error message about a missing or cor-
  rupt driver file can sometimes be corrected by closing all programs and
  restarting the computer.

If a software error is displayed every time you try to capture video, your video-capture
software or Webcam driver software is damaged. Remove the software or driver, reboot,
and then reinstall it from the original CD-ROM. Then check for an update online at the
Webcam vendor's Web site to be sure you're working with the most up-to-date driver or
software.

Webcam Picture Is Fuzzy

If your Webcam displays and captures video, but the video is fuzzy, check the following:

■ Camera out of focus—Webcams, unlike point-and-shoot or single-lens-reflex film or digital cameras, generally have manual-focus lenses. Turn the dial until the part of the picture you want in focus is as sharp as possible.

 Because of an optical phenomenon called *depth of field*, it's impossible to get all the objects at widely different distances from a camera lens in sharp focus at the same time.

■ Dirty camera lens—If your Webcam is on a computer that is used by curious children with sticky fingers, there might be "gunk" on the camera lens. Moisten a lens-cleaning tissue with a bit of lens cleaning fluid and wipe with a circular motion to clean the lens.

 Close the shutter or lens cap on the Webcam when it's not in use. If you have young children who like to fiddle with things, slide the Webcam out of its holder and store it when you're not using it.

■ Low-resolution video viewed in a large window—Whereas high-end Webcams are designed to capture a 640×480 window, low-end and older Webcams are designed to capture a much smaller area. If you set the playback window size larger than the camera's resolution, the video player must enlarge the pixels to fill the window, and the playback quality will be reduced. Note that today's monitors are often set to 800×600, 1024×768, or higher resolutions, so that even high-resolution Webcams can't create a full-screen image.

■ Camera optimized for frame rate, not image quality—To create an acceptably sized video e-mail file, you must choose between high-quality images or a fast (at or near 30 frames-per-second) frame rate; optimizing for fast frame rate reduces image quality.

 If you want to optimize for image quality without a lot of jerky movement in your video e-mails, remind your subjects to sit or stand still and avoid fast, jerky movements.

Also, make sure the room is well-lit. Because Webcams use manual-focus lenses, they use a small aperture to increase the depth of field. However, small apertures let less light through to the sensor which creates the image. More light allows for faster frame rates and high image quality.

Webcam Can't Save Video Clip

If you can't save the video clip to disk after you have captured it, check the following:

- Not enough space left on the target drive—By default, Windows programs save everything to the C: drive, even if you have additional drive letters. If your software lets you select the drive to use for saving files, save your clip to a drive letter (such as a CD-RW drive set for read/write access or a removable-media drive) with enough room to hold it.

- Software problem—If you see a software error onscreen, retry the operation. If it is displayed again, reinstall the program and try again.

- Network drive not available—If you use a shared drive on a home network and don't log in to the network when you start the computer, you can't access the drive. Save the video clip to a local drive, log off the computer, and log back on; don't press the Esc key when asked to logon!

- Drive not ready—If the computer with the shared drive isn't turned on or hasn't finished booting, you can't save to it until it's ready. Make sure a local drive has media with enough free space for your video clip inserted.

Webcam Can't E-mail Video Clip

If you're ready to e-mail your video clip and you can't send it, check the following:

- No connection to the Internet—If you use a one-way cable modem, don't forget to dial up your connection first. If you use a two-way cable modem, check to see if you can ping a Web site or display a Web page you haven't looked at today.

- E-mail server down—If your video e-mail program delivers mail to a special e-mail server, it might be down. Look for an error message with details, and try again later.

Remember: Save your video e-mail before you send it in case the sending process has a problem.

- E-mail client not properly configured—If your video e-mail program uses your normal e-mail client to send video e-mails, make sure you can send regular e-mail. Check the documentation to see if you must create a special e-mail account or settings for sending your video e-mails.

Sending an e-mail to yourself is a great way to see if your e-mail software is working. Even though the e-mail is addressed to you, it still has to be sent out of your system to the outgoing e-mail server. That server sends the email to the incoming e-mail server, which then delivers it back to you. If this doesn't work, your e-mail client setup or the software itself has a problem.

Webcam Can't Deliver Video E-Mail

If your video e-mail is sent, but can't be delivered, check the following:

- Incorrect address—You will know this has occurred if the e-mail *bounces* back to you as undeliverable. If your video e-mail program uses its own e-mail server instead of your normal e-mail client, check with the vendor to find out what the software does if you specify an incorrect address.

- Recipient mailbox full—Many home users use e-mail servers that can handle only 1–2MB of e-mail total. If their mailbox already holds the limit, or if your e-mail (including the video clip) is bigger than the amount of space remaining in their e-mail box, your messages will bounce back as undeliverable.

- Video clip too large for e-mail service—Many e-mail services enforce a 1MB maximum size per message including attachments. Check the size of your video clip after you prepare it for mailing; if it's too large, trim away some of it to reduce its size or create a shorter video clip.

Keep your e-mail box as empty as possible to avoid messages bouncing back to your friends and co-workers. If your e-mail server has a capacity limit or a per-message size limit, let friends, family, and co-workers know.

- Recipient can't handle file attachments—Some e-mail only services are for text e-mail only. If you can send messages without attachments and they arrive, but attachments bounce, the e-mail service can't handle them.

You can create a text e-mail message that can be sent to people who can't accept file attachments if you UUEncode the file; the receiver must use a program that can perform the Uudecode process to re-create the file. To learn more about how to use the popular WinZip file archiving program to create Uuencode files and convert them back to their original form, see the Web site www.winzip.com/uuencode.htm.

Webcam Can't Open Video E-Mail

If your problem is that you can't open a video e-mail file, check these solutions:

■ **File was created with the uncompression option disabled**—Some video e-mail programs allow you to disable the inclusion of the uncompression program to save a bit of disk space. This works if you have previously received video e-mail in the same format and still have the files on your system, because the new video e-mail uses the uncompression program included in the previous files. However, if you have never received files in this format before, or you have deleted previously received files, you won't be able to open the video e-mail.

Always include the decompression program with any video e-mails you send, and keep at least one video e-mail of each type of video e-mail you receive.

■ **File was damaged in transmission**—If the file was corrupted during the trip from the sender's computer to yours, you won't be able to open it. Windows Explorer uses distinct icons for different types of .EXE files, depending on the contents of each file. If the video e-mail file has a plain blue-and-white icon instead of an envelope or other stylized icon, it might have been damaged in transit. Ask the sender to re-send the file and remind him to make sure the uncompression program is included in the file.

■ **Mismatch between computer types**—PCs can't read Mac files, and Macs usually can't read PC files, especially if they're self-extracting .EXE files. Make sure the sender is using a compatible system to yours, or ask them to send you just the video file in a format such as .AVI or .MPG, because major media players can read these.

Webcam Can't Be Viewed by Other Party in Videoconference

Webcams are popular for video chat and videoconferencing, but if your computer is behind a firewall or connected to the Internet via a router or connection-sharing software, you may have problems with TCP port settings. Check these solutions:

■ **Set up TCP ports for use with your software**—Check your Internet sharing software or router manual for the details on how to set up the correct TCP ports for use with your chatting or videoconference software. See Chapters 15, 16, and 17 for details.

- Download the latest version of your conference or chatting software—Some vendors have improved their support for video behind firewalls or routers

- Make sure you and your chat partner are chatting with compatible programs—For example, Microsoft Windows Messenger, its replacement for NetMeeting in Windows XP, can perform audio and text chats with the latest version of MSN Messenger, but can't connect with NetMeeting. Similar incompatibilities exist between other chat software. For the most trouble-free results, both parties should use the same version of chat software.

Troubleshooting Media Players

As you learned in previous chapters, media players such as Windows Media Player and RealPlayer provide the foundation for multimedia excitement online. Without them, you can wave goodbye to real-time audio, streaming video, and Internet radio. Use these tips to help keep your broadband multimedia excitement at its peak.

Troubleshooting Windows Media Player

Many problems with Windows Media Player can be traced to the use of an outdated version. My number one solution for Windows Media Player problems is to install the latest version (7.1 for Windows 98 and above, 6.4 for Windows NT 4.0 and Windows 95; Windows XP includes version 8.x). Because Windows Media Player and Microsoft Internet Explorer share some software components, you should also upgrade to the newest available release of Internet Explorer for your computer.

Connection Problems

If Windows Media Player is having problems with a reference to an online media file, you might see messages such as these:

- The specified server could not be found—The server name is incorrect or no longer online; check the URL for spelling errors.

- Unable to establish a connection to the server—This actually means the server can't find the file you want; it might indicate an incorrect URL or an outdated link.

Tip

Use the Media Guide to find Windows Media Player-compatible files; the Media Guide is less likely to have outdated links than other Web search tools.

Windows Media Player Error Messages

If you see any of the following error messages referencing Windows Media Player

- Error code 80040200
- Error code 80040218
- Error code 80040255
- Error code 8004022f
- Error code 80040265

you can search the support Microsoft.com Web site and specify Media Player and the code # to find the specific article for each error code. The article for each code will provide a detailed troubleshooting process. In general, the most common causes for these errors are as follows:

- Trying to open an unsupported file type
- Damaged or missing Windows Media Player files

Tip

The Microsoft Knowledge Base Article #Q234019 provides an overview of various invalid file format error messages and provides a detailed process for solving the problem. Search for it at Support.Microsoft.com.

Webcam Can't Play Web Content, But Local Content Plays

If Windows Media Player can play content stored on your hard disk, but it has problems with some files retrieved from Web sites, your browser's cache (which stores files for use and re-use by both Internet Explorer and Windows Media Player) might be corrupted. To clear the Internet Explorer cache, do the following:

1. Choose Tools, Internet Options.
2. Click Delete Files (on the General tab).
3. Click OK.

After you clear the cache, reconnect to the media you want to play.

No Sound

If Windows Media Player connects and appears to be playing audio media, but you don't hear any sound:

- Check the speaker connections, power, and on/off switch
- Check the master volume control

Can't Connect After Setting Up a Home Network

If you can't connect after you install a home network, check to see if you're using a proxy server, which requires special settings for browsers and other Internet software (ICS and routers don't use proxy servers). If you are, choose Tools, Options, Network, and set the Proxy settings for HTTP Protocol to match what your Web browser uses or any special settings required by the proxy server. See the proxy server software documentation or online help for details.

Audio or Video Playback Choppy or Stops and Starts

Windows Media Player performs buffering (downloading part or all of an audio or video clip) before it starts to play a clip. However, if the Internet has a lot of traffic and you're trying to listen to or watch a big clip, the buffer might run out of data. When this happens, playback must pause until the buffer is full again.

This is normal, but irritating. Try a lower-bandwidth version of the clip, try listening or watching the clip at a different time of the day, or switch to RealPlayer if the clip is available in both formats.

Getting Updates to Windows Media Player

Windows Media Player is designed to check for updates and install them automatically. You can also check for updates at any time, following this procedure:

1. Click Help, Check for Player Upgrades.
2. Select components listed or click OK if no upgrades are available.
3. Restart the computer after installation is complete.

To view or change the settings for automatic updates, choose Tools, Options, Player. By default, Windows Media Player checks weekly for upgrades. Other options include once a day or once a month. Also, Windows Media Player will automatically download compression/decompression (codec) programs needed to support new audio and video file types.

Troubleshooting RealPlayer

As with Windows Media Player, one of the best solutions for problems with RealPlayer is making sure you have the latest version installed.

If you have a Plus (paid) version installed, you should install the latest Plus version to avoid losing features; don't use the free Basic version. Contact Real.com to see if you need to pay for an upgrade.

Connection Problems

Because RealPlayer is used primarily to play streaming media off the Internet, online connection problems will prevent you from getting your broadband media. Common error messages that indicate network problems include the following:

- Unable to locate server—The URL to the media has an invalid server name or IP address; if you entered the name yourself, check your spelling.

- Requested file not found—The server can't find the file you want; try a different search engine.

RealPlayer's own search tools are less likely to provide outdated information than other Web searches. Use them to find RealPlayer-compatible media.

- A general error has occurred—The file might be damaged or not compatible with your player.

Other Problems

The most common problems and solutions for various versions of both the basic and Plus versions of RealPlayer can be found online at service.real.com/help/faq.

Getting Updates to RealPlayer

By default, RealPlayer notifies you of updates available from the RealNetworks AutoUpdate server, and you can check for updates at any time. To check for updates, to disable notification of updates for 30 days, or to change other settings, click View, Preferences, Upgrade.

Troubleshooting IM Clients

Most of the problems you might have with a particular IM client can be solved by downloading and installing the latest version of your favorite IM client. This is particularly effective if you're seeing software error messages or if some of the features don't work correctly. For other types of problems, see the following Web sites:

- AOL Instant Messenger for Windows—Check out `www.aol.com/aim/faq/winerrors.html`.

- AOL Instant Messenger for Macintosh—Go to `www.aol.com/aim/faq/macerrors.html`.

- MSN Messenger—To reach the correct Web site, click Help in the MSN Messenger main menu.

- Yahoo! Messenger—Try help.yahoo.com/help/mesg/use.

Summary

Problems with Internet webcams, multimedia player software, and instant-messaging services are frequently caused by damaged or out-of-date software. Installing the latest version of the software for the product In question frequently solves these problems.

Webcams can also have problems caused by USB port configuration problems, incorrectly focused or dirty lenses. The Windows Device Manager can help determine if USB ports are working correctly.

Both media players and webcam video chatting can have problems with special Internet sharing configurations. Proxy servers such as WinProxy may require you to specially configure the server to allow media players to work. Routers and sharing software might need to map TCP ports for use by NetMeeting and other video chatting software.

Automatic-update features provided by many Internet multimedia and instant-messaging programs can help to automate the process of keeping software updated and working properly.

22

KEEPING YOUR CABLE INTERNET SERVICE UP-TO-DATE

*C*HAPTER HIGHLIGHTS:

- How to switch to a new PC and keep your cable Internet connection information intact

- Why switching network cards might require a call to your cable ISP

- What it takes to upgrade your browser or other Internet software

Switching to a New PC

Although cable Internet service is inherently fast, changing to a newer, faster computer will make the speed at which Web pages are displayed on your computer, online gaming, and other cable Internet features even faster.

Although the setup CD that most cable Internet ISPs provide will make setting up your new computer for online access easier, what about the e-mail and Web favorites/bookmark settings you have already accumulated? What about the other software you have installed, such as media players and Web camera utilities? It would be really painful to manually transfer all that stuff, and you might lose something along the way. Fortunately, it's now much easier to "take it with you" when you change PCs.

Following are some of the programs you can use to move your software and settings to new machines:

- Aloha Bob's PC Relocator—Macmillan Software (www.macmillansoftware.com). This program includes a parallel file-transfer cable. This program is for Windows 95 and above.

- Desktop DNA—Miramar Systems, Inc. (www.desktopdna.com). This program uses a TCP/IP network connection that is designed for experienced computer managers. This program is for Windows 95 and above.

- PC Upgrade Commander—V Communications (www.v-com.com) uses TCP/IP network, parallel file transfer cable (included), or removable hard-disk type media. This program is for Windows 95 and above.

- PCsynch 2.0—Laplink.com (www.laplink.com). This program uses USB, parallel, or serial file-transfer cables (all included). Optional PCMover Plus program supports more than 40 specific programs' settings. This program is for Windows 95 and above.

Windows XP contains its own Files and Settings Transfer Wizard, which, although it won't move programs between PCs, will handle transferring data files and settings after you have installed the programs you want to use on your new computer. This wizard also allows you to choose which data files and settings to transfer. By contrast, some of the programs in the preceding list are all-or-nothing propositions.

Changing Network Cards

If you change computers, you might wind up changing your Ethernet network card, especially if your new PC ships with a 10/100 Ethernet card or has a 10/100 Ethernet port built in. Depending on your cable ISP's configuration, you might find that this change could cause you problems when it's time to move to the new computer, or even if you keep your old PC and replace just your network card.

Some cable ISPs tie your service to an obscure feature of every Ethernet card, its media access control address, or MAC address. This value is unique for every Ethernet adapter, regardless of whether it's a card, a USB Ethernet adapter, or a built-in Ethernet port. Some cable ISPs record this number and use it to verify your connection. If your ISP matches the MAC address to your cable modem, and you change network cards (and thus change your MAC address), you won't be able to connect to the Internet through your cable modem until you notify your cable ISP of your new MAC address. The MAC address is built into the hardware of your Ethernet adapter and usually can't be changed.

Should you panic about the MAC address issue? Probably not. Although some cable ISPs state that they match the MAC address to your service, in practice, it's often the cable modem hardware that looks for a particular MAC address when you turn on your computer. So, if you change Ethernet cards and you can't connect to the Internet, use the reset feature on your cable modem to clear its memory of your old Ethernet card's MAC address. After the reset, cable modems that are MAC-aware will pick up the new MAC address from your new Ethernet card and work properly.

Tip

According to Scot Finnie's Broadband Report, some of the cable ISPs who use MAC address matching in some of their markets include:

- AT&T Broadband
- ComCast
- Cox Communications
- MediaOne
- RoadRunner

If you use one of these cable ISPs and you install a router for Internet sharing, you should use the router's MAC address cloning (also called *spoofing)* feature to have the router report the MAC address of your network card.

To learn more about this issue, see Scot's report at: `content.techweb.com/winmag/ columns/broadband/2000/35.htm#macaddress`.

If you change your network adapter or change to a new computer with a different network adapter, and none of the preceding steps get you back online, you may need to call your ISP's customer support personnel to ask them to update their database with your new network adapter's MAC address.

Ethernet adapters aren't the only types of network devices that have MAC addresses. Your cable modem has one as well (check the identification sticker on the rear or bottom of the unit if you're curious). If you get a replacement cable modem, you might need to provide the new modem's MAC address to your cable ISP to keep your connection working.

Displaying the MAC Address of Your Adapter

If your cable Internet ISP tracks the MAC address of your Ethernet adapter and you need to provide it to restore service after upgrading your network card or system, it's easy to look up this information. To find the MAC address, run WINIPCFG with a Windows 9x/Me computer, IPCONFIG with a Windows NT/2000/XP computer, or use the Info Button on the TCP/IP Control Panel on a Mac. Depending on the program, the MAC address might also be called the Adapter Address or Hardware address, but it is always a group of six two-digit hexadecimal numbers. Figure 22.1 shows you the Adapter Address as displayed by WINIPCFG.

FIGURE 22.1

The Adapter (MAC) Address is displayed directly under the Ethernet adapter name by WINIPCFG.

If you use a router to share your Internet connection, you should configure the router to report the MAC address of the Ethernet card you originally connected to the cable modem. Many popular cable modem/DSL routers support this feature, called MAC Address Cloning or Changeable WAN MAC address. For more information, see Chapter 17, "Router Your Way to Internet Sharing."

Installing Browser Upgrades

As you learned in Chapter 12, "Speeding Up Your Cable Internet Service," you can change to a number of different Web browsers, but if you're like most users, you probably feel most comfortable with a particular Web browser's features and layout. However, as time goes on, you need to refresh your Web browser with new features and security updates.

Two major reasons exist for installing a new version of your favorite browser:

- Improved encryption—Many banks and financial institutions are abandoning the older 40-bit and 56-bit encryption standards and requiring their users to access their Web sites with browsers featuring 128-bit encryption. If you use a browser lacking the proper level of encryption, you can't access your financial data.

- Improved compatibility with the latest HTML and XML standards and extensions—Hypertext Markup Language (HTML) and eXtensible Markup Language (XML) are the page description languages of the Internet. If your browser displays some pages badly, or can't display some pages at all, you probably should update to the newest version of your browser.

You can check the browser version and encryption (cipher) strength of your Internet Explorer browser by clicking Help, About. Figure 22.2 shows how a recent version of Internet Explorer reports this information.

FIGURE 22.2

This installation of Internet Explorer 5.5 has 128-bit encryption and has been updated with Service Pack 2 (SP2).

With Netscape Navigator/Communicator 4.x, click Help, Software Updates, Your Installed Software to see the version of Netscape you're using and its encryption strength.

Because encryption standards for browsers were changed before the introduction of Netscape 6.1, Netscape 6.1 is available in only a 128-bit version. If you have this version of Netscape, you already have the highest encryption level available in a Web browser.

At one time, upgrading your browser was a pretty straightforward process, although it took a long time with a dial-up analog modem:

1. Download huge (10 to 20MB) file.

2. Install over old browser.

3. Wait until another security breach or feature is announced.

4. Repeat steps 1 and 2.

Today, the process is extremely different, especially if you use Windows and Internet Explorer. With Windows and Internet Explorer, the Windows Update feature discussed in Chapter 6 is the way to go for painless IE updates for several reasons:

- Windows Update checks your system (and Web browser) configuration to determine which pieces of Windows and IE need to be updated.

- Windows Update can install small patches if that's all you need (a process often called updating), or install a brand-new IE version (a process often called upgrading) if that's more suitable.

- Windows Update also fixes problems with IE-dependent features such as Outlook Express e-mail.

- Windows Update can be set to check automatically for system updates with Windows Me and newer versions.

Updating software—Installing improvements to your software that don't change the software version; normally performed to fix software bugs or patch security holes.

Upgrading software—Installing a new version of the software; adds significant new features.

Other browsers, such as Netscape Navigator, rely on you to check for updated versions, but Netscape has also improved its installation process with Navigator 6.1. Rather than downloading the entire program to your drive and saving it, you normally download a small installer program, save it, launch it, and it gets the latest components directly from the Web.

Thus, both Microsoft and Netscape use your PC to call up just the files needed, instead of the all-too-common past practice of downloading obsolete components that might clash with newer software on your system.

Microsoft has made it difficult to bypass Windows Update, which deletes the setup files from your computer as soon as you install the updates. However, if you prefer to keep downloaded files for re-use on other machines that lack fast Internet access, see the following Web site for tips on how to store IE or other files you download with Windows Update after they are installed: `www.pcforrest.freeserve.co.uk/win98_updates.htm`.

Netscape offers the full Netscape 6.1 installation for download at `Home.netscape.com/download/full_install.html`.

Installing Other New Software

What other types of software will you need to update to keep your online experience running as fast and enjoyably as possible?

- ActiveX controls and plug-ins—Development tools for multimedia Web content such as Macromedia Flash also change over time. Don't be surprised if at some point you will need to install a new version of the Flash player or other program to make a particular Web page fully viewable.

- E-mail clients—E-mail clients need frequent updates today because of the huge security risk they pose. In fact, as I was writing another chapter in this book, the SirCam virus tried to attack my system through two e-mail messages. Unfortunately, many current e-mail clients (including Outlook Express) don't properly display the true file type of potentially dangerous attachments, so up-to-date anti-virus software is absolutely necessary as a second line of defense.

If your e-mail client is integrated with your Web browser, as Outlook Express is integrated with Internet Explorer and Netscape Mail is integrated with Netscape Communicator or Netscape 6.1, upgrading or updating your Web browser can also upgrade or update your e-mail client.

- Antivirus software—As you learned in Chapter 14, "Stopping Computer Viruses," keeping your anti-virus software up-to-date in both its program code and virus signatures is absolutely necessary. Fortunately, the latest anti-virus programs work hand-in-hand with your cable Internet high-speed connection to keep you as safe as possible. For example, Norton AntiVirus 2002 checks for updates every four hours, which isn't too often, given the increasingly dangerous world that we (and our computers) live in.

- Unzipping utilities—Although the basic principle of lossless file compression for single-file archives has been around for years, programs such as WinZip, PKZip, and StuffIt sometimes change how they archive files to keep up with changes in maximum allowable file sizes, long filenames, folder storage, and other options. If you can't open a particular compressed file with your favorite version of an unzipping/uncompressing program, check for an update.

Summary

As time passes, both hardware and software components that make your cable Internet experience may need to be updated.

A variety of third-party transfer programs can be used to move data files and software settings or even the entire contents of the hard drive to a new PC. Windows XP's Files and Settings Transfer Wizard performs a similar task for users moving to (or from) a Windows XP-based system.

ISPs which use your Ethernet adapter's MAC address might require you to report the MAC address of a new adapter or of a new computer's network adapter. To avoid problems caused by using a router with cable ISPs which use the MAC address to control Internet access, you can set most broadband routers to report your Ethernet adapter's MAC address instead of the router's actual MAC address.

Web browsers and e-mail clients require periodic updates for security reasons. Microsoft Internet Explorer and Outlook Express in particular are frequent targets of hackers, and your system's vulnerability increases if you don't install the latest security fixes. Both Microsoft and Netscape use dynamic installation to keep their Web browsers and integrated e-mail clients up-to-date, installing only the files required for your system. Internet Explorer and Outlook Express can be updated through Windows Update, while Netscape 6.1 and Netscape Mail require you to manually check for updates.

Install updates to software such as ActiveX controls, Netscape plug-ins, antivirus software, and unzipping utilities as required. Antivirus software should be updated daily for maximum protection, while other types of programs should be updated when the current versions installed on your system no longer work with some types of Web content.

Index

USB

adapters, troubleshooting
cable Internet service, 58
cable modem connection, 54
connections, troubleshooting,
305-309
Ethernet adapters
connecting, 55
*ICS (Internet Connection
Sharing), 223*
*troubleshooting cable
Internet service, 58*
hubs, 308
ports
*adapters, two-way cable
modems, 21*
connection lights, 308
disadvantages, 307
system BIOS, 309
troubleshooting, 307-309
Type B cable connector, 55

Use

a Proxy Server box, 66
DHCP for WINS Resolution
option, 239

**users (ICS (Internet
Connection Sharing)),**

networks, 222
security, 223

using

Sygate Home Network, 259
WinGate, 249-251
WinProxy, 254-255

utilities

hard disk error-checking, 51
Mac, 312
Ping, 312

**UTP (unshielded twisted-pair)
cables, 42**

V

v-mail (video e-mail)

creating, 136
editing, 138-139
picture quality, 138

recording software, 137
sending, 139-140
viewing, 141
Web sites, 99

vendors, Webcams, 97

versions, identifying

MacOS, 34
Windows, 33
Windows NT 4.0, 34

Versions tab, 34

**video. *See also* streaming,
video**

cards, 3D, 161-166
e-mail. *See* v-mail
game, adjusting, 161-165

**View menu commands,
Preferences, 71**

viewing

documents, 81
file types, 81
graphics, 81
multiple Web sites, 84-85
photos online, 90-91
spreadsheets, 81
v-mail, 141

**virtual private network
(VPN), 49**

viruses, 206-207, 215-216

antivirus software, 208-209
Norton AntiVirus, 210
online, 212
Web sites, 212-215
online checkers, 78
Trojan horse programs, 206
Web sites, 207
worms, 207

volume controls, 85

**VPN (virtual private network),
49**

W

**WANs (wide area networks),
266, 273**

warning, security, 79

Web

addresses, sending, 80
browsers
Opera, Web sites, 180
proxy settings, 64
synchronizing, 183-185
programs, routers, trou-
bleshooting, 325
servers, troubleshooting,
router connection, 323
sites
2Wire, 57
@Backup, 91, 154
antivirus, 212-215
*AOL Instant Messenger,
88*
Bandwidth Place, 57
Belarc, 38
bigVAULT, 91, 154
CableModemHelp, 58
*Copernic Technologies,
Inc., 87*
cprextreme, 89
disabling TCP Ports, 194
Discovery Channel, 18
*Distributed Intrusion
Detection System, 190*
Dogpile, 86
download managers, 183
Drive Plus, 154
firewalls, 196-198
game servers, 170-171
gamespy, 89
gaming, 89
Google, 18
GoSearch, 86
ICQ, 88
*Internet Connection
Sharing (ICS), trou-
bleshooting, 320*
Internet radio, 116
iTools, 91, 154
Jasc, 81
Java, 113
*Macintosh Security, 195,
199*
*MacOS, third-party shar-
ing programs, 261-262*

X – Y – Z